Singers of the Century

Conchita Supervia

# Singers of the Century

## VOLUME 2

J.B. Steane

Duckworth

Second impression 2000
First published in 1998 by
Gerald Duckworth & Co. Ltd.
61 Frith Street, London W1V 5TA
Tel: 0207 434 4242
Fax: 0207 434 4420
Email: enquiries@duckworth-publishers.co.uk
www.duckw.com

A catalogue record for this book is available
from the British Library.

ISBN 0 7156 2842 9

Chapters 1-18, 20-3, 28-9, 32, 37 and 50 appeared first in *Opera Now*.
Chapters 39, 40 and 45 are adapted from articles that appeared first in
*International Classical Record Collector*. Chapters 24 and 26 are based on
record notes compiled for Nimbus and Romophone respectively.

**Sources of illustrations** (numbers refer to the pages of this book)

Ingmar Bergman: 84. George Burr: frontispiece, 3, 13, 15, 20, 25, 26, 29, 39,
49, 51, 56, 64, 74, 76, 79, 81, 86, 95, 104, 131, 145, 151(left), 157(left), 159,
162, 165, 168, 172, 177, 187, 189, 195, 217, 219, 235, 239, 245, 255, 257(left).
Danacord: 223, 225. Colin Deane, 227, 229. Decca, 35(above), 249, 251. EMI:
44, 59, 99, 257(right). Gramophone, 115, 139, 197, 199, 207. Metropolitan
Opera: 19, 179. Nimbus: 9, 69, 89, 119, 121, 129, 135, 137, 151(right), 213.
Houston Rogers, 117. J.B. Steane: 4, 11, 35(below), 47, 61, 65, 71, 91, 97, 101,
105, 109, 111, 124, 125, 141, 144, 153, 157(right), 169, 174, 183, 185, 193,
203, 204, 209, 215, 233, 241, 247.

*Jacket illustrations* Turner and Journet: Nimbus; Callas: EMI; Corelli: J.B.
Steane.

Typeset by Ray Davies
Printed in Great Britain by
Redwood Books Ltd, Trowbridge

# Contents

Foreword vii

To John Karran and George Burr
with gratitude

# Foreword

Questions arising out of the first volume concerned inclusions and omissions. The singers found most conspicuously absent were Maria Callas and Enrico Caruso, the first of whom now brings this Second Volume to its conclusion, as (all being well) the second will do for the Third and last. A larger question was then raised as to the whole principle of 'who's in, who's out'. Part of the answer to that must be that the singers chosen had some quality which I personally valued, so that writing about them was a pleasure. This personal element brought advantages, I hope, but it certainly may be true that as a result some readers will consider particular favourites of their own to have been slighted. It may help if I say, quite sincerely, that omission does not necessarily imply anything more than a consciousness on the author's part of not having anything very worthwhile to contribute. On the other hand, critical priorities are operative too.

A word must also be said on the question of order or, if preferred, disorder. As explained in the Foreword to the First Volume, these essays took shape following a commission from the then Editor of the British magazine *Opera Now*. A word-limit for each article was set at 1500, and for the rest I was allowed a free hand. The object was to provide an introduction to the singers and at the same time to come up with material, whether of fact or idea, that might hold readers who were already interested and knowledgeable. No scheme of ordering, chronological or otherwise, was imposed, and when it came to collecting the first fifty for publication in book-form it was decided to preserve the random order of the originals. This had the primary aim of encouraging readers to go beyond their more exclusive preoccupations ('singers of the Golden Age', 'singers of today', 'tenors only' and so forth). It may also have been influenced by such frivolous considerations as the pleasure of a surprise. As a result, one reader, who liked it, related the experience to that of browsing in a friendly, old-fashioned bookshop. If it is not bad manners (or simply injudicious) to say so, then it must be admitted that this is very much the kind of reader for whom I have written.

# CHAPTER 1

# Franco Corelli

'It is an appetite,' said a friend from long ago and far away. But to get the flavour of his speech you have to hear the long vowels of a Brazilian accent with a little spicing of central European origin, and the *con sordino* of a large man who knows that anything louder would make the cutlery dance and fracture the wine glass. 'Eet ees an appetite.' He was talking about the interest we shared in voices and singing. 'A craving, a sensuality, two songs a day, that will do, but those you must have.' 'It's a thirst,' I said, and we began to catalogue the voices for which we thirsted. When it came to those of our own time, high on the list was Franco Corelli's, and even while invoking the name and summoning the sound the thirst arose: a craving, almost a medical condition. I once discussed it with a doctor. 'Ah yes,' he said, 'it's a well-known complaint. Several of my patients have it. In the profession we know it as corellidipsia.'

The thirst, as the man said, is sensual; it is not a brainy thing. The voice we want to drink is a sound, not an expressive system or a stylistic exercise, and what stimulates the thirst for one voice rather than another is its timbre. My belief is that it has much to do with vibrato, the fast vibrato, that is, and something quite distinct from wobble (almost its opposite in fact – have the two ever been known to co-exist?). Over the last 50 years or so this has been reduced almost to the point of elimination even among the Latin races with whom it was once popular; but in a modified form, and especially in his early years, Corelli preserved it as a constituent of his timbre. To my mind, it is a great flavourer; officially blacklisted, it is the ingredient that gives an operatic voice character, excitement, dramatic tension. Power, range, body, resonance: these, of course, are qualities that go to make a good voice, but timbre has much to do with the nature and degree of the voice's vibrancy, and it is in this that the sheer sound of Corelli's voice first exercised its special fascination.

Interestingly, it is a feature which, according to his own account in conversation with the bass Jerome Hines (*Great Singers on Great Singing*, New York, 1982), Corelli set about systematically to reduce. Hines remarks that when he first sang with Corelli, at La Scala in 1957, there was this fast vibrato no trace of which could he detect since the tenor's Metropolitan debut four years later. Corelli replies that he regarded it as

1

the result of faulty breath-management. He also gives it the name by which he says it is known in Italy: *Caprino*, 'little goat', in other words a bleating sound. The evidence of recordings provides a rather different commentary, for the vibrato appears not to have been eliminated after 1961 by any means so completely as they thought and in the early years it never amounts to anything remotely goat-like or bleating.

In any case, I think it observable that a fast vibrato tends to diminish with age. You can't go for long in a discussion of Corelli without mention of Lauri-Volpi. Giacomo Lauri-Volpi was a tenor with many similarities of timbre, and the fast vibrato which is a notable feature of his early recordings in the 1920s has grown much less insistent by 1930, and ten years later (at the age of 48) has all but disappeared. The two singers were, in fact, closely associated, Lauri-Volpi having had a strong influence on Corelli's development and helping him through a critical time in mid-career when his voice was being over-driven, the repertoire itself in need of reassessment. In the second edition (1960) of his book *Voci parallele* (Italy, 1955), the senior tenor refers to Corelli's having at one time seriously lost his way ('grave smarrimento'), and he gives some technical diagnosis of the problems. The 'parallel' and the reasons given for it, incidentally, are not entirely flattering to Corelli, for the tenor brought up for comparison with him is the almost forgotten Rinaldo Grassi, Lauri-Volpi's conclusion being that Grassi, never a top name, lived in an age rich with tenors, while Corelli 'through the scarcity of voices that now afflicts the operatic stage, has no one seriously to trouble him'.

If he had a rival among contemporary Italians it was in Carlo Bergonzi, who became very much the critics' favourite. Accepting 1921 as the date of Corelli's birth, we find Bergonzi three years younger, making his debut in the same year (1951), coming to La Scala in 1953 (Corelli 1954), the Metropolitan in 1956 (Corelli 1961), the two of them succeeding Di Stefano and Del Monaco as the principal Italian tenors in recordings, with Domingo and Pavarotti to follow in due course. At the start we also find Lauri-Volpi a name associated with Bergonzi, whose earliest recordings have something of the same quick vibrato and whose London debut in 1953 caused Harold Rosenthal to cite Lauri-Volpi in comparison. *Voci parallele* has something to say about Bergonzi too. The 'parallel' now is with Domingo, along the lines that both incorporate a baritonal element and that they have in common 'an exemplary sobriety and control, with spontaneity of technical emission thanks to correct breathing'. There must have been a conscious sideward glance towards Corelli in that, and on the face of it it would be to Corelli's detriment. 'Sobriety and control' are not the most exciting of virtues, however, and Corelli (like Lauri-Volpi before him) was nothing if not exciting.

With excitement goes a sense of danger. Corelli's was a career of great brilliance, but it did not run smooth, and, as for the critics, every performance risked censure. It is true that glowing things were said, as in *Opera*

2

Corelli as Don Carlos (Vienna 1963)

Corelli as Radamès in *Aida* (Metropolitan 1961)

magazine: 'a lovely, warm and powerful voice, handsome physique and intelligent expression' (Riccardo Malipiero on *La vestale*, Florence, 1955); 'His tense control and richness of tone are phenomenal, as is his power, yet there is never a hint of strain' (Patrick Turnbull, *Turandot*, Monte Carlo, 1960); 'the most impressive example at hand of that vanished breed,

4

the *tenore robusto*' (Richard RePass, *Il trovatore*, Metropolitan, 1961). But many strike a note of sheer exasperation: 'If he persists in this sort of adolescent ostentation he will shortly ruin his voice, or be unable to sing in any other way' (Elliott Stein, *Norma*, Paris, 1957); 'His now familiar version of Flash Gordon playing Manrico, striding about the stage, boldly defying Cammarano's stage directions, and, in Act I, looking straight at the audience when he throws back his head and sings (to Di Luna) "Ravvisami! Manrico io son!" ' (William Weaver, *Trovatore*, Rome, 1963); 'so insensitively sung that I could hardly believe my ears' (Harold Rosenthal, *Carmen*, Chicago, 1964).

With performances capable of arousing such extremes went a volatile temperament. His cancellations became proverbial (Domingo tells in *My First Forty Years*, London, 1983, how he owed to Corelli's indispositions his first Andrea Chénier, his part in the recorded and televised Verdi Requiem at St Paul's Cathedral under Bernstein, and his Met debut, Corelli having cried off at 7.20 pm). But the most noted, surprising and significant characteristic was his extreme nervousness. Magda Olivero, who sang with him in *La fanciulla del West*, reputedly said she had never met so nervous, and nervy, a tenor: they rehearsed their Act II duet for two hours, singing passionately enough, but hardly ever would he look at her and when she once touched him he literally jumped. Agonies in the wings as he waited to go on recall the similar ordeals of Rosa Ponselle, and a similarity of cause may be worth pondering. Like her he also withdrew at the height of his fame, making the last of his 365 performances with the Metropolitan company on 28 June 1975 in *La bohème*. Occasionally he has given masterclasses, broadcasts and hints of a return (as Otello); but on the whole it has been a very retiring retirement. Efforts were made to involve him in the Metropolitan's centenary celebrations of 1984, but he could not be persuaded.

Corelli is remembered now for two striking attributes, his thrilling voice and his good looks. That does him less than justice. It has to be remembered for one thing that he was an athlete and a boxer, and that, with these good looks, and in the age of films and (already) pop stars, he went into opera. He also sang in a larger and more varied repertoire than is commonly recalled. After all, when Jerome Hines met him as a colleague it was not in *Trovatore*, *Pagliacci* or *Tosca* but in Handel's *Hercules*; he also sang the role of Sesto in *Julius Caesar*. Operas that came and went but still required learning were Guerrini's *Eneo* and Allegri's *Romulus*. The Maggio Musicale at Florence brought rarities such as Spontini's *La vestale* and *Agnese di Hohenstaufe*, while among his Verdi operas was *La battaglia di Legnano*. He had a Russian repertoire too, including *Boris Godunov*, *Khovanshchina* and (in its first performances outside the Soviet Union) Prokofiev's *War and Peace*.

He could also be a genuine artist, fully involved in his work, imaginative and even refined. We hear this probably best in recordings made live from the stage, as in the Metropolitan's *Ernani* of 1965 where his solo has a phrase in which it is as though you see him close his eyes, relish the moment and live the emotion, then hold a diminuendo and affectionately soften the notes that lead back to the melody. The famous 1961 *Turandot* with Stokowski conducting has also lovely touches absent from the studio recording: hear the 'Non piangere, Liù' and the indrawn rapture of wonderment in 'meraviglia'.

It was in *Turandot* that I myself heard him on one of his rare visits to London. I recall thinking that the good looks did not really help him so very much on stage, and that the height (he was 6′2″) seemed principally to make him self-conscious. He cut a curiously isolated stage figure, a somewhat awkward one, lending itself to Philip Hope-Wallace's sketch of him as 'a bewildered recruit clutching an imaginary tea-tray with his bearskin fallen down over his nose'. In the first performance critics reported his singing as 'under-nourished' and 'little more than adequate'. I can't say I remember that. What I do remember is the immediate purchase of a ticket for the second performance and after that another for the third. I must have been thirsty, corellidipsia having already set in.

# CHAPTER 2

# Emmy Destinn

There are milestones on the road to extinction. For singers, the first is retirement; the second, death; and the third the death of the last generation that heard them. In my youth, Destinn-worshippers were still quite thick on the ground, so that she herself retained a kind of life. At any rate, her memory haunted the corridors of Covent Garden, where aged heads, their tongues a-talking, would nod reflectively to the tune of 'Ah, but you should have heard Destinn.' The last opportunity to hear her came in 1919, but for years afterwards her Aida and Butterfly set the standard at which other singers were admonished to aim and to which they would never attain. 'Destinn was our idol,' Alec Robertson once wrote to me. Melba, he explained, had a cold perfection, while Destinn's singing was passionate, very human, and, for that matter, perfect too. 'She lives vividly in my memory,' he wrote in his autobiography (*More than Music*, London, 1961): 'the one and only perfect interpreter of Butterfly, Tosca, Minnie, Aida and Senta.'

This was typical, not merely of starry-eyed youth up in the gallery but of connoisseurs and critics whose own puppy-love had had for its objects Patti and Tietjens. Right from the start, in 1904, they recognised an excellence that had all the potential for greatness. The *Daily Telegraph* reported on her debut as Donna Anna: 'She has a powerful and well-controlled voice, filling easily the ample spaces of our opera house and satisfying the ear by its roundness and timbre.' Two nights later, as Nedda in *Pagliacci*, she confirmed this first impression with 'beauty of delivery and dramatic truth', to which they might have added evidence of versatility, especially when her next role was to be Elsa in *Lohengrin*. Her Nedda appears to have been something special. When she returned to the part in 1906, the *Times* critic wrote: 'This fine artist is always splendid in everything she does, but in Nedda she surpasses herself; quick, sensitive, and alive to her fingertips, she sang and acted last night to perfection, playing with a passionate intensity and a sense of beauty that are rarely found combined in opera singers.' She was probably in her absolute prime during these years. In 1907 she added Venus in *Tannhäuser* to her London repertoire, and again *The Times* wrote: 'Small though the part is, she made it one of the most brilliant she has ever undertaken; her voice comes

7

pouring out in a continuous stream of beautiful melody, and the way in which she was seductive, passionate and defiant in turn was a triumph of the art of acting.' We gain a more vivid picture of this side of her art in the description of her as Senta in *Der fliegende Holländer*. 'Her homely costume and at times almost ungainly attitudes speak as eloquently as her gestures of the girl who is possessed by one idea. Even her back, as she stands gazing at the Dutchman's picture, tells us that there is not, and never has been, any hope for Erik's suit. A more pathetic and living representation has rarely been seen, and each character in which the great singer is seen shows how rapid and sure is her progress to the topmost position in her art.'

The seasons went by and Destinn became as much of an institution as Melba. She lived with some style in Nash's terrace overlooking Regent's Park, enjoyed the social life, and after 1906 had no rival in her roles at the opera house throughout those long summer months in which London society maintained what it would never quite recover after 1914. During these years she sang in a variety of roles, which included also Tess of the D'Urbervilles in a forgotten opera by Frédéric D'Erlanger, Armide in a rare revival of Gluck's opera and, in the London premiere of *La fanciulla del West*, the title role which she had 'created' the previous year in New York. Supreme, in the memory of those who heard her, remain her Aida and Butterfly.

As Butterfly she had perhaps some advantage in that people learned the opera through her performances: that is so often the way in which a role becomes in the listener's mind inseparable from a particular voice. Many years afterwards, Alec Robertson still found the memory of Destinn colouring his review of a new complete *Butterfly* on records: 'When shall we find again the glorious voice, the incomparable *mezza voce* she possessed, the tragic power and intensity of her art?' (*Gramophone*, March 1940). And 20 years after that, in his memoirs, he recalled first hearing her and the impact of that experience: 'It was Destinn's singing in *Madama Butterfly* which gave me a lasting love for the lyric-dramatic soprano voice. I had not heard the opera before and so was unprepared for the magical moment of Butterfly's entrance. Above the lovely melody on the muted violins came, from the distance, the sound of that clear, rich, vibrant, unforgettable voice, ever approaching nearer and, as Destinn appeared, soaring rapturously up to the high point of climax. I was enthralled: and it was at this very moment that my unimaginative neighbour chose to whisper, "What a large Butterfly," a remark that immediately awoke in me a criminal impulse.'

The Aida (where largeness was less likely to be a subject of remark), given every year from 1906 onwards and again on Destinn's return in 1919, was by general consent the crown of her remarkable achievements. *The Times* (30 May 1907) held that no singing could be technically more brilliant, yet there was more to it than this: 'Her Aida is a living figure.'

Destinn as Tess of the D'Urbervilles (Covent Garden 1910)

The greatest thrill of an operatic lifetime might be the Nile Scene in *Aida* when Destinn sang with Caruso and her lover Dinh Gilly. Most fondly remembered of all were the high As, *pianissimo*, which would appear in the air as if from nowhere and would then float effortlessly to the back of the gallery. There was never again, for her admirers, anything quite like it.

Now, sadly, the modern listener who goes to Destinn's records to recapture all this tends to come away disappointed. The famous 'floating' notes are there but inaccessible: we hear them but cannot, except with an almighty tug on the imagination, capture what was heard at Covent Garden. The old recording in the box-like acoustics produces a pipey sound, just ever so slightly flat. At full voice she sounds more convincingly herself, though the 'self' may not be quite what is expected. Sometimes on lower middle-notes there seems to be something dangerously like wobble, though elsewhere there has probably never been a 'straighter' voice, or one more firmly ruled. As for expression, that too is present, but not subtlety: direct, passionate, but elementary. She made a great many records, collected recently on the Czech Supraphon label, on eleven CDs; so she was, in her time, reckoned a successful recording artist. Yet hearing, say, four or five arias in succession, one is likely to emerge in a bewildered mood, perplexed by sounds in which it is hard to take pleasure, yet haunted by something urgently individual to which one may have to return.

The answer lies with that last word. It is a case where familiarity breeds, not exactly respect but more an affectionate fascination. The voice-character is immensely strong, its timbre concentrated, almost in the way of a baby's crying; there are times when it sounds thick and even lazy, and yet even then it is liable to blaze forth with a passionate energy. Therein lies the fascination.

Affection grows, though in a strange way, as one thinks of the woman and relates that to the voice. 'Appetite' is the word that comes to mind: not a particularly lovely one, but right at the centre of life, human and animal. To take it at what I suppose we have to call the lowest form, she certainly liked her food: hence the 'largeness'. Doctors went unheeded, her blood-pressure rose and in January 1930 she suffered a stroke which proved fatal. She was within a month of her 52nd birthday and had been in virtual retirement for six or seven years. Her sexual appetite was also legendary. The Algerian baritone Dinh Gilly (known at the Metropolitan, we are told, as the 'forza del Destinn') had what seems to have been a deep and true love-affair with her over many years (she literally fell into his arms during a mishap on stage in *La fanciulla del West*). Later, as a respectable married man, he spoke bitterly about 'these prima donnas' whose desires knew no bounds, calling if need be on stagehands and startled draymen from the vegetable market.

Her other appetites were for work, her country and her art. The early years in Berlin involved her in an immense work-load: she could sing

Theme from Smetana's *Dalibor* with Destinn's signature

anything from Mignon to Salome, and at a moment's notice. Her patriotism was equally intense, generous, outspoken and strong: it touched her art also, and she championed the operas of Smetana abroad and at home, taking Destinnova, the Czech form of her name, for professional use after the war. It is appetite, too, that we sense in her voice on records: for the homeland in *Aida*, the imprisoned lover in *Il trovatore*, the motherless child in the finale of *Madama Butterfly*. And perhaps by this time we are not so far, after all, from Alec Robertson and his contemporaries, who found in Destinn a singer never to be replaced and never to be forgotten.

<br />
CHAPTER 3

# Conchita Supervia

Towards the end of her tragically shortened life, Supervia married a businessman who was also a specialist in orchids. In London, just a step away from the Wigmore Hall, he had a florist's shop at which his beautiful Spanish wife would sometimes call. When she did, so they say, it was as though a hundred twinkling lights had suddenly been turned on, and the place became all smiles. It is the same now when one of her records is played. Of course it depends a little on which record it happens to be and what kind of equipment is involved; also whether other persons present can cope with so much vibrancy. But generally, when Conchita Supervia sings, life quickens. She would challenge and cajole, charm and sigh, wheedle and scowl. The voice would rattle with alarming Southern stridency, yet none could sing a sweeter lullaby. She mixed the colours of her song with daring and intuitive skill: its scents and shades, flashes of scarlet amid pastel tints and delicate half-tones, were a florist's shop in themselves, and rivals were soon out of business.

Perhaps it was fortunate that in one branch of her singer's business there *were* no rivals. Londoners, at least, reckoned to have heard nothing like her. It was the coloratura that most intrigued them. Coloratura sopranos, yes, those remained extant, though by the 1930s an endangered species with few conservationists to protect them; the coloratura mezzo, or contralto, that was something else. Nowadays of course they are two-a-penny, and Rossini revivals are no longer astonishing. But when Supervia introduced Cenerentola's aria into her concert programme in 1931 she created something of a sensation. By 1934 it was still considered a bold venture on the part of the management that *La Cenerentola* should have been mounted for her debut at Covent Garden, though two performances only were permitted, those being the first the house had seen since 1848. In the event the opera itself met with a mixed reception (for one thing, the audience, religiously reared on Wagner and accustomed to being told by Sir Thomas Beecham to shut up, failed to laugh and applaud as apparently they should have done); but there was no doubt about the success of the heroine, nor that she would be invited back for the next season.

Even so, the Rossini association was not entirely to her benefit. The *Musical Times* of January 1934 carried a long and thoughtful review of her

<br />
<br />
<br />
<br />
<br />
<br />
<br />
<br />
<br />
<br />
<br />
<br />
<br />
<br />
<br />
<br />
<br />
<br />
<br />
<br />
<br />
<br />
<br />
<br />
<br />
<br />
<br />
<br />

Supervia in her London home, c. 1934

recent song recital at the Aeolian Hall, revealing much about the methods and effect of Supervia's singing, and serving as a useful reminder to readers at this later date of the low esteem into which the coloratura's art and repertoire had fallen. 'It is well, of course [wrote their critic, "HJK"], to have a long-range singer at hand for occasional performances of such works as *The Barber of Seville*, but neither the music nor the type of singer to whom such music is manna warrants more than passing attention ... While Supervia continues to sing the music in which she has earned her fame she can never be regarded as more than a "stunt" singer ... If Rossini's music were nowadays the fashion, it would, of course, be imperative for singers to study length of range ... But it happens that most composers manage to get along without asking singers to be both larks and ventriloquists. The proper place for the performance of vocalises is in the singing studios.' What we have seen in the last 30 years, and particularly in the last decade, has been the reversal of this position: Rossini's music *is* nowadays 'the fashion' (insofar as it is heard, admired and rarely attacked), and the coloratura with extensive range and practised fluency has returned to favour. Supervia, to that extent, was born out of her time.

The *Musical Times* critic went on to discuss what he considered the real gift of this exceptional singer to be: 'for it is in the more difficult realm of what may be called "straight" singing that Supervia shines.' Her programme of *arie antiche* and folksongs, he thought, was 'little short of perfection'. The real *bel canto* was to be found in the Italian songs and 'the real Spanish "juice" in those Catalan and Andalusian melodies'. He identified a particular skill by which, in songs of question-and-answer, her range of contrasting tones could be effectively employed. It makes me wonder whether at that concert she had sung a delightful dialogue-piece called 'Lo frare' by the Catalan composer Juan Manèn, in which a meek little home-going peasant meets a great big robber dressed up as a priest, the voices being marvellously characterised by Supervia in her recording. As the critic remarked, she makes 'other deep-voiced singers leaden by comparison'.

The review ended with a hope that she would soon be singing Carmen. She might indeed have sung the role at Covent Garden later that year, for it had long been in her repertoire and in recent times had been the talk of Paris. Instead there was further controversy because of the schedule which arranged for the performances of *Carmen* to precede *La Cenerentola*, whereas Supervia wanted them the other way round. It was a question of the demands the two roles made upon the singer, particularly in respect of tessitura; and when the management offered a re-ordering but with the loss of one performance, she withdrew. There were newspaper headlines and letters of explanation to the *Morning Post* and *Daily Telegraph* in which Supervia quoted a letter of support ('Dear great and lovely artist – Certainly I am absolutely of your opinion') from the great Emma

Supervia as Cherubino in *Le nozze di Figaro*

Calvé. So the 1934 season saw only Supervia's Cenerentola, and the Carmen had to wait till the following year.

When it was eventually seen and heard, reaction was equivocal. Some found it too Spanish, others too kittenish, domesticated and under-powered. Ernest Newman, listening carefully to the card scene, found that 'the voice was beautifully modulated and inflected from moment to moment, but one thing I could not feel was the fatality that should brood unselfconsciously over the scene'. The production itself may have been partly to blame. We tend to assume that in those days there was no such thing, so that at least the singing could go ahead unimpeded, but on this occasion it seems there

15

was some attempt at a revolving-stage effect (Cardus in the *Manchester Guardian* reported 'an interior [scene] projected out of the wings before our very eyes' and Newman saw it as 'the sudden sliding of a room half-way across the stage'), while in Act I Carmen was shut behind the barracks wall and had to sing the Seguedille through a grille. The modern age had begun.

It is curious that the reports differ so much from the evidence of recordings. In those, there is strength of every kind and no suggestion of the very limited attainments perceived by these experienced reviewers (Cardus, for instance, summed it up by saying, 'She is a soubrette of genius; and Carmen ought, without loss of her style and charm, to be more than that'). One wonders about various things – whether, perhaps, it was simply that Covent Garden was the wrong house for her Carmen (in Paris her triumphs had taken place at the Opéra-Comique), or whether, just possibly, there was a concealed health problem. She was on the one hand (according to interviewers) very conscious of health – a teetotaller, non-smoker and so forth; but she was also a determined slimmer and (according to the late Ida Cook) proud of her figure in an advanced stage of pregnancy. It was a very shocked world that learned of her death after childbirth. *The Times* carried a note that she had gone into hospital, and on 30 March 1936, she died.

Reports of her age differed rather widely. Most of the reference books gave 1899 as the year of her birth, but this proved difficult when it was pointed out that in the November of 1911 she sang Octavian in the Italian premiere of *Der Rosenkavalier* at the Costanzi in Rome. The date generally accepted now is 1895, with some difference as to whether the birthday was 8 or 9 December. At any rate, the prospect of a not-quite 12-year-old Octavian can be revised to accommodate the notion of one just under 16. The Italian press described her as 'practically a debutante', which no doubt she officially was though there exists a photograph of her allegedly dressed to appear as one of the smugglers in *Carmen* at the age of four. Her early career, nowhere very completely documented, is said to have taken her to Buenos Aires, Russia, New York and Havana by 1914. She was with the Chicago Opera in 1915 singing Charlotte in *Werther*, Mignon in Thomas's opera and then Carmen. In the 1920s she appeared at La Scala in *Hansel and Gretel*, *Rosenkavalier* and *Le nozze di Figaro* (as Cherubino, under Richard Strauss). Rosina, Cenerentola and Isabella in *L'Italiana in Algeri* were the Rossini roles, which brought her, via Paris, to London.

She remains, through her records, one of the most vivid and enchanting of all singers. The fast vibrato deters some, as it never appears to have done 'in the flesh'; to others, it adds relish and flavour. As Desmond Shawe-Taylor wrote, in an essay that deserves reprinting in this her centenary year,* 'She was incapable of dullness; even in the most trivial

---

* This article was published first in *Opera Now*, December 1995.

song there will come a phrase so personal and so completely genuine that the listener feels something akin to physical contact' (*Opera*, January 1960). She conveys, as he says, a sense of extraordinary joy in the sheer act of singing. She also more than half convinces us that there may be more life in this voice from beyond the grave than there is in any of our day-to-day encounters, on record or off.

# CHAPTER 4

# Louis and Gino Quilico

'Bald as a coot and shiny brown as a milk chocolate egg' was how one London critic described Amonasro in Covent Garden's new (1960) *Aida*. Memory has it that the chocolate was darker than that; also that as skinheads had not yet come into fashion the appearance was really rather impressive. Moreover, if ornithology is to be invoked, this potent arrival on stage was no harmless water-fowl but rather a fierce old predator and not one that would take kindly to captivity. Anyway, on the particular evening I have in mind, the sight of Amonasro was nothing to the sound of him. As another of the critics remarked, and quite rightly, he had no sooner uttered his first words, 'Suo padre!', than 'one sensed an electric thrill run round the house'. It was the thrill that accompanies recognition of a real voice, a voice rich with colour and resonance, firm in focus and powerful in its ring. It was, in fact, the baritone we had been waiting for.

Louis Quilico came to Covent Garden at a time when the resident company had a number of stalwarts who never put a foot wrong and never missed a note of their music; but the Italianate *cantabile* baritone was something we had not known on a regular basis for years, probably not since the prime of the young Paolo Silveri. Quilico, making his debut as Germont père in *La traviata*, brought this greatly desired quality; the pity was that he left us so soon. He was with the company for less than three years, from 1960 to 1962, and though he returned occasionally in the 1970s, by then it was not quite the same. On the other hand, he had done something no other baritone of his time could match; he bequeathed us a first-class baritone son.

Gino, on his arrival in 1983, fulfilled a different need. By this time a good number of baritones had come and gone, and the kind of richness we had heard from Louis had become familiar again in the opulent tones of Renato Bruson. Others were still with us, none more esteemed and loved than Thomas Allen. But a certain type of baritone sound, sampled on the rare visits of Yuri Mazurok from Russia, proved elusive: it was the timbre known on records through Battistini and perhaps the young Galeffi, a clear, high type of baritone, not (as some might say) a lazy tenor, but possessed of a shiny transparency, most at home in the upper octave (say, G to G), characterised less by roundness than by an easy freedom, supple,

Louis Quilico as Rigoletto (Metropolitan 1973)

slender and cleanly defined. This is what we heard first from his Valentin in *Faust*, then as Rossini's Figaro and a little later as Rodrigo, the Marquis da Posa, in *Don Carlos*.

It is this that comes to mind most readily if I try now to recapture the sound of the young Quilico as heard, not on his records, but 'in the flesh'. Certainly his voice was an ideal instrument for 'Per me giunto il dì supremo' in the scene of Rodrigo's death, but most characteristically it had the grace and clarity for his first solo, 'Carlo, che sol' è il nostro amore', lightly accompanied and pure *cantabile* in style, lying comfortably in the best part of the voice. In this, too, Yuri Mazurok had been memorable, but

19

Gino Quilico

20

to his practised elegance Gino Quilico added a more Italianate glow of warmth.

The two voices, father and son, are heard together in a Christmas record, where comparison of the voice-types is complicated by the disparity in age: only memory can compare like with like, for few of Louis' recordings that I have heard do full justice to his prime. At least the *Adeste fideles* disc shows Gino taking a fine top B flat in the Gounod 'Ave Maria', and Louis following suit in 'Gesù bambino'. On stage they have sung together many times. As a student at Toronto, Gino played Marullo, to whom Rigoletto cringes in the great scene with the courtiers. At Cincinnati he graduated to one of the great roles in which baritones prepare for bigger things, Paolo in *Simon Boccanegra*, the title role being played by his father. Toronto saw the remarkable duo again in 1988 in *Don Giovanni*, but now the father played Leporello to a still boyish-looking Giovanni who had already an international reputation of his own. A year before that they had appeared together at the Metropolitan, Gino as Rossini's Figaro and Massenet's Lescaut, Louis as Don Bartolo and the Comte des Grieux. And, said Louis, on the first night that happened it was as though, if he had been struck dead at that moment, he would have gone with the sensation of having had more than his fair share of life's good things.

As always with such a happy outcome, one reflects that it could so easily never have happened. Louis, who had no music in his family background, might well have gone into his father's bicycle business and never have sung at all; Gino might well have found too much music to ignore entirely (it was part of his life from the start) but have turned to pop rather than opera. That Louis developed a love of music and singing is due, as is so often the case, to his having joined a church choir. That in itself was a matter of chance. The choirmaster came along to his school asking for volunteers, and the six-year-old Quilico put up his hand. He left school at 14, worked in the shop, and, when his voice broke, would sing along with Robert Merrill, John Charles Thomas and Ezio Pinza on the radio. Best of all he liked Tino Rossi and reckoned to turn in a very passable 'Violon dans la nuit' or 'J'attendrai'.

As for Gino, his upbringing had been so cosmopolitan (Montreal, London, Paris, Rome, New York, Toronto), that he hardly knew where he was. At 17 he wanted simply to go his own way, try this and that until he found what he was good for, whether as garage mechanic, worker in the coal mine at Wawa or salesman for Tip Top Tailors. He also played the guitar and like every youngster at that time tried to form his own group. At least it brought him a step nearer to music and singing.

Perhaps the first nudge towards opera came to Louis from a radio programme. Still in his teens, he would sometimes tune in to an opera transmission from New York introduced by Ruby Mercer – who many years later was to write the whole story in her book *Les Quilico* (Les Editions de l'Homme, Quebec, 1991). What this book also makes very clear is that there were not two Quilicos, but three.* Lina Pizzolongo had been an infant prodigy, a pianist who played in public at Montreal when eight years old, later studying with Cortot and Marguerite Long in Paris. She met and married Louis Quilico; she also heard him sing, knew at once that he was for opera, and from that time subordinated her own career to his, working with him on repertoire and giving the help and encouragement without which, as he repeatedly said, he would not have had a career. On one grand occasion in 1984 all three Quilicos appeared as soloists with the Montreal Symphony Orchestra under Dutoit. The vast Maurice-Richard arena was packed, and the ovation threatened to last till dawn.

Gino's career is still in full flight. Within a short time he has become one of the leading baritones of the age. From his first three years at the Paris Opéra ('this young man has a ringing high baritone and considerable acting talent', wrote *Opera*'s correspondent in 1980) he has gone on to Covent Garden ('strikingly lithe and youthful stage presence ... matched by a superb voice ... elegantly focused ... supple musical sensibility', *Daily Telegraph* reporting on his debut), La Scala, Vienna and the Met, followed by a notable Salzburg debut as Dandini in *La Cenerentola* ('The real star was Gino Quilico, visibly enjoying himself when playing his master's role and milking every one of his phrases for all the sensuousness they could provide,' Horst Koegler, *Opera*, Festival number, 1988). The recording companies took note more promptly than is often the case, and the visual side of his work, which has always caught its share of attention, is there on videos, such as the lovely San Francisco *La bohème* of 1989 with Freni and Pavarotti and the rather less lovely *Ghosts of Versailles*, in which the big virtuoso solo is sung in mid-air holding on to a rope with one arm.

Louis has been less fortunate with recordings, one of the few eminent singers of his time to have suffered serious neglect. A live recording of his favourite part, Rigoletto (sung at the Met as recently as November 1995), under Julius Rudel at the New York City Opera in 1973 shows something of the fine tone and dramatic conviction, but only as part of a performance sadly lacking in refinement. What we want are recordings of his triumphant concerts in the Soviet Union or, better still, of the early days at Covent Garden. One performance particularly he recalls in his memoir with Ruby Mercer: a *Lucia di Lammermoor* with Sutherland and Alain Vanzo. Everything went well that night, and the sextet (almost uniquely in the theatre at that date) was allowed an encore: 'The house seemed to explode. It was the most formidable ovation I have heard in my life.' A pity, he reflected, that none of the critics were present, and the only written report, as far as he knew, was in a book. Well, there may be two books, but I hope not, for it would be nice to think that the book (*The Grand Tradition*, p. 482) was mine.

---

* See also under Quilico in 'Dates, Books and Records', pp. 266-7.

CHAPTER 5

# Mary Garden

Actress, singer, personality; American, Scots, Parisian; gregarious individualist and hard-headed aesthete; New Woman and Eternal Female;
journalist's delight, Billy Sunday's fury: that was Mary Garden. She was
also a great (if unintentional) instigator of lists.

Here is Harold Schonberg's: 'Sir Thomas Beecham, Maria Callas and
Geraldine Farrar rolled into one: lively, indomitable, glamorous, witty,
imperious, publicity-minded, capricious and a great artist on top of all
that' (*New York Times*, 15 January 1967). And here one of James
Huneker's many: 'a line of Pater's prose, the glance of one of Da Vinci's
strange great ladies; a chord by Debussy; honey, tiger's blood, and ab-
sinthe; or like the energetic pallor we see in renaissance portraits, cruel,
voluptuous and suggesting the ennui of Watteau's *L'indifférent*. She is all
things to all critics' (*Bedouins*, New York, 1920).

Schonberg never heard or met her: he says that for somebody of his
generation it didn't matter (he 'knew' just the same). Huneker saw her
first in Paris at the turn of the century, and could scarcely take his eyes
away save to explore the depths of his deep purple inkwell. Others
managed to resist. The New York critic Richard Aldrich was also the 'R.A.'
who in the third edition (1928) of *Grove's Dictionary of Music and Musicians* concluded that 'Miss Garden's personality has counted for more in
her performances than her vocal art, which is defective, or her histrionic
skill, which is limited and vitiated by many mannerisms.' Even so, it was
enough to hold captive not only a few million Americans (who reputedly
knew her as 'Our Mary') and a few thousand of the more fastidious French
('C'est la perfection même', *Annelles du Théâtre*, 1902), but also the
composer of *Pelléas et Mélisande* who wrote to André Messager in London
that her timbre exercised a tyranny over him so powerful that he found
himself utterly unable to forget it.

For Debussy, there was no 'Mary', only 'Mélisande'. It was a point she
liked to make years afterwards when people asked – or came as near as
they dared to doing so – whether they had been lovers. She recalled it in a
talk given at the Edinburgh Festival of 1950, back in her native Scotland
– where there was not much heard of 'our Mary' either, for few of her
countryfolk had any idea who she was. She had developed into a fine art

the brushing aside of importunate questions about lovers: she never loved anyone, she said. Men, of course; men, she implied disparagingly, were plentiful as flies in summer and for the most part just about as tiresome. On 3 April 1909, it was reported that she would marry a Prince Mavrocordato; a few days later the story was that he had proposed but been rejected in favour of three further years of devotion to spinsterhood and art. On 4 October, she was about to take the veil, and then on the 24th she was not. There was also the Pasha. An engagement-ring was flashed at reporters to demonstrate the existence of the Pasha who would shortly be arriving from Turkey to claim his bride, with, as a delighted reporter for the *Chicago Tribune* put it, '78 Turkish ladies in bifurcated hobble skirts' who would plead with her not to marry him. It was all part of the fun of her fame. She enjoyed the press conferences and the reporters loved them. Moreover, she never married.

Yet, for all this extravaganza and pantomime, her art was genuine enough, and so was she. A brave little slip of a woman – she was only 5′4″ in height but everybody who saw her on stage thought of her as tall, and she kept her weight steady at 112 pounds – she had what Shaw would have seen as the Life Force within her. She wanted to be at the top, and so she was, throughout her professional life. She arrived with the new century and with the opera which, at that time, seemed to embody it. Charpentier's *Louise* – the story of working-class people and the teenage couple who defy parents and convention in the pursuit of free love – had its premiere at the Opéra-Comique on 2 February 1900 and on 13 April (a Friday) the heroine fell ill halfway through. The unknown, untried understudy took over – with the big aria, 'Depuis le jour', immediately ahead of her. The sensation, the triumph, is all part of history. She, 'la petite Garden', became the talk of Paris and followed *Louise* with *La Marseillaise*, a short-lived opera in which she played the fiancée of Rouget de Lisle, making everyone laugh – though good-naturedly – when she suddenly stood up and cried 'Je suis française!' Gabriel Pierné's *La fille du Tabarin* came next, then *La traviata*, then Manon, and, in 1902, the world premiere of *Pelléas et Mélisande*.

It seems that her foreign accent even worked in her favour with the Parisians in this. As the authors of *Dieux et Divas de l'Opéra* (Roger Blanchard and Roland de Cand, Paris, 1987) write: it 'added to the foreignness of the character, the unknown girl lost in the forest who knows neither who she is nor whence she has come'. Debussy later said that he had scarcely to tell or teach her anything; it came naturally and of its own accord. In her autobiography (Mary Garden and Louis Biancolli: *Mary Garden's Story*, Michael Joseph, 1952) she recalls her audition, when Debussy played the piano and said not a word. Eventually she was called into the office, where he was sitting. He rose, took both of her hands in his and asked where she was born. 'Aberdeen, Scotland.' 'To think', he said, 'that you had to come from the cold far North to create my Mélisande,

Garden in the title role of Février's *Gismonda* (Chicago 1919)

because that is what you are going to do, Mademoiselle.' And he added: 'Je n'ai rien à lui dire.' (I have nothing to tell her.)

There, again, is what Shaw might have recognised as the Life Force. She was a vessel for the idea of the time. 'With her,' wrote Huneker, 'the

25

THÉÂTRE NATIONAL DE L'OPÉRA-COMIQUE — SOIRÉE DU 1er JUIN 1907

# Pelléas & Mélisande

Drame lyrique en 5 actes, tiré du théâtre de M. Maurice MAETERLINCK

*Musique de M. Claude DEBUSSY*

Décors de MM. JUSSEAUME et E. RONSIN. — Costumes de M. Ch. BIANCHINI

| | |
|---|---|
| Pelléas. | MM. Jean PÉRIER |
| Golaud. | DUFRANNE |
| Arkel . | VIEUILLE |
| Un médecin . | GUILLAMAT |
| Mélisande . | Mmes Mary GARDEN |
| Geneviève . | BROHLY |
| Le Petit Yniold. | De POUMAYRAC |

Acte I. — Scène 1 : Une forêt. — Scène 2 : Une salle dans le château. — Scène 3 : Devant le château.

Acte II. — Scène 1 : Une fontaine dans le parc. — Scène 2 : Un appartement dans le château. — Scène 3 : Devant une grotte.

Acte III. — Scène 1 : Une des tours du château, un chemin de ronde passe sous une fenêtre de la cour. — Scène 2 : Les souterrains du château. — Scène 3 : Une terrasse au sortir des souterrains. — Scène 4 : Devant le château.

Acte IV. — Scène 1 : Un corridor dans le château. — Scène 2 : Une terrasse dans la brume. — Scène 3 : Une fontaine dans le parc.

Acte V. — Un appartement dans le château.

L'orchestre sera dirigé par M. RUHLMANN

---

play-instinct is imperious; it dominates her daylight, it overflows into her dream-life.' The New Opera was to unfrock the posturing heroines, depose the swaggering tenors, unweave the brash melody and banal confrontation to remake them with kaleidoscopic subtlety. Debussy accomplished this in *Pelléas et Mélisande,* and in 1902 he had for his essential medium the intuitive receptivity of Mary Garden.

The trouble was that the New Opera could go no further in this direction than Debussy had taken it. For Garden, it was a matter of finding a new public. It was not there for her in London, in the Covent Garden of Lady de Grey and Nellie Melba. There a new opera, and a native one, was indeed tried out in the first of Garden's two brief seasons in the house. Sanguine expectations were aroused in 1902 by Herbert Bunning's *Princess Osra*, based on a novel by Anthony Hope; but first, despite the fact that author, composer and principal singer were all English-speaking, it had to be translated into French, and interest was soon lost. Better prospects seemed to lie in the New World. Oscar Hammerstein was the man to make things stir; he saw Garden's value with intuition sharp as her own, and he was willing to take a chance on the new repertoire. In the second season of his Manhattan Opera Company he introduced New York to Massenet's *Thaïs*. The opera had a mixed success with the critics, but Garden, from her first entrance scattering the rose-petals, inspired them to unprecedented flights of lyricism: 'At moments it seemed as if this creature of supple frame, slender as a sapling, pliant as a willow, wore only the garment of Eve as she moved along the boards with the stride of a tigress and the tortuousness of a serpent' (*New York Press*, 26 November 1907). No wonder the bible-belts were tightened at news of this advent. When the Paris of free love and *Louise* invaded, the whale-bone corsets (Garden let it be known that she never wore them) rattled ominously; when she sang Tosca in white satin to the Scarpia of Vanni Marcoux in black, the passions left either too little or too much to the imagination and Boston ladies turned their backs on the stage. When Salome was announced, the Chicago police decided to attend, and Billy Sunday, a popular evangelical, told her 'Miss Garden, that's a very sinful opera.'

The little woman survived all this, and more (including a dreadful year as Director of the Chicago company in which she gave America its first *Love for Three Oranges* and ran up a debt of one million dollars). She died, aged 92, in the Scotland she had left first as a girl of six. In its obituary notice, the *New York Times* drew, inevitably, upon Huneker and came up with the dizziest list of all. She was: 'A swan, did I say? A condor, an eagle, a peacock, a nightingale, a panther, a society dame, a gallery of moving-pictures, a siren, an indomitable fighter, a human woman with a heart as big as a house, a lover of sport, an electric personality, and a canny Scottish lassie who can force from an operatic manager wails of anguish because of her close bargaining over a contract; in a word, a Superwoman.' Recordings, incidentally, also suggest that, despite rumours to the contrary, she was not at all a bad singer.

# CHAPTER 6

# Friedrich Schorr

'He was the greatest!' stated the young man when the conversation turned to Friedrich Schorr and Wagnerian bass-baritones in general. There can scarcely be a proposition which I would normally feel less inclined to challenge, but one of the unwritten laws of dialectics instructs us that the surest way of making somebody think again is to shout at him in its most uncompromising form the opinion which you know to be already his own. It is in articles of faith, moreover, that the shouting tends to be loudest, and all such questions as this are bound to involve an element of faith in what we ourselves have not heard or seen. Neither I nor the young man had heard Schorr in the flesh; nor could we have heard his principal rival among contemporaries, Rudolf Bockelmann, still less his great predecessor Anton van Rooy. Among later singers in these roles there were, heaven knows, several eminent specimens of whom we had no direct experience, though between us we could probably have mustered a respectable company of Wotans and Sachses from Ludwig Hofmann to John Tomlinson. But then, of course, the compiling of even so brief a list of singers as this complicates the issue, for much depends on criteria and priorities.

Schorr was indeed one of the most honoured singers of his age. His memory is perpetuated by recordings, mostly from the late 1920s, which capture him in his prime and show a voice of unsurpassed beauty in this music. In that respect, hearing him in these, one can be very tempted, like the lady in *Hamlet*, to cry, 'O confound the rest!' Scarcely any others have that beauty of tone, enriched, as it is, by a gentle glow of warmth and humanity. The criteria, then, are emerging. Beauty, gentleness, humanity: but what if sheer blazing power is wanted as the first essential, or a darker majesty of tone, or a subtler flavouring of words? And what also if one refuses to select 'the greatest' by sound alone?

If stage-presence is placed high among the priorities, we may have to recall that for the post-war generation in our own time the standard was set by a Wotan not mentioned so far, and one of mighty physical stature: Hans Hotter. He looked the god, and it was not simply a matter of height and bearing, for a nobility of character spoke both in his acting and in the amplitude of his voice. Schorr, by contrast, was of only average height and I cannot recall any report suggesting the presence of that charismatic

Schorr as Hans Sachs in *Die Meistersinger von Nürnberg*

quality which can sometimes create an illusion of physical dominance. A vivid disappointment, in fact, was registered by P.G. Hurst, author of *The Age of Jean de Reszke* and *The Golden Age Recorded*. In *Gramophone*, July 1936, he wrote: 'I have been immensely impressed by Schorr's volume as

29

Schorr as Wotan in *Die Walküre*

broadcast, only to find disillusionment on hearing him at Covent Garden; moreover, he cuts an unimpressive figure on stage'; Van Rooy, he added, 'was in a different class altogether'. Contemporary critiques bring other surprises. In the comparison with Bockelmann, for instance, it seems on records that Schorr is, among other things, the more refined and thoughtful artist, yet a review by Ernest Newman of *Die Walküre* in 1930 says of Schorr 'his reading of the part lacks the fine intellectuality of Mr Bockelmann's'. Of his Hans Sachs, renowned (one would say) for its mellow geniality, we read in *Musical Opinion* (also 1930) that it 'just lacked a little of the easy gestures and mellow geniality required for the part'. He was of course most regularly celebrated as arch-enemy of 'the Bayreuth bark', so we do not expect to read of his 1925 Kurwenal in the *Evening Standard* that 'the bluffness of the character made him bark a bit at times'.

'Oh well,' people will say. 'Critics ...' And the rest of the sentence is understood. Still, we give those critics plenty of credence when they say what we want to hear, and so cannot quite dismiss them when their comments do not fall into line. In fact, the vast preponderance of commentary praises Schorr in the highest terms, and we will restore the balance before long. Meanwhile: some points about his remarkable life and career.

He was the son of a well-known cantor, who brought his family from Hungary to Vienna in the early 1890s and did his best to persuade the young Friedrich to take to law instead of the stage. Yet the boy had always sung, in the synogogue, at school and at home, and on a trip to America in 1912 had his first taste of life backstage and on, making an unlikely debut as the Second Monk in *I gioielli della Madonna* with Andreas Dippel's company in Philadelphia. Later that year he returned to Austria and created something of a sensation with his official debut as a 23-year-old Wotan in *Die Walküre* at Graz. 'The baby Wotan' they called him (affectionately), and it took him a few years to live that down. Prague and Cologne led to Berlin and the State Opera in 1923. Berlin led to the USA with a touring company that same year (scenery and costumes were confiscated by the American Customs on arrival as there was no money to pay duties); and then the Manhattan Opera House, where they performed, led to the Metropolitan the following season. For London he was an essential part of the great 1924 generation – Leider, Lehmann, Schumann, Olczewska, Melchior, Schorr, they were all new to Covent Garden that year.

The doors closed to him in Berlin and Bayreuth when the Nazis came to power in 1933; Vienna followed shortly afterwards. Shameful to say, Covent Garden excluded him too rather than risk their relationship with the Berlin State Opera. Schorr stayed with the Metropolitan until 1943, in his last seasons probably to help out the management, eventually retiring with a performance of *Siegfried* in which the Wanderer's staff broke in the wrong place or time and was heard to be flung aside by an exasperated god in the wings on his way out.

• By then he was already transferring a large part of his interests to teaching. In 1940 (*New York Times*, 1 December) he was urging strongly that schools should incorporate music into the essential curriculum: 'General culture today, as in great periods of the past, demands musical literacy for all.' He is sometimes named as the teacher of the baritone Cornell MacNeil, but by implication MacNeil repudiates this in his talk with Jerome Hines (*Great Singers on Great Singing*, 1982) when he names Louis Margolis, having left a previous, unnamed, teacher with whom he felt he was not making progress. Schorr's main contributions in this part of his work were probably made in his time as adviser on the German repertoire to the New York City Opera and as head of the school of music

31

in Hartford, Connecticut. He had sadly little time left, for he died of cancer in 1953. Newspapers gave his age as 64, the reference books confirming this with 2 September 1888 as his date of birth. According to Alfred Frankenstein (*Record Collector* XIX, 1971), the younger brother, Dr Eugene Schorr, stated the year to be 1889, which would tie in with the 'baby Wotan' debut late in 1912 at the age of 23.

More widespread than his personal teaching was the influence his singing had by example and reputation. His great principle was that Wagner should be sung, as far as possible, following the best Italian methods of voice-production and style. He insisted on the primary importance of the vowels, and said that he himself would approach a performance of Wotan's Farewell with as much care for the cantilena, the legato singing-line, as if it were one of the baritone solos in *Un ballo in maschera*. It is a principle to which most subsequent Wagnerian singers will at any rate pay lip-service, and some will conscientiously aim to practise it. James Morris, for instance, has said something very similar in comparatively recent times, and has recorded a Verdi-and-Wagner recital to demonstrate the unity of method.

Schorr himself had not the easy upper register of the typical Italian baritone, yet he did sing in both Verdi (*Aida*) and Puccini (*Tosca* and *Il tabarro*). In a New York concert in 1926 he included an aria from *Macbeth*. The programme had shown him (said the *New York Times*) at his most splendidly resonant in Schubert's 'Dem Unendlichen' and with his most tender *mezza voce* in Schumann's 'Du bist wie eine Blume', but the *Macbeth* aria was reported as 'the highest artistic achievement of the evening'. On records he sang the bass solos in Bach's Mass in B minor, and the 'Quoniam' is an object-lesson in the fine sonorous evenness of semiquaver runs. His *Elijah* solos, too, are treasurable examples of masterly technique and deeply felt expression. As for his Wagner, the London critics testify: 'the best Wotan in the world' (*Morning Post* 1931), 'Mr Schorr's Dutchman is even greater than his Wotan' (*Sunday Times* 1930), 'What effortless power and command of colour and varied expression! What mellow richness of full-bodied tone and infinite tenderness in the soft passages! And what nobility of style! Truly a consummate and commanding artist is Friedrich Schorr' (*Daily Telegraph* on *Die Meistersinger von Nürnberg*, 1929).

Better testimony even than that comes from the records: from the Dutchman's 'Wie aus der Ferne', Wotan's Farewell, Sachs's monologues. A special beauty of texture, a very personal character of timbre and enunciation – for whatever causes (and these are among them), the records establish themselves very quickly among the irreplacables. And, yes, it is time to make a proper response to the young man whose conviction about Schorr provoked the question-mark. He was indeed the greatest. Almost certainly. Probably.

# CHAPTER 7

# Peter Pears

In a circle of Hell not visited by Dante, singers lie wedged within grooves of the longest-playing record there ever could be. Whirled in perpetuity, they see the icicle stylus move nearer and nearer but never quite arrive, and what they hear is worse: an eternal distortion, a sound which inescapably reproduces the singer's own voice and yet is subtly, agonisingly wrong.

Sir Peter Pears rarely listened to his own records with pleasure. The magnified presence, unsolicited intimacy, unsparing close-up, went against the taste of a man in whom taste itself was a most finely developed faculty. A personal disinclination of this kind did not preclude his involvement in the recording process. Even so, it is an opinion that can be risked as a statement of fact, that Pears on record and Pears heard live were two very different things.

Readers, I am sure, can 'play' Pears' recorded voice in their heads. It comes out more or less in the tones of Dudley Moore's famous parody of Pears and Britten in a folk-cum-art song version of 'Little Miss Muffet'. Or, freeing the voice from its most readily parody-prone self in association with Britten, we might summon up the sound of it in something different, a song by Schubert perhaps, 'Im Frühling' or 'Auf dem Wasser zu singen' let's say. Here, again, there rises that highly characteristic sound, not quite a wobble and yet not quite steady; not (maybe) describable as pallid or effete yet hardly robust, resonant or forthright; not deficient in volume but not full-bodied in tone; not throaty yet making you think of the throat; not exactly 'mannered' (to use the modern jargon) yet suggesting neither the voice, nor yet the manner, of nature.

Now, the records are unmistakable Pears: there never was a recorded voice more immediately identifiable. But 'in the flesh' the balance of forces, the total impression, was different. Most crucial, perhaps, was the difference in perceived *quality* of sound. Pears' voice was remarkably pure, and even to the end it betrayed no signs of coarsening, no accretion of surface-scratch, no scrape or rattle of metallic alloy. Heard in the concert hall, it was a voice which you could settle to listen to as sound: not that his singing ever encouraged that (because sound without sense was not his line of business at all), but the quality of the voice was a pleasure in itself. It was

33

also a much more virile sound. I heard him first in *La bohème* and as the stuttering Vašek in *The Bartered Bride*, and the year would have been 1945 or '46. His voice then was slender, like his figure, clear-cut, not rich but fresh. At Covent Garden in the early years he needed more power, but later the volume increased quite remarkably, so much so that in his final and probably greatest role, as Aschenbach in *Death in Venice*, his voice impressed in all parts of the house as being ample and even full-bodied.

One vocal quality which the records do capture faithfully is what one might call the silver-grey of the voice. It is movingly present in much of the Evangelist's narration in the Bach Passions, or those songs in which the voice needs to have the experience of thought and spirituality within it, songs such as Schubert's 'Nachtstück' or 'Der Müller und der Bach'. In *Peter Grimes* it was (and is) there in 'What harbour shelters peace' and in the tormented half-consciousness of his final scene. When in *Billy Budd* Captain Vere looks in memory through the mists to the year 1797, that, too, brings back Pears as he truly and unforgettably was; and as Aschenbach, with his 'delight in fastidious choice', the mind beats on through a voice which has grown old as though specially to come to maturity for this crowning achievement.

That was in 1973: *Death in Venice* had its premiere at the Maltings on 16 June, a week before Pears' 63rd birthday (and we remember that he was to make his debut at the Metropolitan a year later still). He had, by then, a venerable, almost episcopal appearance and an authority in his own right which after Britten's death grew so as to give him a position in the world of music very rarely attained by a singer. Its justification lay not simply in past achievements but in present activity. He devoted his unabating energies to the Aldeburgh Festival and the newly founded Britten-Pears school. Additional money for this had to be raised, then courses to be organised, workshop masterclasses to be run, and until 1980 he was still singing in public. In the December of that year he had a stroke yet still remained active, and, indeed, took a Bach class at the school the day before he died. In his last years, the emotional centre of his character, which, like the good patrician he was, had been so controlled, was less firmly under restraint. People (often friends of many years) would say, after his death, that they sometimes felt they had never really known him, that there was always a point at which the reticence, the restrictions or perhaps sheer good manners, intervened. But in the last years, when the beauty of a Schubert song or of a poem by Hardy took him, he would weep; and if he heard what seemed to him a fundamental wrongness in perform-ance he could be passionately angry.

For myself, I always find it hard to think of him as old. He was so very much the young singer of our youth (I had even, as a sixth-former, collected his autograph and thought how the educated handwriting, with its neat Greek 'e's, befitted the man). At Cambridge, he gave a recital with Joan Cross, in which they included excerpts from Verdi's *Otello* (the love duet,

# PETER PEARS

JOAN CROSS
*Soprano*

PETER PEARS
*Tenor*

PETER GELLHORN
*Pianoforte*

*Programme*

I.

| | |
|---|---|
| Duet from 'L'Incoronazione di Poppea' Idole del cor mio | |
| Lament from 'Orfeo' Ah! Tu sei morta | MONTEVERDI |

Air de Margot from 'Les Troqueurs' — DAUVERGNE

*Dido and Aeneas* — PURCELL
  The Sailor's Song
  Duet and Lament

II.

| | |
|---|---|
| Divinités du Styx | |
| Bannis la crainte | GLUCK |
| Duet from 'Iphigenie en Aulide' | |

| | |
|---|---|
| Zeffiretti lusinghieri from 'Idomeneo' | |
| Serenade from 'Il Seraglio' | MOZART |
| Duet from 'Cosi fan Tutte' | |

III.

| | |
|---|---|
| Duet from Act I 'Otello' | |
| Tu! Indietro! Fuggi! from 'Otello' | |
| Desdemona's Scena | |
|   Willow Song | VERDI |
|   Ave Maria | |
| Fenton's Aria from 'Falstaff' | |
| Duet from Act IV 'La Traviata' | |

Programme for a recital at the Guildhall, Cambridge, 27 February 1949

35

the 'Ave Maria' I think, and, amazing to relate, Pears singing the 'Ora e per sempre addio'). It stood, for me, as the fine product of a properly nurtured, freshly relished, civilisation. Their encore was the duet for Tormentilla and her lover in Vaughan Williams's *The Poisoned Kiss* – 'Blue larkspur in a garden', which I've never heard since and had not heard before: a lovely piece, I thought, to be able to pull out of the hat, and, in those young days, an emblem of limitless discoveries to be made in the byways of music. At the same time his recording of Britten's *Serenade for Tenor, Horn and Strings* became an obsessive care of listening-hours, though even then one noted that the idiosyncratic, eminently imitable voice and style came out of the record as a kind of distorted magnification of certain elements in the singing one had heard 'in the flesh'.

The young singer of one generation became the almost legendary veteran of another. Alan Hollinghurst's novel, *The Swimming Pool Library* (Chatto and Windus, 1988) has a vivid and moving description of an evening at Covent Garden in which *Billy Budd* is performed, and in which the narrator sees Pears take his seat in the stalls, his 'stroke-slackened but beautiful white-crested head' evoking a powerful emotion, a sense of history, a sense, too, of the poignancy of reminiscence in the singer's mind reflecting that of the Captain Vere on stage: 'seeing other singers performing it; on the same stage in the same sets as he had done decades before, under the direction of the man he loved'. The narrator in the novel and his friend share the emotion that the presence of the singer has induced, while the grandfather, whose box they are in, remarks, 'Many people, understandably, didn't altogether care for the Britten-Pears thing.' The 'thing' – the love of these two men – was, of course, the subject of many a knowing joke, yet my impression is that most people found this moving too, and when Britten's final illness brought him to unconsciousness I think there was an overwhelming sense of rightness, and of sanctity, in the understanding that he died in Pears' arms.

Many singers have at some time been close to a composer, but there is probably not one whose closeness has been as lasting and productive as that of Pears to Britten. The special nature of Britten's writing for the tenor voice is – I won't say inseparable from Pears' voice, as singers have now come along and made the separation – but it is inconceivable as a creation without the fact of Pears having been there to inspire it. The notes in head-voice, the intervals with a particular kind of portamento linking them, the call sometimes for a greyed colouration, the implicit assurance of a singer able to respond to delicate, ambiguous shifts of harmony: all of these features have Pears for their fulfilment.

The very choice of literary texts implies a tenor of fine sensibility and rich cultural resources. 'I loathe what people normally call a beautiful voice,' Britten once said, adding that it was like over-ripe fruit, without flavour or meaning. He did consider Pears' voice to be beautiful, but its supremely distinctive feature was the inexhaustible capacity for expres-

sion. Donne's *Holy Sonnets*, Hardy's *Winter Words*, the language of me-
diaeval poets and the King James Bible: from a composer's point of view,
the performance of his settings was half-way to fulfilment if the singer
already had the literature within him.

Pears had this background, and also the receptivity of spirit to extend
it. Finally, he was one of the great originals among singers, and, like others
in that small band, he is one to learn from but not to copy – especially in
that strange mixture of truth and distortion that is found in his records.

37

# CHAPTER 8

# Walter Widdop

Widdop and Pears were – and, because of their recordings, are – antithetical: at least that will do for a start as a working proposition. Primarily, Widdop's power lay in power itself: he was a Siegfried, a Tristan, a Radamès and a Samson. His style was forthright where Pears' was subtle. He delivered with the directness of his northern working-class ancestors, while everything about Pears declared the patrician public-school and university southerner. One can no more imagine Widdop singing Britten's 'Queen and huntress chaste and fair' than one can Pears in Siegfried's Forging Song or, for that matter, Maccabeus' call to arms.

To today's listeners they offer quite different kinds of pleasure (and I don't see, though some do, that they need be mutually exclusive). To students they teach quite different lessons (and here a certain amount of picking and choosing is certainly advisable). Records have also served them very differently: Pears will long be remembered independently of his records, or almost in spite of them, whereas Widdop's reputation gains steadily on their account, and indeed without them his name might today be almost entirely forgotten.

In terms of years, they were not so very distant, Widdop, born in 1892, being 18 years the senior, rather less than the difference in years between, say, Alfredo Kraus and José Carreras. They seem, nevertheless, to be an age apart. Pears remains distinctly a modern singer, musically educated in the complexities of a modern idiom, while Widdop is seen essentially as a traditionalist who would probably have been much happier in the company of his elders such as Edward Lloyd and Sims Reeves. In kind, Pears was the musician-singer who today is found in those terrifyingly expert groups which can faultlessly sight-read anything from Machaut to Messiaen. Widdop, under other circumstances, would have led the tenors in some northern choral society's annual *Messiah*.

Yet perhaps even at this point it is time to refine a little on these blunt antitheses. Widdop was no musical clod. Simply in the matter of repertoire he extended himself far more broadly than the main lines of this account would suggest. In 1934, for example, he took the part of the Drum-Major in the first British broadcast of *Wozzeck*, and in 1936 sang the title role in Stravinsky's *Oedipus Rex*. At Covent Garden his appearances included the

Widdop as Siegfried (Covent Garden 1935)

world premiere, in 1929, of Eugene Goossens' *Judith*. He sang in Mahler's Eighth Symphony and was frequently on call for *Das Lied von der Erde*. His oratorios included *The Dream of Gerontius* and *The Kingdom*, and he was among the sixteen soloists chosen for the first performance of Vaughan Williams' *Serenade to Music*. When last involved in a studio

recording it was as Aegisth in *Elektra*, and, if the mastery of difficult scores is in question, we have to remind ourselves that the Wagnerian roles in which he specialised are hardly child's play.

The unsophisticated background does, of course, make such an achievement all the more remarkable. Widdop left school at 12, which you could do in those days, and he went into the local woollen mill. This was at Sowerby Bridge near Norland in Yorkshire where he sang in the choir at St Luke's. When the war came in 1914 he joined the army, and it was not until 1922 that he started to think in earnest about singing. Much earlier, one of his workmates had told him: 'If ah 'ad tha' voice, lad, ah'd mak messen some brass,' and even before that the organiser of a chapel concert to whom he had protested that he couldn't sing said: 'Tha can and doesn't know it.' By the age of 30 he began to think that there might be something in it after all, and took advice from the bass Norman Allin.

Somehow, 'brass' in sufficient quantities was obtained for lessons with Dinh Gilly in London, and when that was all gone he presented himself to Allin again. Luckily there was an opening: dramatic tenors can not have been too plentiful in those days any more than now, and he was engaged to sing Radamès and Samson (Saint-Saëns' version) on tour with the British National Opera Company, whose winter season, early in 1924, took them to Covent Garden. Widdop's London debut, as both Siegfried and Siegmund, took place on 25 January and it has a place in the annals on three counts. Its rehearsal was held in a London drawing-room set up as Mime's cave and with the fire-irons for props. The event itself took a still more remarkable turn as the Brünnhilde failed to arrive for Act III of *Siegfried* so Act I of *Die Walküre* was substituted. And the third count is that out of this farrago there emerged a new and notable *Heldentenor*.

What followed was an important and successful career, yet not so successful and important as it should have been. Listening to the best of his records, one thinks, 'Surely this was international,' and to some extent it was: he sang opera in Spain, oratorio in Holland and songs in America. Yet the career remained homebound and limited. Its limitations no doubt owed something to those of his own nature and capacity. He seems, for one thing, never to have been much of an actor. Sometimes a review would offer encouragement, and when in 1925 he sang in the *Ring* at Manchester the *Musical Times* went so far as to say that his Siegfried 'embodied the Wagnerian ideal of sensual life in its natural and joyous fulness'. That could not be said of his portrayal of the Chief Eunuch in *Judith* (the part was apparently supposed to be a comic one, but Widdop seems not to have seen the funny side of it and was said to have looked more like Siegfried with a beard). In Gluck's *Armide* in 1928 the *Star*'s critic described his acting as 'sincere but a little too restrained', though the singing was fine, filling the theatre 'without a trace of effort'. The following year, Alfred Kalisch, writing of his performance in *Die Walküre*, observed that he had made 'strides in acting'. Yet a certain stiffness persisted, and with it an inhibition of temperament or imagination: he 'lacked subtlety of inflexion' reported *The Times* of his Tristan in 1933, while Cardus found his Parsifal 'not spiritual enough' and noted that in the drinking songs of *Das Lied von der Erde* 'the English habit of mild geniality' ensured that 'the mouth was never purple-stained'. Despite hard work and what they called 'a certain facility', his pronunciation of German betrayed its origins, and that, too, was reckoned a handicap for a tenor whose speciality was Wagner.

Against these quibbles must be placed two tributes from people who really knew about singing and whose praises may be worth all the rest. As crabby a critic as you could find when he felt like taking a post-golden-age singer to task was P.G. Hurst, who, writing in *Gramophone* (July 1936), contended that 'Walter Widdop is worlds better than any visiting German tenor since the war, and yet we have to put up with imported Teutons who turn our thoughts to murder.' This found an echo in the bosom of another writer who surveyed the next year's season in retrospect (*Gramophone*, August 1937): 'There are two hundred opera houses in Germany to whom Widdop would be a godsend ... It is waste in an era of famine for a singer with his material and skill to go round the country year after year singing in *Messiah* when he could be singing Lohengrin, Tannhäuser, Siegfried and Parsifal. After two years routine on the German stage he would be one of the four leading heroic tenors in Europe.' The author styled himself 'Beckmesser', but I believe that to have been a pseudonym of Walter Legge.

Apart from making one wonder who at least two of the three European rivals might have been (Max Lorenz and Franz Völker perhaps), Beckmesser's pronouncement sends one on one's way rejoicing, back to the records. These were made mostly between 1924 and 1930. They have been re-emerging for some time now on compact disc, the surfaces nicely freed from the gunge and crackle that seemed inseparable from so many of those old brown-label records on 78s. They include plenty of Wagner, but it isn't primarily the Wagner that draws me, fine as much of it is. Treating myself to a home-made programme of Widdop, I think it would begin and end with Handel. 'He that dwelleth in Heaven shall laugh them to scorn,' promises the recitative, and then, with fine Old Testament relish, comes the aria, 'Thou shalt break them.' Beckmesser seemed to think it a fate worse than death for a tenor of Widdop's kind to 'go round year after year' singing *Messiah*; but I must say I would go to hear that great work a good deal more often if I thought there was a chance of hearing singing like this. It is forceful and smooth in just the right proportions and places – the opposite, one might say, of the modern school, which hasn't the virility of tone to provide the force, or (generally) the technique to sing the runs with this evenness.

That would be followed by more Handel, the *Jephtha* solos, which make eloquent contrast and alert one to something else about Widdop, again providing commentary on those blunt antitheses with which we started. One of the critics complained of a lack of spirituality: not here, however.

I'd go then to *Elijah*, sung out good and strong, and with a soul to it. Gounod's 'Lend me your aid' and a few other grand nineteenth-century things would come next – and be played twice, for their sheer magnificence. Then some songs – 'Tom Bowling' perhaps, and even 'I know of two bright eyes': tender, restrained and very, very much of their period. For Wagner, some *Lohengrin*, and a two-minute silence to remember that Widdop died a singer's death: he sang Lohengrin's Farewell at a Promenade Concert in 1949, collapsed in his dressing-room immediately afterwards and died the next day. And finally I revive him with the best of all: 'Sound an alarm' from *Judas Maccabeus*, after which who shall say that he was not already 'one of the four leading heroic tenors in Europe'? And why stop at Europe?

CHAPTER 9

# Irina Arkhipova

It seems strange and perhaps not very respectful to find oneself saying about a distinguished singer that she has dissolved into a smile, yet that, for me, is what the great Russian mezzo-soprano Irina Arkhipova has done. It comes about as a result of her recent appearances in London, in which she combined the role of singer with that of grand old lady and benevolent teacher, pupils in tow. She gave a concert at the Wigmore Hall in 1994 commemorating the 150th anniversary of Rimsky-Korsakov's birth and introducing the young Bashkirian bass, Askar Abdrasakov. Programmes and articles are somewhat reticent on the subject of her own birthday, and the encyclopaedias lack unanimity – Kutsch and Riemens' *Dictionary of Singers* has 2 January 1925, while the *New Grove Dictionary of Opera* agrees about day and year but transfers the event to December. Either way, at the time of this London recital she was in her 70th year, and older again by 15 months when she returned in February 1996.

On that occasion the pupil was a soprano, and a strikingly good one, Natalia Datsko. As before, teacher and pupil sang duets, and then there were smiles all round. Arkhipova's is a wonderful face for smiles: it has something to do with the high cheek-bones and still more with a light in the eyes. One almost felt that when she left the platform, her smile remained behind – like the Cheshire cat in *Alice in Wonderland*, except that there the expression was a grin, which is knowing, just slightly sinister and suggestive of complicity, whereas here it expressed nothing but delight and good will.

Of course one has only to play some records to summon back the rest of her, the most important part, which is the sound of her voice in earlier years. And what a voice it was! Recently re-issued, the original recording of Prokofiev's *War and Peace* under Melik-Pashayev has Vishnevskaya as Natasha, Lisitsian as Napoleon, and a number of others who were well established in what was then the Soviet Union and not entirely unknown over here, even if only as recording artists. But the first voice to make one sit up and consult the cast-list is that of the Countess Hélène who, in the second scene, has just two lines to sing; and this is the young Arkhipova. The recording dates from 1961, not long after she had come to enviable prominence at the Bolshoi with a Carmen sung opposite Mario del

43

Monaco: that, too, is on record, but not for the faint-hearted. Better for sampling are some Russian arias recorded in the Sixties, such as a tender and increasingly passionate farewell to the forests from Tchaikovsky's *Maid of Orleans*, and a beautifully even, deeply felt song from Prokofiev's music for *Alexander Nevsky* in which a bride on the eve of battle tells how she will walk over the field of the slain and kiss those who have died for Russia. There are also some excellent song-recordings from this period, including Tchaikovsky's Serenade, the one set to words by the Grand Duke Konstantin, with a delightful accompaniment, haunting melody and beautifully shaded singing.

In all of this, though the expressiveness of her art is also considerable, it is the health and fine focus of a completely steady, wide-ranging voice that attracts: splendidly firm, excitingly vibrant on high without a hint of tremolo or spread, and full-bodied though never plummy. This was the sound that, a little bit late in the day, reached the West on records, and (in advance of the other houses) La Scala in person.

It is sad, unjust too, that the wider reputation of a Russian singer should have depended so largely on appearances abroad. Arkhipova's career was centred on the Bolshoi where she sang first in 1956. Though habitually listed among the great opera houses of the world, the Bolshoi was still remote, little up-to-date news of its achievements reaching us; and if we tried to follow even so prominent a singer as Arkhipova in the columns of *Opera* magazine, this primary source is simply not there. Only when the Bolshoi visits Milan or Paris does news permeate concerning its singers. As it happens, Arkhipova's European debut as Carmen in Naples, 1961, went unreported too, but only because at the covered performance she was indisposed.

In 1967, however, with the Bolshoi at La Scala for *Khovanshchina* and *Boris Godunov*, we read of a 'splendid' Marfa and a 'splendid' Marina. In Paris three years later, Arkhipova was 'a splendidly firm-voiced and regal-looking Marina', and at the Orange Festival of 1971 she shone as 'the real star of the evening' in *Il trovatore*. At Buenos Aires in this same opera she was accounted 'the only singer who deserved the applause received' (July 1974), while at Covent Garden 'she pierced beneath the context of a star-studded performance to what Verdi and the music really mean' (January 1975). At this point she should have gone on to a debut at the Metropolitan in New York and a regular and prominent place in the Western recording-lists. That never happened, and though she sang on for many more years in opera at home and abroad, her career probably peaked about this time, with a celebration of her 20th anniversary at the Bolshoi, singing Carmen, the opera of her debut.

It was at the Covent Garden *Trovatore* of 1975 that I myself heard Arkhipova for the first time. She made a strong impression though the voice was not entirely what recordings had led one to expect. The cast was indeed a distinguished one, with Montserrat Caballé producing in the last act some of the most heavenly sounds ever heard ('Gemente aura', and that last phrase of recitative lifted, vertiginously, to a glimpse of Paradise). Sherrill Milnes was the powerful Di Luna, and it is possible that had I been sitting not in the front stalls but up in the gods the balance between him and Arkhipova might have been reversed – he generally seemed to me better heard close-to, and she, one gathered from others present, had projected well throughout the house. Still, it was not a Bumbry voice, or a Rita Gorr or Cossotto – that point was emphasised by comparison with the fully competitive singing on another occasion of Cossotto and Carlo Cossutta, who was the Manrico of this performance also. In her duets with this very ample tenor, Arkhipova sounded, not small, but (say) compact.

In fact her real distinctions struck me as lying elsewhere. One distinction was visual: she was rather wildly be-wigged and favoured the grand gesture yet still gave a genuine acting performance. The other was in sheer musical scrupulousness and refinement. All the detailed markings in 'Condotta ell'era in ceppi' and later in 'Giorni poveri vivea' were not only observed but absorbed, to such fine, concentrated effect that she held the attention in a way that could not have been commanded by mere volume.

Her other role at Covent Garden was less succcessful. Ulrica (or Madame Arvidson), the fortune-teller in *Un ballo in maschera*, needs to have steely-strong low notes in her first solo and then an opulence in the upper register for the triumphant 'E lui!'. But this performance took place in 1988, when she was already over 60, and, as she told John Allison in an interview for *Opera* (April 1995), it was never a favourite part ('I adore the difficult notes in Amneris; Eboli and Azucena I love doing, but Ulrica I find hard'). The great Russian roles were missed over here: we never had a chance of hearing her Joan of Arc in Tchaikovsky's opera, or (and from recordings this sounds magnificent) Lyubasha in *The Tsar's Bride*. Marfa in *Khovanshchina* was at any rate sampled in recitals, Paulina (of *The Queen of Spades*) too, and, most recently and vividly (in 1996), the old Countess.

And like the Countess in this respect at least, Arkhipova has become something of a legend in her lifetime. In Russia her status is unique among living singers, partly because in spite of her international fame she has stayed back there with them. The comparison with her almost exact contemporary, Galina Vishnevskaya (born 1926), is inevitable. Neither of them can have had an easy upbringing, the Arkhipovas leaving Moscow for Tashkent when the war started; but the horrors of Vishnevskaya's childhood and wartime seem to have no counterpart. Arkhipova's autobiography, *My Muses* (Moscow, 1992), tells of an altogether more equable nature, less sharp-minded, less contentious. She came through the Stalin era and the regimes before perestroika without apparent bitterness (fully aware nonetheless, of the KGB on her tail when she would have liked to to get to know her Italian Don José better). Equally, she has learned to live with the new times, though none too happy about their effect upon the arts

46

and the conditions for young singers. She is, one feels, positive in outlook, a believer in getting on with the job and using her senior authority for the good of the younger generation. Hence the teaching, the adjudicating, and the institution of the Arkhipova Fund for the furtherance of Russian culture. Hence, also, the pupils in tow at her concerts in London.

It was in respect of them that her smiles on these occasions were broadest. They warmed, too, as she sang; and well they might, for despite some tatters in its mortal dress, this was still a voice to reckon with. I remember wondering which other mezzo in history could parallel this at the age of 70 – and a name did occur to me, an illustrious one too. 'She was the most beloved of singers,' said the wife of a famous New York critic in 1935 on hearing of the death of Ernestine Schumann-Heink. She, too, was a great smiler, and she sang almost to the day of her death at the age of 75. In the interval of Arkhipova's last concert at the Wigmore, some Russians came up and chatted. They talked of her voice and its marvellous preservation, of her accomplishments as a painter and architect (some of the buildings she designed can still be seen). And then one of them added: 'In Moscow she is simply the best loved of all.'

CHAPTER 10

# Mattia Battistini

Turning out a bottom drawer with the idea of transferring some of its contents to the so-called filing system, I am waylaid by a bundle of envelopes addressed in the carefully formed, shaky handwriting of the very old. In the top left-hand corner of the uppermost, my own hand of 15 years ago affronts the dignity of the correspondent's fountain-pen with a ballpoint inscription reading, 'BATTISTINI'. The letters came from an old man who, some 40 years earlier, had heard him.

He was not the first or the only person of my acquaintance who had heard Battistini 'in the flesh', but none of the others seemed to remember anything. To this 83-year-old it was as clear as yesterday (and probably clearer). The year was 1922, and the great man – 'King of Baritones', as legend has it – had not sung in London since the golden summer season of 1906. His operas then had been *Don Giovanni* (Destinn and, yes, Caruso in the cast, Messager conducting), *Rigoletto* and *Traviata* (with Melba and, again, Caruso), and *Eugene Onegin*, given with such success that the work was never heard again at Covent Garden until 1971. At his reappearance in London, Battistini was 70: the Queen's Hall was filled to capacity.

'When he appeared,' wrote my correspondent, 'we saw an elderly man, solidly built, slightly on the stout side, but of enormous dignity. We were almost back in Victorian times, for he wore white kid gloves and carried a piece of sheet music. To great applause he bowed graciously – almost, I should say, royally ... and we waited expectantly.' His opening aria, apparently, was from Saint-Saëns' *Henry VIII* (this, I think, places the event as the second recital, on Friday 12 May, and, incidentally, accounts for the 'capacity audience'). It was an unexpected selection, and was taken for a sort of 'warm up'. But, says the writer: 'After a dozen bars we sat back (at least I did) and knew that nothing could go wrong.' A dozen of the most testing nineteenth-century Italian arias followed. 'And then came the encores. The audience would not let him go. His voice was even better than when he started and one sensed he truly loved singing for its own sake.' He gave them the Prologue to *Pagliacci*, 'Largo al factotum', 'Quand'ero paggio' and ('light as thistledown') 'La danza'.

In his next letter (the writing now more arthritic) my correspondent reported on the other Battistini recital he attended: 'most vividly I remem-

48

Battistini as Valentin in *Faust*

ber a glittering rendering of Gluck's "Spiaggate amate". It wasn't Gluck by a long chalk but technically marvellous.' And he concludes: 'The greatest singer I ever heard', doubly underlining 'singer'. Then he goes on, as I think I must have asked him to, to tell of the other famous baritone who appeared in concert in London that very same week: Titta Ruffo. The coincidence of these two major exponents, representing the younger (Ruffo) and the older (Battistini) generation (there were 21 years between them), led to much comparing, contrasting, shaking of heads and estab-

49

lishing of preferences. Most took sides – the critics being all for Battistini. My man revelled in both. Again he gives a lively account of the scene. All of Italy in London was there and the noise of their preparatory enjoyment was already an uproar. 'Finally the moment came. The pianist walked on with his music and then we heard the opening bars of "Largo al factotum". The applause rather spoiled Ruffo's entrance for he had obviously arranged it carefully. A man of medium build with a large head and mouth bounced – literally – on to the platform beaming with jollity. However, the reception was such that, despite the huge voice, not a note could be heard and the whole business had to start again!' Those were the days. His high G brought the house down, the encores were innumerable (Tosti, Denza and 'a big group of Neapolitan tunes'), and 'when he finally was allowed to go I remember feeling stupefied by so much power and richness of voice – not the exhilaration I was to feel later after hearing Battistini'. The press, he says, praised Ruffo, 'but the criticism was not on the same level that greeted the concerts of Battistini'.

Actually, such press reports as I have read came down rather heavily against Ruffo, and, sincere as I'm sure was their regard for Battistini, they also used the veteran baritone as a stick for beating the noisy upstarts of modern times. A lengthy essay by Herman Klein in *The Sackbut* (Vol. 2 No. 10) expounds the view of 'the establishment':

> Battistini came out of the ordeal with higher honours. His first audience was not half the size of Titta Ruffo's nor half so noisy and ill-mannered. Yet by force of rare freshness and beauty of tone – unequalled in a man of his years since the days of Sims Reeves and Santley – consistent elegance and finish of style, coupled with a consummate mastery of phrasing and expression, it was easily the elder exemplar of the *bel canto* who won the real triumph.

Klein (himself a veteran almost of Battistini's years) went on to tell of technique and repertoire, and then located his comparison of styles and schools in the 'page' song 'Quand'ero paggio' from *Falstaff*, which both singers included as an encore (Ruffo, he says, 'no fewer than three times'):

> No more eloquent illustration could have been furnished of the contrast between the method of the two men – the one sustained, suave, polished, clear as crystal; the other staccato, crisp, half murmured, half sung, with a headlong rush at the end. Herein by the test of diction, Battistini gave us the perfect union of word and tone; we could hear every syllable; his tempo and accelerando to the ultimate 'gentile' were actually as Maurel was shown by Verdi. Titta Ruffo juggled with his words until we lost them, and mouthed with tone so that melody vanished and only rhythm remained ... One, then, was a piece of true singing, the other a trick of rapid speech in the same genre that made of the 'Largo al factotum' a noisy, vulgar medley of shouting and patter.

The whole article is worth turning up, for it has a good deal more to say

BATTISTINI

about Ruffo; and, as I suggested, it is fairly representative of the 'establishment' viewpoint. At least one dissenting voice was raised, and though it took some time to make itself heard (for the owner was then a teenager) it became a very powerful one. To young Walter Legge, Ruffo was a miracle, a *non-pareil*; and years afterwards (spoiling for a fight) he said to me, rhetorically, 'Tell me, did Battistini make *any* good records?'

Indeed he did, though the sound of them may fall strangely upon modern ears. Return to them in a moment, but first (it must be a question in younger readers' minds) – who *was* he, this 'King of Baritones', this

51

septuagenarian celebrity who commanded such honour among connoisseurs?

He was born near Rome in 1856 and his career dates from 1878 when he sang in *La favorita* (50 years later he prepared to celebrate his golden jubilee in the same role, but within a few months of the event he fell ill and this final triumph was denied him). Throughout his career he remained associated with the so-called bel canto repertoire, which was becoming ever more old-fashioned, but he kept up with Verdi, too, and sang also in *Tannhäuser* and *Lohengrin*. He was a famous Don Giovanni, and Massenet adapted the role of Werther specially for him. Many of his greatest triumphs took place in Moscow, St Petersburg and Warsaw, where he had indeed a colossal reputation. In those years he travelled around Europe like a prince, with 30 large trunks in tow, containing his costumes and stamped royally with the initials MB.

Such was the legend who appeared before Londoners in 1922 and again in the following two years. He had by no means renounced his operatic career, and was still to be heard in *Traviata, Un ballo in maschera* and *Tosca* as late as 1925. He gave his last concert in 1927 and died on 7 November 1928. Though he sang in South America during his early years, he developed (so it was said) a horror of the Atlantic crossing and refused all invitations to the States. He remains one of the few great singers not to have sung at the Met.

His records are still with us, the earliest made at Warsaw in 1902, the last ones just on the brink of electrical recording in 1924. They tell a fascinating tale, of the refinements of another age and sometimes a forceful anticipation of the very style which critics such as Klein set him up to oppose.

If I close my eyes now and open my 'inner' ears I can hear him very clearly from records, just as my correspondent said he could do, to that day, from hearing him 'in the flesh'. It is a voice of extraordinary beauty in the upper middle register: the purity, flawless texture and firm production create a thirst to hear immediately and not with just the 'inner ear'. More than that, he had the panache and accomplishment of a virtuoso always ready to hand, with the firm support of a fine Italian school behind him.

More still: he sings from his soul. Tagged with the somewhat abstract loveliness (vaguely anti-intellectual, anti-expressive) of 'bel canto', he is misrepresented. He was, in fact, highly expressive and by no means given to abstract loveliness. When my correspondent doubly underlined the word 'singer', he must not be misunderstood. 'His singing was a good deal more than just *bel canto*,' he remarks: he was also a singer-actor in whom 'the real acting came through his voice', and in these terms, we remember, not merely 'King of Baritones' but 'the greatest singer I ever heard'.

CHAPTER 11

# Maria Jeritza

Jeritza is the subject of a particularly delightful chapter in Nigel Douglas's second volume, *More Legendary Singers* (London, 1994): he says most of what needs saying and tells all the best stories. That, plus the fact that she has never (through her records) been a favourite of the present writer's, might have ensured her exclusion from these pages. Yet here she is, and here, I fancy, she will always be when singers of the twentieth century are extensively discussed. She has, for one thing, an impressive list of 'creations' to her name – the first Ariadne in Strauss's opera, the first Empress in *Die Frau ohne Schatten*, Austria's first Minnie in *La fanciulla del West*, Turandot in the American and Austrian premieres of that opera. In Vienna she was the star of stars; at the Metropolitan she commanded a salary as large as Caruso's had been just before her. She brought an excitement into the opera house such as better singers (Elisabeth Rethberg, for example) failed to generate. She was also astonishingly beautiful.

But one comes back to those records of hers, the only extraordinary feature of which is their ordinariness. Her fame, after all, was that of something sensational. Like or dislike a performance of Jeritza's in the theatre, one could not (we understand) be indifferent. She was, for example, a sensational Carmen – and by most accounts sensationally bad – yet her recording of the Habanera is as dull as any ever made. Neither in timbre nor expression is it in the least seductive, and all that can be called exotic is her pronunciation of French. On the other side of the original disc was Carmen's *Chanson bohèmienne*, 'Les tringles des sistres se tintaient', and here the voice has more body, the singing more energy, but still she provides nothing that amounts to character. In a whole variety of roles (Agathe, Elsa, Santuzza, La Gioconda, Fedora) she seems in these solo studio recordings to be innocent of any notion that, these being individual women, the tone and style of her singing might in some way reflect their individuality. And when it comes to her most celebrated role of all, that of Tosca, whose 'Vissi d'arte' she so famously sang from the floor, the ordinariness is at its height. She did, indeed, record the aria twice, the first time in 1914, where there is a hint of pleading and pathos at the start. But in the second, from 1928, scarcely a distinguishing feature emerges, whether of power or quality, phrasing or feeling. Posthumously (since this constitutes part of her memorial), the Tosca *prostrata* is brought low in a different sense, for one scarcely looks at her. In a sequence of recorded 'Vissi d'arte's, this would pass virtually unnoticed.

Now, there are better elements in Jeritza's studio recordings but the general observation remains true, that they tell nothing exciting about this woman who so evidently could be an exciting artist. That she *was* an artist, not just a personality and a beauty, seems beyond dispute if one reads contemporary accounts. For instance, when she sang first at Covent Garden in 1925, there sat in the audience a man whose praise counted for something if only because he had heard practically every Tosca of note, at any rate in London and New York; he was also habitually critical, not exactly a dyed-in-the-wool 'golden ager' but a veteran who reckoned to have high standards, for which, in turn, his word counted for much in the world where singers' reputations were won and lost. He also had heard Jeritza's records and, while having reservations, was by no means dismissive about them. The sound of her voice in the theatre, however, became quite a different matter and in combination with her acting and stage-presence impressed him deeply. 'Magnificent,' was Herman Klein's word for her acting (*Gramophone*, July 1925), and 'an intensely striking and superb performance,' was his summary of her Tosca. 'Tenderness alternates with jealousy in the church scene; anxiety, charm and resentment with burning rage, despair, gloating, satisfied vengeance in the terrific duet with Scarpia.' And in the 'Vissi d'arte': 'she half murmurs, half weeps the bitter plaint ... with an intensity of emotion such as no Tosca off the stage has ever yet dared to put into a gramophone record.'

Not all the London critics were as captivated as Klein, and no doubt (quite apart from a knee-jerk reaction to the hype which preceded the debut) they had good reasons. But 'PP' of the *Evening Standard* was probably not far wrong when he wrote: 'There is nothing like an electric emotional success for the complete annoyance of the superior person, and the superior person in music is so very superior. So there are – and would inevitably be – those who were mildly funny about Jeritza as La Tosca, about her wonderful blonde hair, her hysteria before Scarpia, her dresses, her panther movements. But ... the calmest and most merciless judgment could give no verdict but a favourable one on the voice. She is incomparably the finest dramatic soprano Covent Garden has known for 25 years.'

In New York, Klein's oracular counterpart (but with a sharper edge to his utterances) was W.J. Henderson of the *Sun*. Reporting on the new *Tosca* (1 December 1921) he wrote: 'It was more significantly unconventional in the larger sense, in that it put a new and enthralling vitality into the role which has threatened to become restrained by routine. Mme. Jeritza does not look the ideal Tosca [Tosca is described as 'bruna' and has 'occhi neri'] but she sang and acted the part entrancingly. Her singing was her principal histrionic asset, as singing always must be with a really

Jeritza as Turandot (Vienna)

Jeritza with Gentleman Jim Corbett

great operatic artist. The short recitative passages, which have so often gone without apparent meaning, she read with luminous intelligence giving every phrase, every word, every syllable a value.'

'Luminous intelligence,' we note. That has to be stored up against a whole battery of aspersions that, if not exactly the dumb blonde of convention, she was at any rate the 'dumme Ganz' (or silly goose) of Strauss's (not unaffectionate) rebuke during rehearsal.

Certainly Jeritza was not noted for the accuracy of her singing, and one wonders what those celebrated Strauss premieres were like, for her great rival Lotte Lehmann, though generally credited with more in the way of brains, was often none too sure of the details herself. The two of them have a good old laugh about it in a post-war broadcast which was supposed to have effected a reconciliation. They admit to not having been always note-perfect, 'but we gave the public what they wanted,' says Lehmann. That won't really do for us nowadays (nowadays we are all superior persons), but it accords with a feeling that comes strongly as one listens to the few 'live' recordings. With Jeritza they go far to bridge the credibility-gap between studio-sound and opera-house experience. They are also a reason for writing about her just now.

An exciting and valuable collection of 'historical' recordings has recently been issued on the Koch-Schwann International label containing fragments of performances at the Vienna State Opera House from as long ago as 1933. Jeritza is heard in short but vivid excerpts from *Die Walküre*, *Salome* and *Cavalleria rusticana*. They make an immense difference to what we can learn of her with our own ears. She is almost another singer. The voice projects, a good house-filling sound, and it is now one that proclaims its identity.

But more than that, there is a kind of rapture in the singing. With the superb Friedrich Schorr, she gives heartfelt intensity to the passages from *Walküre*, Act 3. Her Salome has the seductive magic of long-drawn phrases and concentrated feeling. The *Cavalleria rusticana* duets have moments of quiet, indrawn tenderness and (with Alfio) a crowning top C, (with Turiddu) a curse to carry to the grave.

At the time of these performances, Jeritza, born in 1887, had reached the mid-forties, just a few years past her prime. Still, hearing, we can believe. And, although the style is of its period (or perhaps earlier), it is that of a fully engaged artist – she is not a joke.

Her memory, it's true, has a smile, a laugh even, attached to it. There are so many stories: 'Gigli not nice to me tonight,' for instance. These were her words, vouched for by attentive long-stayers after the show was finished and Jeritza came before the curtain at last to take her curtain-call. She said them between sobs, and the rights and wrongs were debated over a period of ten days (12-22 February 1925) in the *New York Times*. Some thought it a publicity stunt (another one); others held that Gigli was a terror for contriving curtain calls for himself alone, and that it was enough to make any self-respecting (and modest) prima donna weep.

This was the singer to whom Strauss repeatedly entrusted demanding roles, dedicated one of his *Four Last Songs* and wrote another called 'Malven', discovered in manuscript after her death. She was one whose beauty of voice can be discerned in some early records (from *Ariadne auf Naxos* and Goldmark's *Das Heimchen am Herd*, for instance). Her beauty of face and figure is captured in countless photographs and, fitfully and flickeringly, in a film called *Grossfürstin Alexandra* in which she plays, with charm and restraint, opposite the great Leo Slezak. She is at last captured convincingly in sound by those precious fragments from the stage in Vienna. And perhaps best of all, the impression she made 'in the flesh' is defined by another woman – and one who was not too jealous. 'She had a Wagnerian type of voice,' said the 90-year-old soprano Mary Ellis in a broadcast earlier this year, and 'she was just like a sunrise, golden and slim and beautiful.'

CHAPTER 12

# Ljuba Welitsch

For those who heard Ljuba Welitsch in her prime, the news of her death (31 August 1996) will have recalled a sudden brightness that quickened the pulse and, in post-war London, proclaimed life beyond the Age of Austerity. A shining, indomitable voice, a centre-stage personality, a radiant tousle of sunburn hair, a flash of eye and lithe, unpredictable movement: with these came the solid virtues of a technique that guaranteed absolute firmness of tone and an even, well-bound singing line. She was also the most elementally exciting new singer of the decade.

Unfortunately, that was it. When I myself first heard her, the year was 1953, and the decade had passed. She sang Lisa in *The Queen of Spades*, and I remember listening intently through that packed first scene, with its soldiers and children and nursemaids, for the voice which was to penetrate with a thrust of timbre instantly recognisable. It should have come to us, up there in the gallery, like sunlight on the golden onion of a Moscow church. But no: here was the quintet, and that mild soprano, identifiable indeed but principally on account of the foreign accent (the performance was in English), singing as to herself, gleamed more like a very small candle on a very large birthday cake.

Disappointment became blank acceptance in the second scene, which opens with the two girls in duet. Years later, Monica Sinclair, the Paulina of those performances, told me how she had to sing *mezza voce* throughout and play the spinet accompaniment as softly as possible; yet it was her voice that reached us easily and amply, while the soprano (one would have said) had a voice for another, and smaller, house. It was a pure sound, and a pretty one, with something of a special character that progressively focused attention; but tiny.

What had I expected? No doubt the voice as heard in the recordings made only a short time before, where Lisa's solos, sung in German, have the characteristic incisiveness and which rise gloriously in climax. Yet, listening to them again now on the old Decca 78s, one can recognise, too, the presence of those softer tones as heard on that evening of disillusionment at Covent Garden. We think of Welitsch as bright and steely, which was the 'image' of her voice as it had been in the days of her greatness; yet, as the records show, much was gentle and even velvety. Perhaps there was

58

more of the true Welitsch in her undervoiced Lisa than I appreciated. *Opera* magazine's critic, William Mann, went through the same process, and wrote most faithfully and understandingly of his experience. First he recalled 'the tornado that plunged on to the stage of Covent Garden in September 1947' as Salome, and 'the soaring thread of confident, silvery tone that bestrode the orchestra in the closing scene'. Then, turning to the diminished present, he reported the beauty of her appearance, and vouched that throughout the performance 'there was not an ugly note nor an unmusical inflection to be heard from her'. But the projection of voice had gone, and when he returned to the theatre for a later performance 'the haze was slightly more pronounced'. He concluded: 'I hope that the incisive edge in her voice is not vanished for ever; that is a part of Welitsch's vocal personality. The flexibility, the melting purity of tone and the artistry are perhaps even more mature than before. Even if the voice proves to have lost its carrying power, I would rather hear and see Welitsch in her own repertory than any other living singer' (March 1953).

The critic's rueful gallantry has something loyal and almost boyish about it; but that is a measure of the affection Welitsch inspired in those years, and indeed later, when her voice had almost completely gone and she herself gamely kept going with 'character' roles and a second career in films and stage plays. What the post-war audience probably overlooked was that, new to them as she was, Welitsch had been singing in public since 1934. She made her debut that year in Sofia, at the National Opera House of her native Bulgaria. From there she had moved to Graz and Hamburg, making guest appearances in Berlin and then joining the Munich company in 1943. In 1953 she was 40, no great age, but one at which several famous sopranos had retired and others would have been well advised to have done so. There is some similarity with Callas, born ten years later. Everyone lamented her premature decline, and brought forth clichés (as they still do for both Callas and Welitsch) about 'blazing meteors' yet she, too, had been singing for longer than people remembered (the Santuzza of a student performance of *Cavalleria rusticana* in 1938, and Athens' *Tosca* in 1942). In both instances, the war years slowed progress, and those now exist in a kind of limbo of operatic history; yet for Welitsch they were years in which the world should have been hearing her, with the voice we ourselves can hear in that thrilling record of Salome's closing scene salvaged from the Vienna of 1944.

This was the decisive year in which her career turned. She had previously made a great impression as the Composer in *Ariadne auf Naxos*, not least upon the composer himself, who saw in her his ideal Salome and prepared her for the gala performance to be given in Vienna on his 80th birthday. She duly became a leading member of the company, with which she first visited London in the famous mini-season of autumn 1947. This introduced a brilliant generation of singers, particularly rich in sopranos, Welitsch, Schwarzkopf, Seefried, Jurinac and Gueden in the lead, with Welitsch as the brightest of voices and most fascinating of personalities. Later she was to add Aida and Musetta to her Covent Garden roles, and for years the cleaving sound of her voice in the ensembles of *Aida* was remembered, while, as for the Musetta, that appears to have been one of those delicious opera-house occasions when good taste and propriety (with rebukes in the columns of *The Times* next morning) were thrown to the winds while everybody rejoiced.

At the Leeds Festival of 1947 she sang in Beethoven's Ninth Symphony and Verdi's Requiem under Barbirolli; at Edinburgh in 1948 there were more Donna Annas and (I remember a thrilling broadcast of this) Amelia in *Un ballo in maschera*. Her New York debut as Salome that same year

*Tuesday, 3rd November, 1953*

*The 39th performance at the Royal Opera House*

*of*

# SALOME

OPERA IN ONE ACT

## CHARACTERS IN ORDER

## OF APPEARANCE

NARRABOTH, a young Syrian, Captain of the Guard     EDGAR EVANS

PAGE TO HERODIAS     ..    ..    ..     MONICA SINCLAIR

FIRST SOLDIER    ..    ..    ..    ..     MICHAEL LANGDON

SECOND SOLDIER    ..    ..    ..    ..     GORDON FARRALL

JOKANAAN (John the Baptist)    ..    ..     OTAKAR KRAUS

A CAPPADOCIAN    ..    ..    ..    .. HUBERT LITTLEWOOD

SALOME, daughter of Herodias    ..    ..     LJUBA WELITSCH

A SLAVE     ..    ..    ..    ..     VERA HODDINOTT

HEROD, King of Judea    ..    ..     THORSTEINN HANNESSON

HERODIAS, wife of Herod ..    ..    ..    ..     EDITH COATES

FIRST JEW    ..    ..    ..    ..    ..     WILLIAM MCALPINE

SECOND JEW    ..    ..    ..    ..    ..     DAVID TREE

THIRD JEW    ..    ..    ..    ..    ..    ..     WILFRED JONES

FOURTH JEW ..    ..    ..    ..    ..    ..     EMLYN JONES

FIFTH JEW    ..    ..    ..    ..    ..     RHYDDERCH DAVIES

FIRST NAZARENE    ..    ..    ..     MARIAN NOWAKOWSKI

SECOND NAZARENE ..    ..    ..    ..     ANDREW DANIELS

probably stands as the high point of her career – unless, conceivably, it was surmounted when 24 years later she reappeared at the Metropolitan as the formidable Duchess of Crakentorp in *La fille du régiment*, receiving an ovation of unprecedented length without singing a note.

Of her decline the explanations were various and unauthenticated. One spoke of an operation, which I mention now merely as reporting the talk of the time. Singers had their own ideas. Irmgard Seefried in conversation with Lanfranco Rasponi (*The Last Prima Donnas*, London 1984) said: 'She gave too much of herself, and nature is fierce, for the price to be paid is high.' Elisabeth Schwarzkopf, observing more technically, feels that the price may have been exacted by an excessively open method of production in the upper register, exciting at the time but risky in the longer view. Maybe she was simply unwise in singing with a sore throat. Whether the loss was sudden or gradual is also hard to ascertain (an account in *Opera* of the Covent Garden *Tosca* of June 1951 noted that the voice 'was crystal clear and often of most beautiful quality, but its size seems to have been reduced'). 'Nobody loses their voice,' Leontyne Price remarked when, she having said that it was a performance of *Salome* with Welitsch that made her decide on an operatic career, I ventured, not very cleverly, the remark that that must have been before she lost her voice. Personally, I felt I knew all about loss of voice: as a boy chorister, just about the time of the 'break', I could produce a strong alto that would last until the Benedictus (Matins) and Nunc dimittis (Evensong), after which the edge disappeared, leaving a sound that was probably pure enough but lamentably ineffective. Sitting up there in the gallery at that *Queen of Spades*, I duly extended a choirboy's sympathy.

Anyway, one should not think of Welitsch's career in too tragic a fashion. She herself survived in fine style, with stage successes in *The Killing of Sister George*, *Arms and the Man*, and (as Signora Palpiti) in Nestroy's *Lumpazivagabundus*. A vivid glimpse of her in 1969 was provided by Philip Hope-Wallace writing under the heading of 'The Most Beautiful Woman I Know' in the *Guardian* – he found her in Vienna, cooking a goose for Sunday lunch and listening to one of her records playing at an angle 'like the rings round Saturn', while she cried 'Geschossen!' (bull's-eye) as a high note went ping to the centre. She has also left us records, the incomparable Letter Scene in *Eugene Onegin*, an adorable 'Valse de Chopin' by Josef Marx, and the waltz of Musetta, its phrases carried through such a generous, sustained legato. And there is that tribute of Lord Harewood's, with its strangely prophetic coda: 'Welitsch is one of the most remarkable singers of our day – I do not think there could be any doubt about that, even if she were suddenly to decide to stop singing tomorrow' (*Opera*, February 1953). The day after tomorrow the singing did indeed stop, but now, with her death some 40 years later, we can amend the sentence to cover not just 'our day' but our century.

# CHAPTER 13

# Lawrence Tibbett

So many of these singers, it seems, have a glory in their art and an almost proportionate sadness in their lives. All public figures doubtless are subjected to abnormal stresses and strains, though in many professions age brings protection with a skin grown thick over the years. Singers usually come through well enough having approached old age, but before that the process of ageing has to be faced and with it a suppressed dread that the voice itself may fail. This happened with Ljuba Welitsch, but she managed to cope. Tibbett did not.

The new biography, published to commemorate the centenary of his birth, tells of a meeting with the popular hero among baritones of an earlier generation, Titta Ruffo. It happened in Spain where 'at a party in their mutual honour, the two baritones sang together and praised each other's vocal accomplishments'. One wonders, first, and incidentally, what it could have been that they sang. Duets for baritones are not plentiful, and at the moment all that comes to mind is 'The Two Gendarmes', which hardly seems a likely choice. 'Suoni la tromba' from *I puritani* perhaps. Anyway, one lingers a little with thoughts of the event, the friendly emulation, the good luck of those privileged to be present, the speeches of mutual admiration. But from any competitive angle the odds must presumably have favoured the younger man, for the year was 1932 and Ruffo had all but arrived at the end of his career. His autobiography, we remember, is called *La mia parabola*, and, though the book was written in 1924 when he was only in his mid-forties, the downturn was already in sight. At that date, Tibbett's career had barely begun (he joined the Metropolitan, without operatic stage experience, in 1923), and the chapter of *Dear Rogue* which mentions this meeting is headed 'To the Heights'. When the two baritones met in Spain, the summit of Tibbett's fame had in fact been reached, while the artistic heights were scaled also in these very years with performances of *Simon Boccanegra* and *Emperor Jones*. In 1932, when Ruffo's magnificent voice approached the condition of a noble ruin, Tibbett must have felt himself to be, as he was, a man in the prime of life. Yet within the coming decade the decline of his own parabola had begun and by 1942 had reached a point at which colleagues, such as Eleanor Steber, saw in him 'a mere shadow of the giant he had once been'.

Tibbett (right) with Dino Borgioli and Claudia Muzio
(*La traviata*, San Francisco 1933)

Exactly what Tibbett 'had once been' was perhaps more accurately not
so much a giant as the embodiment of a very human ideal. He was a singer,
to be sure, gifted with a rich and ringing voice over which he had at that
time absolute mastery. He was also a man, physically a fine specimen, 6'2",
well-built and athletic, handsome (with a trim Clark Gable moustache) in

the manner of the age. The voice itself betokened manliness, with its vibrancy, its capacity for thrilling top notes and sturdy low ones but settling in the middle where singer and listener could feel most comfortable. More than that, he was a human being, one who mixed naturally with chorus, film extras, young folk. In their midst he was distinguished, but wore his distinction with an easy grace. This is the Lawrence Tibbett who for some 15 years, perhaps 20, stood as one of the most renowned and admired of living Americans.

He rose to fame in true American style, rapid and sensational. From California he came to New York at the age of 25 without the assets of wealth, influence or experience. Within a year (almost to the day of his arrival) he secured an audition at the great national opera house, and then, when that failed, a successful second. In November 1923 he made as inconspicuous a debut as possible (in the role of Levitsky, Jesuit monk in the last act of *Boris Godunov*). Roughly a year later rehearsals were called for a revival of *Falstaff*, and with some misgivings Tibbett was cast as Ford. On the first night, 2 January 1925, the house rang with his name, and the next day he was front-page news. 'American Baritone stirs Opera House,' ran the *New York Times* headline. Subheading: 'Unprecedented scene when Lawrence Tibbett fails to realise he's made a hit.' Third announcement: 'Gets roars of applause.' Below, the critic Olin Downes gave details. Tibbett's ovation followed the scene between Ford and Fal-

A Tibbett recital at Sydney, Australia, 1938

65

staff who was sung by the veteran Antonio Scotti. This, says the critic, 'Mr Tibbett delivered with a quality of vocalism and interpretation which constituted one of the highest points and one of the strongest individual performances of the evening'. At the end, the relevant principals took a bow together, then Scotti and Tibbett. Then: 'At last it was evident that the audience wished Tibbett and none other for its attentions. But this singer did not come before the curtain alone. The commotion in the theatre increased. Cries of "Tibbett!" came from various parts of the house. There was no response. For a while no one appeared before the curtain; the lights were lowered, and Mr Serafin, the conductor, raised his baton for the next scene to begin. He found it impossible to proceed. Pandemonium grew. Even the elect in the boxes began to take more than a polite interest.' Eventually Serafin sent a member of the orchestra backstage, Tibbett took his bow, and the most famous sixteen minutes of continuous applause the house had known came to an end. Tibbett, reflected the critic, had certainly made progress: 'He is evidently one of the most important acquisitions of the Metropolitan company.'

Soon he was to become an important acquisition in Hollywood too. *The Rogue Song* (1929) found him battling against the elements with the assistance of Laurel and Hardy. In *New Moon* (1930) he subdued a regiment of Russian officer-eaters and won Grace Moore into the bargain. *The Prodigal* (renamed *The Southerner*, 1931) had him shunning the hunt-ball in favour of the black folks' barbecue. *Cuban Love Song* (1931) challenged his manhood to the utmost by co-starring the tempestuous Lupe Velez. These were not cinematic masterpieces, but they brought something like worldwide fame to the singer, who during the course of them (but not too often, for producers had learned at this stage that the public preferred action to music) was given opportunities for song. These recurred in his last film, *Metropolitan* (1935), in which the Toreador's Song from *Carmen* afforded illustration of the energy and physical panache of his stage performances.

Through all this time, and in spite of the financial rewards of film, concert and radio work, he remained loyal to the opera. In 1932 the American premiere of Verdi's *Simon Boccanegra* centred upon him. The following year came *Emperor Jones*, the adaptation by Louis Gruenberg of Eugene O'Neill's play. This, too, made front-page news ('instant and sweeping success', 'the audience listened, absorbed, deeply moved') and Tibbett's performance was hailed in *The Times* as 'a great masterpiece of dramatic interpretation'. After the premiere, the critic, describing it as 'the work of a true artist who has developed from small Metropolitan roles to a position which makes him an ornament of the lyric stage', reflected that, while repetitions might prove more authoritative, 'it seems questionable whether he will ever sing it with more of the artist's tension, the excitement, the electric thrill that he gave it yesterday'.

A recording, pirated from an abridged version broadcast in 1934, shows quite enough of this for us to imagine the rest. It is an astonishingly vivid, powerful and moving achievement, and very easy to understand why several critics ranked it with Chaliapin's Boris. It also fuels speculation on the causes of Tibbett's vocal decline in the next decade. By comparison, the singer of Boris Godunov has a comfortable evening, spending more time in his dressing-room than on stage, and provided with numerous passages for unbroken lyricism. Brutus Jones is on stage throughout and his style of part-sung part-spoken declamation is brutal. Tibbett gives not just of his voice but of his whole being, and does so with such intensity that it comes upon us as an almost inevitable reaction to exclaim at some point, 'But this man must burn himself up!' In some degree one feels it when listening to Tibbett in other recordings, whether in the studio or 'live'. He could sing softly and preserve a scrupulously smooth vocal line at any volume, but the intensity, and the acting quality within the singing, is never completely relaxed – it is a condition of his identity as an artist.

Another condition, in the period of his absolute vocal prime, was a vibrancy of tone, the intensifying or relaxing of which became also an essential means of expression. Sometime in the late Thirties the voice began to respond less keenly to such demands. In 1940 he appears to have experienced a crisis, though exactly of what sort and with what cause is still unsure. The consciousness of it preyed upon him and he turned to a treacherous ally. In a remarkably short time this splendid man became an alcoholic, and he died in a deplorable state at the age of 63. He was the first of a notable line of American baritones; he was the singer upon whom the hopes of a national school of opera were built; he was one of the first American singers to travel widely and gain a resounding international reputation. He gave good service to musical life in other respects, organising the American Guild of Musical Artists, arguing on behalf of American composers in the Armed Forces, promoting any number of deserving causes. But essentially he was the singing actor we see so vividly through our hearing when we play his records: one of the irreplaceables, an artist as expressive and individual in sound as a well-loved actor is by sight, and as unforgettable.

CHAPTER 14

# Jussi Björling

Turning from the recent biography of Lawrence Tibbett to that of Jussi Björling, we read his wife Anna-Lisa's summary of her subject: 'an immensely gifted singer, a conscientious artist, a loving husband and father, and a kind and good man caught up in a lifelong struggle with a disease – alcoholism – that he could contain at times but was unable to conquer.' It sounds familiar.

Actually, the life-stories, the characters, the circumstances, are very different. Rather like a teacher who will chalk up on the blackboard a triangular shape called in turn India, Africa and South America, so the outline here (singer, citizen, alcoholic) tells little about the real identity. Nationality itself is a factor. Tibbett was American through and through: at the age of six, for instance (and this is not to suggest that the experience is part of a typical American childhood, only that there is something very American about it), a schoolmate came to him with news that his pa, the deputy sheriff, had been killed in a shoot-out. Björling's upbringing was certainly not that of a typical Scandinavian child (he became a professional singer of a kind, international too, at about the same age as Tibbett was when he learned of his father's death), but Sweden, its people, scenery and language, was home to him, the place to return to throughout his life. For him, the family was always the centre of his being; for Tibbett, neither of his marriages appears to have provided that centre, though he also had children for whom he cared. Nor was the alcoholism really the same thing. A naturally sociable, out-going man, Tibbett drank (it seems) in a normal way till the troubles began with his singing; Björling, private and even shy by comparison, was known to 'have a problem' even in mid-twenties at the time of his marriage. If ever there was a singer free of vocal problems, it was him, and when he died, at the age of 49, the voice was still in superb condition.

With a singer, voice is character, or rather, the 'sound-image' is perceived character, the artistic fact. Björling and Tibbett (to extend the comparison just a little further) are alike in the mental 'picture' we have of them as vibrant, magnificently healthy voices. A difference lies in the nature of the vibrancy. Björling's is purely that of a singer, Tibbett's that of a singing actor. When Tibbett, in his recording of Tchaikovsky's 'None

but the lonely heart', sings 'My senses fail; a burning fire devours me', he uses the resonance of vibrations (and its absence) as a Shakespearean actor might. With Björling, the thrill of his resonance is never emotionally neutral, but it remains essentially as pure song rather than the musical reshaping of an actor's declamation. On stage they represented two different kinds of artist, Tibbett a very active physical performer, sometimes overdoing things, Björling one whose acting was largely accomplished through the voice and even then in a way which expressed emotions but hardly created characters.

Rather as with Carlo Bergonzi in more recent times, Björling was generally welcome as so fine a singer that the limited interest of his character-portrayals could be relegated as a side-issue. Even so, it may in his own lifetime have contributed to the impression of coldness. This is mentioned several times in the biography, usually to be confuted by one of his colleagues who had good opportunity to watch him closely (I have heard as much myself, notably from Victoria de los Angeles, who found it intensely moving simply to see him sing). Yet it is doubtful whether this is what Italians have in mind when they hesitate over Björling. The assessment by Gabriele Baldini in *Le grandi voci* (Rome, 1964) is of a singer admired but not loved. He acknowledges the lyrical sweetness of a tone that could expand towards the heroic. But, observing that Björling sang in Italy on only rare occasions, he suggests that 'the lack of direct contact with the Italian style of singing is felt in a certain rigidity of emission, and as it were a diffidence in "abandonment", or rather in an "abandonment" which catches the authentic style'. Listening deliberately as through Italian ears, one can probably understand this. What it then calls into question (and not for the first time) is the validity of Italian ears. It would be natural that Italians know their own business best, but the progress of Italian singing in the relevant years was hardly such as to reassure the rest of the world. If those who had this feeling about Björling had made a corresponding effort to listen with adjusted ears they might have discovered in this 'certain rigidity' the scrupulous care for musical line which was once the fine flower of their own best bel canto tradition; they might also have questioned the advocacy of this 'abandonment'. A course in Björling might have done a world of good to Italian singers in those years.

His own idol was certainly Italian enough, for this was Enrico Caruso. He worshipped, but was determined not to copy – except in one song. Tosti's 'L'alba separa della luce l'ombra' is a passionate setting of a poem by D'Annunzio, expertly written for the tenor voice and perfect for Caruso's. Björling's introduction to the Caruso recording (which apparently he had previously missed) is recounted in the biography (p. 190). His friend and American manager, Frederick Schang, played him the record ('Just listen') and at the end Björling said 'Play it again'. And again. Then he sang it along with the record and 'with such power that the windows rattled'. It is a good story and the skin shivers at the thought of it. This was the one piece that Björling reckoned to sing in Caruso's manner. But then we play the records, Caruso's of 1917, Björling's studio version of 1949. It is a comparison that can be turned either way, according to the criteria of the moment; both are superb. Caruso sings at one point ('il sole eterno' first time) with such glory that the skin crawls again at the mere recollection. He commands tones both of the utmost sweetness ('Chiudimi, o notte') and of a forward-thrusting, brilliant high fortissimo. Björling cannot offer these wonderful extremes, and with him the 'abandonment' is reined; it is in fact refined (cf. Baldini's judgement that Björling lacked 'a

HAROLD HOLT LTD.

ANNOUNCE

# JUSSI
# BJÖRLING

*WILL MAKE HIS NEXT LONDON APPEARANCE*

## IN TWO
## CORONATION FESTIVAL
## CONCERTS

AT THE

## ROYAL FESTIVAL HALL

*Monday, June 8 at 8*

*Monday, June 15 at 8*

certain stylistic refinement'). Yet the result is not tame. A wise teacher would send likely pupils to both records with a caution that worship may be conducted at the shrine of Caruso but copying (should that be in question) had best be done through the school of Björling.

Björling, of course, never heard his hero in the flesh. And that 'of course' passes easily enough, but in fact it was a near miss. The book tells how, in this extraordinary chapter of young Jussi's life, the father took his three sons to the States for a season of professional engagements as the Björling Quartet. While they were in New York, Caruso was 'on' in *Pagliacci* at the Met, but so was a western with Bill Hart in Times Square. Tickets for the opera matinée had been bought, and they were not cheap; but the sight of the picture-house was too much, the boys would not budge, and to the movies they went.

It was an extraordinary upbringing after all. This quartet (the father a powerful, well-trained tenor, the boys strong-voiced and well-disciplined) toured the States in 1919, and Jussi, aged eight, was already singled out for praise. His party-piece, translated as 'Give me angels' wings', was not among the items recorded, yet even at this date it should be possible to identify Jussi among the soloists in the items extant (I like to think he is the one in Psalm 4 who sounds already on the way to tenor). When next recorded, in 1929, he was a lad of eighteen, and yet the tenor voice is beautifully formed. 'For you alone', made in this first solo recording session, can be moving almost to tears, rather like Di Stefano's juvenile recordings made privately in Switzerland. Soon came those first famous releases, the *Bohème* and *Aida* arias that carried his name around the world, then such things as the *Bettelstudent* song with its youthful exuberance and ringing high D flat; and we can also hear him in excerpts from *Aida* at his triumphant debut at Vienna (1936), the stylish Covent Garden *Trovatore* (1939) and the supreme *Missa Solemnis* under Toscanini (1940). All these recordings are precious mementoes, and so (one comes to find) are the 'live' performances where he sings in Swedish and in which it is not fanciful to detect an extra fervor and freedom of expression.

The years in America followed, and my own memories date from the early 1950s, with concerts in London where the initial reactions were those I had learned to dread in the first hearing of a famous singer known previously on records. The voice was smaller, dryer, than expected; the manner formal, the style in those first songs rather stolid. But soon everything eased. The encores began early and ended late, the patina of tonal impurity wore through, and soon we were hearing 'Ch'ella mi creda libero' or 'Che gelida manina' just as on the records. My last memory was of the *La bohème* in March 1960 when he was already a sick man. Again I recall an initial disappointment (his seemed the smallest voice among the four Bohemians) and then a thrilling fulfilment in Act 3. He died in the night of 8 September. It was bad news and a terrible loss, yet in one way and at this distance in time one can almost be glad, for he died of heart failure in his sleep at home at the height of his powers, in dignity and peace. It could so easily have been otherwise.

CHAPTER 15

# Eva Turner

In her late years – and there were mercifully many of them – everybody knew Eva; and 'Eva' is what she was. She would make that clear at the beginning of an interview ('And I am Eva, dear'), and if you referred to 'Eva' in musically-minded company (in London at least) everybody knew who you meant. She went out to operas, concerts and receptions; she sat on juries at competitions; she taught in private, talked in public, was always ready to add her voice and opinion in any meeting or symposium. And all of this till well into her 90s. And when she talked, how it rang! Was there ever a speaking voice of such clarity? How she would measure out vowels, roll the r's, give to the proper names their utmost span of regal dignity. Her spirit was invincible, her memory prodigious; and that other memory, the one she has left behind, remains infinitely precious to all who knew her in those years. Witness the attendance at her memorial service in Westminster Abbey on 5 February 1991: not a seat to be had.

On that occasion, the Abbey's ancient walls resounded to the enunciation of an unfamiliar gospel, that of the Princess Turandot. In a recording made, very probably, before most of the congregation were born, came the voice about which Ernest Newman wrote: 'On Tuesday we had the impression that the scoring that could drown Miss Turner had not yet been put on paper.' Perhaps by coincidence, possibly by design, the service was held on a Tuesday also; but the one referred to by the *Sunday Times*'s critic was Tuesday 5 June 1928. It was the evening of her return to Covent Garden, where she had sung previously in the rather apologetic winter seasons allocated to the Carl Rosa Company. Now she was appearing at the height of the so-called Grand Season, with an international reputation behind her and in the role that seemed sent by heaven to suit her.

The effect of her singing that night was phenomenal. *The Times* spoke of 'superb singing', the *Manchester Guardian* reported a reception 'enthusiastic to the pitch of frenzy', and more than one commented that there had been nothing like it since Luisa Tetrazzini made her unheralded debut in 1907. 'Her tones were imperious, declamatory, dramatic,' said the *Daily Telegraph*, and the *Daily Express* claimed that 'avoiding all harshness of tone, she sang the tempestuous music as it has never been sung in London before'. The heroine herself said merely: 'I am proud of Bolton,' though

73

Turner as Turandot

perhaps for once she had not made the words clear enough for she was born in Oldham. But everyone was keen to have a share in this event: 'British soprano's triumph' was one headline, 'England finds a Jeritza' another, and (rather more reasonably, since this was where she had been brought up) 'Bristol Lady's Great Success' (*Bristol Evening News*).

Of course, when the cheers died down, questions arose. Nobody doubted the success, but could national pride have contributed to the extent of it? Nobody denied that here was London's best Turandot to date, but how many Turandots had London heard? (The answer to that is two, the second, Florence Easton, being a marked improvement on the first, Bianca Scacciati, who was reputedly dreadful). Then there was another query, one which occurred to Ernest Newman almost on the spot. The role and the voice were perfectly matched and both were exceptional. 'What also strikes one in the voice,' he wrote, 'is its curious impersonal quality.' It was ideal for the icy princess, but what about other roles?

Reassurance on that point might have been sought in the singer's past record. Turner was, after all, well-known in London during her eight years with the Carl Rosa. She had sung in a wide repertoire of roles, such as Leonore (*Fidelio*), Leonora (*Trovatore*), Elisabeth (*Tannhäuser*), Brünnhilde (*Walküre*), Butterfly and Tosca. Critics took notice even then: 'one felt she will make a fine Isolde one day,' wrote the perceptive opera critic of *Musical Opinion* after a performance of *Lohengrin* in 1921. Her Butterfly was noted by the same critic as an emotionally moving portrayal, and it was in this that she had been heard by Ettore Panizza, who recommended her to Toscanini. But still, in its fully developed state, as Newman observed, the voice was that of Princess Turandot, and not easy to imagine in music that called for warmth and humanity. She sang next in *Cavalleria rusticana* ('Miss Turner and Mr Pertile together could challenge a full military band and come out smiling,' wrote Richard Capell in the *Daily Mail*); but it was *Aida*, a little later, that gave her the needful opportunity to show that she was not a one-part singer. Figaro of *Musical Opinion* was not convinced in all respects but noted that she 'surprised us by the sweetness and charm of much of her singing in the Nile scene'. Sweetness and charm: those are the very words one feared not to find in the Turner annals, and their validity is confirmed in reports on this and other roles throughout her Covent Garden career.

The trouble is that that career was all too limited. After such a debut as could not have been more brilliant she was heard in only one new role additional to the three of her first season: Sieglinde in a single performance of *Die Walküre*. Or rather, that is all that the exclusively 'Grand' folk heard: the more significant extensions (Agatha, Isolde, the *Siegfried* Brünnhilde and Amelia in *Un ballo in maschera*) were consigned to the winter months, and totalled twelve performances in all. The great Turandot itself was heard in London only fourteen times in those eleven years. She sang in the provinces and did a good deal of concert work. Even so,

this was hardly an example of England making best use of its natural resources. Perhaps, one might say, it was the penalty of having an international career.

But that raises another question, one which has been asked rather more openly since Eva's death, at the age of 98, in 1990. Just how much of an international career did she have? Her professional leaflet gave as its heading: 'Royal Opera House, Covent Garden, La Scala, Milan, and Principal Opera Houses in Europe and North and South America.' The appearances at La Scala consisted of a debut-role (Freia in *Das Rheingold*), a follow-up in the same season (Sieglinde in *Die Walküre*), and then a return with Turandot in 1929. She sang at the San Carlo, Naples, the Reale, Rome, the Arena at Verona; her first Turandot was given at Brescia, and her last Italian performance appears to have been at Bologna in 1939.

76

Italian companies did not welcome foreigners in those days, and at least it can be said with fair confidence that in opera she was heard as often in Italy as in London. Such press cuttings as I have seen are full of 'grande squillo', 'stupendo effetto' and 'applausi da ogni parte', but, in common with most Italian music criticism of this period, they are so generalized as to signify little more than a big 'bravo'.

North American critics were more specific. For instance, in *Le nozze di Figaro* 'The "Dove son" was a bit of straightforward singing, yet lacked something in grace of line and delicacy of shading' (*Chicago Evening Post*, 4 January 1929). The *New York Times* placed her Turandot, together with Frida Leider's Brünnhilde, as the finest achievement of that season. She returned to Chicago in 1938, singing Turandot, *Walküre* and (with, in turn, both Gigli and Martinelli) Aida. She was also back in America after the war, but then as a greatly loved teacher at the University of Oklahoma.

An area of her career that, as far as I know, has never been documented comprises her appearances in Germany (she would sometimes break into German – as she regularly did into Italian – in speech). Also lying ahead for a future biographer are the further-flung fields of South America. The English newspapers occasionally gestured in an impressive manner towards triumphs in Venezuela, Argentina and Brazil, and she herself gave some details in an interview for *The Record Collector* (Vol. 35, 1990). But again it is my impression that we don't know half. She told me, for instance (and I shall never forget it because of the extraordinary picture conjured up and the gleeful resonance of her telling), that on one great occasion the whole opera company set out overnight so as to sing Rossini's *Stabat Mater* in honour of 'the grrreat patrrriot' Simon Bolivar in the presence of President Mendoza at a dawn Mass on the plain of Carabobo. I telephoned the next day for the joy of hearing her say that last word again. 'Ca-rra-bo-bo, dear.'

I heard her sing just once. That was in one of her performances as Turandot in 1948, and that also I shall never forget. She was by then a sacred name to me as a young record collector, and I was dreading a disappointment. Turandot is a nerve-racking opera in these circumstances, for you have to wait till halfway through before the princess sings a note. I was experienced enough to know how great were the chances, and how fearful the consequences, of hearing a voice that shattered the image. In the chord before 'In questa reggia' I closed my eyes tight and took a deep breath. Then opened them, breathed freely and took in the wonder: for here was this woman of 55, with the voice that on recent broadcasts I had regretfully thought unsympathetic and wobbly, and the voice was that of the record from 1928. Or so it seemed. It was easily the most powerful voice I had heard; the high notes were the most thrilling. More than that, it was perfectly firm; and much more than all of those, it was pure. No surface-scratch, no wobble: just a great, shining beauty.

CHAPTER 16

# Renata Scotto

A 'case' is something which is to a marked degree individual and exceptional yet also sufficiently representative as to be in some way significant. That can probably be shot down as a definition but it will do for a point of reference. The career of Renata Scotto is 'a case'. Plotted in outline, it looks like a *memento mori* writ large. Youth brings the rosebuds: the sweet voice, the pretty appearance, the roles to match. You are everybody's favourite, except possibly for the reigning diva who is not too happy about the applause which the audience bestows upon its new little charmer. But soon, granted such talent, you will be a diva yourself, and the repertoire will expand. More weighty and more dramatic will be the roles expected, contracted or volunteered. The voice grows too, but only so far. The roles exceed that point and then you have to watch out or the voice will suffer. But by now you are an artist, not a mere singer, and you have a vision, almost a sense of mission, strengthened by an awareness of having survived the prophesied dangers thus far. The warning-signs increase but so does your own urge for fulfilment. Then the upward curve turns downward. Things fall apart, but you can still pick up the pieces and carry on. Wise people say, 'You are living dangerously'; you reply, 'I am living.'

On the face of it, it would seem a shame that a career which began in so sunny and hopeful a climate should have run into squalls. Back in 1917, when Scotto made her London debut, Andrew Porter wrote: 'Renata Scotto was, for me, the discovery of the whole season ... Her enunciation is sharp as a razor, her singing clear as crystal' (*Opera*, July 1957). That was of her Adina in *L'elisir d'amore*: 'Her phrase in the first scene, 'Elisir di sì perfetto, si rare qualità', showed at once that, for accuracy, purity and evenness of tone, she can sing the head off any soprano *leggiero* we have heard here since the war'. Of her Mimì in *La bohème* he remarked again on the first notes 'which yielded a thrill of anticipatory pleasure that was amply fulfilled when this delicious little soprano appeared ... There seems to be no doubt that Renata Scotto is destined to go to the first rank of opera singers.' And indeed to the first rank she duly went. But, if that is the first Act of her career, here is a scene from the last: 'Nobody expected much of Scotto in this role at this stage of her career,' wrote Patrick J. Smith (*Opera*, January 1983) on her Lady Macbeth at the Metropolitan. ' "Vieni,

Scotto as Julia in *La vestale* (Florence 1970)

t'affretta" ... was damaged dramatically by her crawling with clawed hands ... thereafter the proportions of wobble and shriek increased.'

So what went wrong? Ask an obvious question, you may get an obvious answer. As in some absurd mathematical proposition, Adina into Lady Macbeth will not go. A singer's life is too short to encompass, without peril, these two extremes, and if the second is feasible in later years there was something wrong with the casting earlier, which appears not to have been 'the case'. So it is to 'the case' that we return, keeping in mind that we are now looking for negatives and must not fail eventually to celebrate the rest.

Reading her autobiography (*Scotto: More than a Diva*, with O. Roca, USA 1984), one can see that hers was always, to a greater extent than usual, a voice with choices before it. She tells how she originally thought of herself as a mezzo, and that even her teacher was not sure. So at her first student concert she sang Aida's 'O patria mia' and Azucena's 'Stride la vampa': next day the local paper reported that she had a bright future as a soprano, and a soprano she duly became. *La traviata* was her first opera, an amateur performance given in her hometown, Savona, on Christmas Eve 1952. When the success was repeated at the Teatro Reale, Milan, in the summer of the following year, it became clear that this was something quite out of the ordinary, and a new offer arrived. She was invited to sing Madama Butterfly, and was warned by the senior soprano, Mafalda Favero: 'Be careful. The role is a voice killer.'

Nevertheless she sang it (with Favero's help) and was soon doing so, as she says, all over Italy. Later she went to another teacher, Mercedès Llopart, whose reaction was 'No more *Butterfly*, no more *Pagliacci*. First you must learn to sing.' This sounds fine: it is what we, the voice-loving public, want to hear. But I am not so sure about the next sentence: 'You will sing *coloratura*.'

*Coloratura* came to mean, first, *La sonnambula* and soon *Lucia di Lammermoor*. Both brought great success, yet even now the more vocally-sensitive critics felt a faint misgiving. Philip Hope-Wallace, hearing her in *La sonnambula* at Drury Lane in 1978, observed that her voice seemed to have darkened a little: 'There was suspicion of throatiness too, and at least one moment perilously near a crack in "Ah, non giunge" ' (*Opera*, April 1958). He also felt that she was imitating Callas. Then, at a *Lucia di Lammermoor* at Rome in 1960, William Weaver noted that 'to ensure projection she forced the former sweetness out of her tone' (*Opera*, January 1961). By 1962, Harold Rosenthal, the editor of *Opera* magazine, writing on a performance of *Bohème* at Covent Garden, inclined 'more than ever ... to the view that she is a lyrical rather then a *coloratura* soprano'. On *Lucia* at Turin in 1964, Giorgio Gualerzi, reporting on a triumph, wondered why she so insistently attempted 'those high Ds and Cs which are beyond her range and are not written'. It sends one back for a further glance at that first review of Andrew Porter's, so full of delight and

enthusiasm. It ends: 'She has it in her power to become a considerable artist, but to do so she must listen scrupulously to herself and draw back (just as Elisabeth Schumann used to do) the moment a trace of shrillness or hardness appears in her tone.'

She can hardly have done so, and throughout the following years words like 'strident' and 'uncomfortable' became ever more frequent in reference to the high notes. In the 1970s another observation became inescapable. 'Though at the peak of her interpretative powers, she did not possess the necessary volume and was forced to make the voice sound bigger and to forfeit the beauty of its sound' (*Opera*, on Bellini's *La straniera*, Venice, 1970). At her first Norma, at Turin in 1974, Gualerzi found that she had 'done definite damage to the radiantly beautiful voice'; at Florence in 1978

81

'the unlovely acid in its higher regions took on a note of desperation' (Max Loppert); and at the Met on the opening night of 1981, amid an infamy of 'catcalls from a boorish claque', she was beset by 'ever more insecure singing, above the stave', a 'lack of breath control' and a habit of fragmenting the music 'into bits and pieces' (*Opera*, November 1981).

The lessons do not need spelling out. But let us put the other side of this 'case'. Scotto was always, right from the first, a singer with exceptional power to move her listeners. Present at her student *Traviata* in Milan was the experienced critic Eugenio Gara, who recalled that by the middle of Act 2, with 'Dite alla giovine', she was 'so steeped in tears and desolation, even the most hardened of them [the audience] were on the edge of their seats' (*Opera*, March 1971). I myself remember her Butterfly as the most movingly sung I have heard in the opera house, her Mimì hardly less so. Nor did she absolutely need a stage: the last time I heard her was in a performance of Verdi's Requiem at the Albert Hall, where an aristocracy of bearing, an intensely concentrated art, made her contribution deeply impressive. On records too, there was a time, in the mid-1970s when she virtually reappeared, with some recital discs on CBS (now Sony), singing from such a rich fund of colour and emotion that one thought back, beyond Callas, to Claudia Muzio.

Now, suppose she had been 'sensible' and limited herself to what did not involve forcing the range or the volume, would she not have kept, imprisoned within herself, a great deal of unused art? Even when they deplored, her critics repeatedly found themselves marvelling. Patrick J. Smith, who chronicled those last years at the Met with full awareness of their faults, wrote of 'characteristic dagger-thrusts of sound that would catch the breath in one's throat' (on *Vespri Siciliani*, 1982). Max Loppert, quoted earlier on the Florence *Norma* of 1978, still judged it to be 'a perfomance of the role on the highest level, delivered without stint'. John Ardoin, reviewing *Un ballo in maschera* that same year, found 'an intensity, authority and beauty of line that placed her in the vanguard of Verdi sopranos'. At *La vestale* in Florence, 1970, William Weaver made another telling observation: that in portraying the emotional pain of the character she 'at times allowed her voice to harden, but this could-be defect was turned into a positive, dramatic contribution'.

Scotto has never played safe, and as late as 1995 was still extending herself – amazingly with an excursion into the Strauss repertoire, singing the Marschallin in *Der Rosenkavalier* at the Spoleto Festival in Charleston. I shouldn't think it was 'sensible'; nor is the thought of a 62-year-old Marschallin particularly edifying. But there is something about it and about the whole of Scotto's headstrong, embattled career that commands a kind of wonder: a spirit of adventure, of commitment, risk, involvement. 'The cistern contains; the fountain overflows.'

## CHAPTER 17

# Håkan Hagegård

Håkan Hagegård has been with us, in London, for the best part of a week, listening to young singers, taking four of them through a public 'Insight' class, standing in for an indisposed colleague at an orchestral concert, giving his own recital the following night, then off on the next leg of his world tour ... What a life it is, this of the modern singer. 'No peace, no rest' as Prince Igor sings in captivity, where his trouble is quite the opposite, life being at a stand-still. Håkan Hagegård looks happy with it. He looks like a happy man: at any rate, he has that qualification for happiness, the purposefulness of someone serious within his smiles, bearing with him, in middle age, the sense that you should do something with your life, meaning that you should leave something behind you at that point where life-in-general and you-in-particular most urgently and uniquely intersect. There is a quotation that stands as an epigraph in John Whiting's play, *A Penny for a Song*, to the effect that we should 'leave some token of pleasure in every place ... else get we nothing'. I fancy Hagegård would agree.

He is concerned for the furtherance of music and of youth. The wheel of European culture is broken (the confined but plentiful span with the Bible, Shakespeare, Rembrandt, Beethoven in its midst). The teeming produce of the Internet, indifferent to goodness, truth, beauty, yet potent in all; the hermetic physical life of youngsters each in their own room with their own computer or synthesizer – these may cause misgivings to most of us, but particularly to a man who himself values, probably above all else in his artistic life, the act of communication. And this (though he would not be doctrinaire about it and deny the value of records, films and so forth) means essentially on-the-spot communication between physically present, living people.

Behind this conviction, of course, lies a memory of childhood. Hagegård, born in 1945, was not brought up in an exceptionally musical household. That was the beauty of it. He felt it was not an unusual home in that respect, but everybody played some instrument or sang, and there would be evenings when they played together: it was the sort of thing people did. Even this mattered not so much for the music as for the relationships, for when they played they communicated, or so it seemed to him. To preserve

Hagegård as Papageno in Ingmar Bergman's film of *The Magic Flute*

something of this, or to make way for something that would provide a comparable enrichment, has been one of his greatest wishes, and it was partly to that end that he founded the HageGarden Music Centre.

This is a place of retreat, also a place where people can make music together in peace and without pressure. It is like a small village, set in woodland by a lakeside, roughly half-an-hour's drive from Karlstad, his native town and the capital city of Varmland. No return-to-nature or yesteryear is on the agenda; on the contrary, the most modern facilities for recording and maintaining international communications are installed and regularly updated. It is not music in the home, but it helps that informal mutuality and experience through music which was among the most valued features of his own home life.

The other, and major, part of Hagegård's professional life is still his singing. Here too he has set out to achieve something special. In London's Wigmore Hall on 6 March 1997, the audience settled to an opening item called 'Nordic Drama'. Critics and others cursed when the lights went down so that it was impossible to read the programme. We then watched, perhaps a trifle sceptically, as a young woman in what seemed to be a kind of mermaid outfit sat in a spotlight cross-legged on top of the grand piano and played her violin. From the back of the hall the singer's voice, softly as could be, took up the melody of a folksong which lasted the length of his slow journey to the platform. The mermaid slid softly from the piano and made ready to play a familiar pizzicato, identified less immediately than it might have been because the drama with which we associated it was definitely not Nordic. Never mind: the quietness and grace wrought their spell, and there at the door, listening to Don Giovanni's Serenade, was Donna Elvira. She proved to be a handy pianist, and songs of myth and magic followed. Then, encapsulating these strange matters, came Sibelius's 'Was it a dream?', and we began to realise that the little 'drama' was soon to end. The mermaid played once more unaccompanied; Donna Elvira vacated the piano stool; Hagegård, singing as at the start, slowly walked to the back of the hall, and the violinist, reseated upon the piano, played softly the closing phrases.

In the interval all shades of opinion were aired, the nearest to a consensus being that 'Nordic Interlude' might have been a better title, that it had all been quite fascinating, but rather too embryonic. It nevertheless provoked thought – nobody was talking about the Schubert group which followed. Similarly in the second half, the programme ended with some lively, strongly characterised songs by Strauss, but the subject of conversation was the semi-dramatic dialogue-piece by Dominick Argento: *A Few Words about Tchekov*. In this, the delightful Charlotte Hellekant, with her clear mezzo and elegant presence, sat on one side of the platform in a glamorous actress's fine dress and pearls while Hagegård-Tchekov in dressing-gown took a chair on the other. The memories of Olga Knipper dated from a performance of *The Seagull* and ended with Tchekov's death at Badenweiler; the interplay of the two voices again held interest of a kind not normally associated with the song recital. How successful (or how good the music) is another matter, but we had been held and sent on our way with something to think about.

All of this may seem a strange development for a singer who is still

85

remembered most widely for his Papageno. It was years ago now, but Ingmar Bergman's film of *The Magic Flute*, sung by Swedish singers in Swedish, charmed audiences throughout the world; and the great charmer, the lovable character whom, of all, as in a pantomime, everybody welcomed back on each reappearance was the birdcatcher. The whole world of the film was young, and he seemed the very embodiment of it. In fact he was already thirty and had been singing Papageno for six or seven years (he then put an embargo on it). All the same, the 'image' was fixed by that film, and even now in every one of his audiences there will be some who will look at and, so to speak, *through* him, to see what they can discern of that Papageno of 1975.

It is not quite true to say that his international career took off from that point for he had already appeared at Glyndebourne, as the Count in *Capriccio* and the better-known Count in *Le nozze di Figaro*. His New York debut followed in 1978 (Malatesta in *Don Pasquale* at the Metropolitan), and he was also heard at Covent Garden, La Scala, Vienna, Paris, Sydney and so forth. He has added roles in modern operas, such as Corigliano's *The Ghosts of Versailles* and Lindholm's *The Dreamplay*. He disclaims any ambition to 'shape' a career, and if he accepts a new role it will be because he likes it or likes the company. Amfortas, he adds, would be something worth thinking about.

Thinking and acting, repertoire, dates and places, personality and style:

86

there seems, surely, to be something missing, something not lighted upon. Voice, of course! And singing. These (it's interesting to observe) are not subjects that attract him. He was a pupil of Gobbi, but Gobbi taught 'interpretation'. In the Stockholm Conservatory, certainly, there were lessons on voice-production, but did he feel, in those early days, that he had to learn to sing, as one might learn a language? It appears not. In the musical evenings at home he had sung as by nature, and the foundation served him well. It is, nevertheless, as a singer that he appeared recently, and afresh, on my own horizons. A collection of recordings from 1971 to 1981 – the golden decade? – had just come out on CD, and I had started to play it, mechanically enough (another record from another pile). But, marvellously, this Prologo, then Valentin's aria, then Rigoletto to the courtiers, shone, soothed, bit, with the exercise of one of those high baritone voices – not exactly Battistini for heaven's sake, not Heinrich Schlusnus either, but a voice that of itself, given a chance, could prove to be a reference-point, like theirs. Wolfram's 'Evening Star', Carlo's 'Per me giunto', and then some songs, among them that favourite of Jussi Björling's, 'Land du välsignade', less thrilling here perhaps but (dare one say it?) more intelligent, and, above all, beautifully sung. So that is what it comes to essentially, beautiful singing. That, in the first place, is why he is here in the book: ideas and dedication yes, but first of all, voice and voice-production.

# Heinrich Schlusnus

Like Håkan Hagegård, Heinrich Schlusnus comes to mind now because of a compact disc. A collection of Schubert songs recorded between 1927 and 1943 has appeared in Nimbus's *Prima Voce* series, and playing it has been a happily fortifying experience: almost (in a broad sense of the word though with a narrow application of it) religious. After all, here we are, in this series of studies (essays, or notes) devoted to singers. Sometimes the singer is a personality or a portent; an extraordinary career or an unusual repertoire may claim attention; a power of acting, a clarity of insight: all of these may occupy us in turn and for a while. But always a thread is there, the common factor, in that all are singers. There must be something of intrinsic worth about this singing-business. What we commonly call 'interpretation' is not singing. The creation of a character on stage – which increasingly becomes the only subject to attract comment when a singer's contribution to the evening's opera receives mention in the newspapers – that also is not singing. Precisely because of this diversification in the singer's art, it is all too easy, even among devotees, to look everywhere except at the centre: which is the voice and its production. With Schlusnus you can hardly miss it: partly because of its excellence, partly (I come to think) because there is not much else. Among all whom we have so far encountered in this series, Schlusnus probably approaches most nearly to the condition of pure singer.

His career was highly successful and distinguished, but not very interesting. Debut as the Herald in *Lohengrin* at Hamburg in 1915 led to an engagement at the Berlin Royal Opera (later the State Opera) the following year, and there he stayed as principal lyric baritone for almost three decades. He appeared in opera elsewhere (Vienna, Bayreuth, Chicago, for example) though never at Covent Garden, the Metropolitan or La Scala. He gave over two thousand Lieder recitals – notable that a statistic should leap out of his biography as vivid and memorable, when one is hoping for something more subtly significant. He toured Europe, the States and South Africa. He gave his last performance in opera in *La traviata* at Coblenz and his final song recital in Hanover, both at the age of 62 and eight years before his death. Life brought its usual complement of contentment and distress – he was badly wounded in the First World War and lost

his son (and his home) in the second – but generally his was a story of happiness and fulfilment. It was also the time of the Third Reich, which he disliked but, as a non-political being, accepted, becoming, as the only singer thus 'honoured', a *Reichskultursenator* in a farcical assembly that sat for a single session. He liked animals, enjoyed a flutter at the gaming tables, was a good family man and a loyal son of his hometown, Braubach-am-Rhein.

The biography, affectionately written by a friend and colleague, Eckart von Naso, with the singer's second wife, Annemay, certainly tells of more than that. The terrors of dictatorship (peremptory warnings and a final command to disassociate from 'undesirable' friends), the onslaught of nerves at a concert or the frog-in-the-throat at a recording session: these come from the life and in turn give life to the portraiture. Particularly moving is the wife's account of the last evening in the singer's life. He suffered from a weak heart and lived as a sick man for months, during which time he had never been heard to sing. His wife tells how she left the door open while she was away from the living-room for a moment, and heard 'this voice'. 'O wie schön ist deine Welt, Vater, wenn sie golden strahlet.' She came back to find her husband standing by the window and, in perfect voice, singing Schubert's 'Im Abendrot'. He had sung it countless times in concerts and in many countries; now, she says, he sang it for himself, and in that moment, though physically a shadow, he seemed again to be strong and great: 'the singer Heinrich Schlusnus as people knew him.'

And yet (it seems almost heartless to say it) 'know him' is what we don't. We feel the love of others towards him and have some picture of a fine and lovable man, yet he is hardly 'seen', his living individuality elusive. And, of this, his singing tells little more.

Take the first seven songs of the Schubert recital mentioned earlier. Perhaps the reader can listen inwardly along with the writer, on this particular playing, which is a quest-session – trying to hear how each song lives in this singer's performance, and for that purpose not paying attention to 'pure singing' (the habitual art which might equally well be exercised in a *solfeggio*) but concerned with what Lotte Lehmann had in mind when she gave to her book on the performance of Lieder the title 'More than Singing'.

'Erlkönig' comes first, with the nightmarish ride of a father home with his young boy, feverishly obsessed by the vision of a spirit-creature intent upon possessing him. Is the father anxious, or even curious, about his son's behaviour? Does the son seem frightened and eventually frantic? Does the spirit-voice entice, intensify and then grab ('so brauch ich Gewalt')? Does the father audibly shudder ('Der Vater grauset's')? Does the child's death (which we know is imminent) shock and impress as a real, unscripted event? After this, on to the two songs with the title 'Wanderers Nachtlied'. In the first, do we feel, as the words say, that the singer is indeed 'weary

Schlusnus as Spielman in *Königskinder* (left) and as Rigoletto

of being drawn onward'? In the second, do we sense from the singer's voice that the promised peace may be the peace of death? 'Im Frühling' is next, with its modulations from major to minor and back again: are these reflected in the voice? Then 'Der Neugierige', where the poet looks to a brook for the answer to his questions: can we tell from the singer's tone that his mood is one of tender, vulnerable uncertainty? And two songs from *Winterreise*: 'Der Lindenbaum' and 'Frühlingstraum'. In the one, do we feel that the invitation to seek peace in the tree's shade has more than literal meaning, and in the other does reality's way of breaking in upon the dream seem real (does it come with an unanticipated ruthlessness, prompting a deeper yearning to re-enter the dreamland of a kinder reality)?

Perhaps the reader, listening alongside, can vary the monotony of a reluctant negative which, in my hearing, attends each of these questions. Perhaps too we would differ (from each other or from the precedent) when it comes to Schlusnus' operatic recordings. But, as we turn to them, we might now listen with another object in view. This scarcely has to be formulated as a quest: it is essentially an acceptance of what is abundantly offered. Only, of course, in order to accept, one has first to recognise it.

Another seven, then, from another compact disc: this, one of the excellent Preiser series, comprising operatic solos recorded in the 1930s (or the singer's forties). Hans Heiling's 'An jenem Tag' is a fervent love-song with

91

a vigorous introduction, just the kind of thing that tempts an unmusical attack and (in Germans especially) guttural emphasis. Nothing of that here, however, and no loss of energy either: simply a fine example of dramatic effect obtained at no expense to the singing tone. Then, from *Zar und Zimmermann*, the nostalgic 'Sonst spielt ich' where the gentler, more relaxed mood brings no flabbiness but the same clean definition, softened in its imprint. No bulges in the line, no intrusive aspirates, no obtrusive consonants, yet with the words as clear as the tone itself. Wolfram's 'Blick ich umher' in *Tannhäuser* is followed by the 'Abendstern', which from the start of his career was the aria most in request wherever Schlusnus sang; and again there is the joy of beautifully even phrases, the contrasts of volume never impeding the flow, and sung with a fine stylistic finish exemplified by the perfect 'turning' of the notes grouped on the first syllable of 'Engel'.

When he sings Verdi it is to show Italians (and the rest of us) what 'bel canto' means. In the easy grace of his 'Il balen del suo sorriso', that most taxing of arias for the Verdi baritone, then in the elegance of 'Di Provenza' and the disciplined force of his way with Rigoletto's outburst against the courtiers: all provide joy for the ear which recognises and values singing.

But now it is time to go back to that Schubert record, and to listen not so much with the 'questing' as with the receptive ear; then to pause, perhaps after 'Am See' or 'Nachtstück' and ask whether any more lovely Schubert *singing* exists on record. Or we could return and finish that opera recital, where the next item would be from *Un ballo in maschera*. There we could pause again to ask whether any finer example comes to mind of the Verdi baritone (even if he sings in German, and even if we recall the great Battistini whom in some purely vocal respects Schlusnus so closely resembles). In his marvellous short story 'The Country of the Blind', H.G. Wells tells of the perfect smoothness to the touch, which is the blind man's ideal of beauty. The singing of Heinrich Schlusnus is an aural counterpart, with a voice so exquisitely smooth that, were it susceptible to touch, even the most fastidious in that sightless land must be moved by its beauty. Such a beauty, moreover, once apprehended for its intrinsic worth, gathers to itself a wealth of emotion which is the product not of 'interpretation' or of 'interest', but of the art proper to a pure, quintessential *singer*.

CHAPTER 19

# Thomas Allen

Thomas Allen has been called the best English baritone since Santley, which is probably true but only the beginning. He is a singer of international renown who has won high praise in the world's leading opera houses and concert halls. In terms of achievement and recognition, services to music and consistent, durable pleasure given to listeners, he belongs to the front rank, irrespective of nationality and predecessors. He is also a singer who is liked (plenty are admired and some are worshipped, but to be liked is a different matter). In all observable and reported ways, he is a man of good humour and good sense; it would be hard to imagine any streak of falsehood or meanness in his nature. A well set-up man too, with a presence to which people warm, as they do to the sound of his voice: the kind of singer, in short, who gets his profession a good name.

In these respects Allen is the all-rounder in whom merit is raised by the necessary degree to gain this front-rank distinction. His special quality is one which ought to be axiomatic, even a truism. He not merely sings, but truly sings – or sings truly. However strange it may seem, this is not a state of affairs that can be taken for granted, as by definition. In true singing, notes are held steadily and linked evenly; a fine quality of tone is preserved throughout the full range of vowels and of the voice's compass. It sounds so simple and is so fundamental. With many famous singers it is not habitual practice; with Allen it is.

This is the real distinction of his singing, whether heard 'live' or on records. Other singers will provide (for example) a more intense or individualised *Dichterliebe* or *Winterreise* but it would be hard to find a version which, in the defined sense, is better sung. His Elijah (to take another instance) has not the dramatic force of several whose recordings can be compared; yet, playing the opening statement of the oratorio in nine or ten different performances, I found only two that conformed fully to the principles of true singing as stated, and these were Allen and the earliest of the singers, the Australian baritone Harold Williams. Sometimes in such comparisons the expressive power of inferior singing will compensate; on the other hand, there is no reason why expression should be achieved at the expense of 'true singing', and often the very fact of fine tone and scrupulous method carries its own authority and gains the readier response.

Certainly the earliest memories of Thomas Allen that come to my mind are of a voice which in quite small roles made one turn to the programme in search of a name. His debut at Covent Garden was as the old seaman Donald in *Billy Budd*, revived in 1971 with Peter Glossop in the name-part. Among the many fine voices in that cast there was still something special about Allen's baritone as it led the crew in the 'Off to Samoa' shanty. Billy was to became one of his own most important roles, and in fact he even then served as understudy for Glossop. His Silvio in *Pagliacci* was the first role to bring him at all fully in focus at the Royal Opera House, and not long afterwards came his Valentin in *Faust*. While that was in repertoire I happened to meet Walter Legge, who had not been to the performance and was, I suppose predictably, rather sceptical. He had witnessed the famous occasion in 1928 when the young American, John Charles Thomas, scored such a success in the role that the Méphisto-phlélès of the not-best-pleased Chaliapin was quite overshadowed. Could Allen have done that, he asked, and of course it was a question with no very satisfactory answer to it. But when we met next, Legge had been to hear for himself and, perhaps having forgotten my original recommenda-tion, praised the new Valentin in terms which could hardly have failed to do justice to the fabled J.C.Thomas or even to Sir Charles Santley himself. I think I answered rather more coolly, adding that Allen made a very good Silvio. 'Silvio!' he said. 'Oh, something much more than that. No, he should be in *Don Carlos* as Posa – and he will!'

Presumably it was Legge who drew the attention of Karajan his way in 1977. Allen had by then become firmly established as a leading singer at home, and when he arrived in Salzburg that August had come from Glyndebourne having given there the first of his hundred-and-more per-formances as Don Giovanni. Karajan auditioned him, with Legge and Schwarzkopf also present. The story is told in Allen's *Singer's Journal* (*Foreign Parts*, 1993). He completed his two arias to Karajan's approval and was then questioned about repertoire. At the mention of *Pelléas et Mélisande* Karajan observed that he would make a capital Golaud and went on to propose the Count di Luna in *Il trovatore*. Allen, very wisely and rather bravely, resisted both propositions, and the more he thought about it afterwards the surer he felt. Golaud was too dark, di Luna too likely to find himself, as he put it, 'among a cast of leather-lunged heavies, all belting away at the top of their voices with a very loud orchestra under Herbert von Karajan's direction to accompany them'. In Verdi, he settled for Rodrigo da Posa (as Legge had prophesied), and in Debussy for his scheduled role of the 'milksop' (Karajan's term) Pelléas in the forthcoming production at Covent Garden: it was one of his greatest successes. The Salzburg episode is interesting in several respects. For one thing, it shows that a level-headed singer is likely to know his own voice best. It also

shows that Allen had the strength of mind to resist the compound of blandishment and bullying in which Karajan was so expert. Something more than 'niceness' is involved here: the temptation to go against one's better judgement and take a short cut to superstardom must have presented itself, and it takes some nerve to stand firm and not be dazzled.

Opera singers nowadays can hardly call their souls their own. If not the conductor, then it is the producer who commands, and at risk to voice, life and limb the singer generally obeys. In his book, Allen gives a charming example, though with no more than passing mention. It concerns the arrangements made for Billy Budd's execution at the Met. In this production, prior to his hanging from the yardarm, Billy 'had to walk the length of a cricket-pitch along a three-foot-wide board, thirty feet above the stage'. They assured him, he says, that the rope was fitted with a device to prevent strangulation should he stumble; what was not explained, apparently, was what would happen if he fell the thirty-foot drop. He went through with it of course and lived to tell the tale, but I daresay most of us would sooner die first.

More insidious and endemic is the power of the producer to distort an opera and the contribution of its singers in order to suit his 'concept'. The most detailed account in Allen's book concerns rehearsals of *Don Giovanni* for a new production at Covent Garden late in 1991. The producer was Johannes Schaaf, whose starting-point appears to have been the notion that Giovanni has 'more in common with the Marquis de Sade than with

Casanova'. Accordingly, he is to stab the Commendatore with a knife instead of killing him in a duel, and he does this out of curiosity, 'avid for each new sensation as it arises'. While the interpretation was not imposed upon the singer by absolute *diktat,* it clearly ran counter to Allen's own (experienced) view of the character and situation. It is an interesting predicament. The singer has respect for the producer and has also the good will and intelligence to welcome an approach that makes all concerned reconsider their preconceptions: 'it seems to me we're doing new and interesting things.' He enjoys exploring character and relates this particular exploration to a novel he has been reading. One can almost see it as fulfilling the idea of opera as an intelligent occupation. Yet for the reader, detached from personalities and the heady atmosphere of the theatre, an immense contradiction looms. One of the points on which Schaaf wins Allen's admiration is his constant reference to the full orchestral score. And, he says, 'since all the answers lie in the music, the score becomes Johannes' vital prop'. But where, asks the reader, does the music (in which all answers lie) tell us that 'Don Giovanni has more in common with the Marquis de Sade than with Casanova'? *Is* there some point at which the music tells of Giovanni's sadism? And, if not, how is it that all these intelligent people, putting their heads so earnestly together in these long, long rehearsals, cannot recognise so evident a distortion and put a stop to it there and then? But this is the modern operatic world, and Allen, like all the singers of our time, is caught up in it. The outcome in this instance was critical dismissal on the first night. Even a critic so sympathetic in principle to new ideas as Tom Sutcliffe of the *Guardian* rejected it: 'Why does Giovanni refuse to fight the Commendatore and instead stab him repeatedly with a stiletto? Is such dishonourable cowardice really part of the Don's game ...? When Giovanni has no nobility, despite a charmer like Tom Allen mugging away, there's no drama in the call to repentance' (7 February 1992). How reduced the singer's status has become! The intelligent and respected artist who knows the role inside out is found 'mugging away' in somebody else's concept. And this after that eternity of 'creative' rehearsal in the best modern fashion.

Sutcliffe's review is a smart one, but worth staying with a moment longer because (what really is rare these days) it actually mentions the singing: 'Allen's sound is growing drier and less generous and the familiar mannerisms are becoming a way of evading vocal limitations.' Whatever the mannerisms, they are not so 'familiar' as to leap to mind, and 'dryness' is a quality I would not myself associate with Allen's voice even now, when he is in his fifties. It is true, however, that for perhaps the past ten years, as heard in the opera house, the voice has been a shining instrument only in the upper register, and even before that, the role which brought out most sheer joy in the voice was the high-lying Pelléas. Elsewhere is a quality which it would be wrong to call cloudy or dull and yet is not quite clear and bright. It may also be true that in this later phase of his operatic

| *Billy Budd* | *Characters in order of appearance* | |
|---|---|---|
| | CAPTAIN VERE . . . . | RICHARD LEWIS |
| | FIRST MATE . . . . | PAUL HUDSON |
| | SECOND MATE . . . . | ERIC GARRETT |
| | MR. FLINT, *Sailing Master* . | RICHARD VAN ALLAN |
| | BOSUN . . . . . | JOHN WOOD |
| | SIX MIDSHIPMEN . . . | GEOFFREY BEDINGFIELD<br>JOHN GIBBONS<br>CHRISTOPHER METZ<br>DAVID O'SULLIVAN<br>JOHN STEVENS<br>CHRISTIAN WILLIAMS |
| | DONALD . . . . . | THOMAS ALLEN |
| | MAINTOP . . . . . | HANDEL OWEN |
| | NOVICE . . . . | ROBERT TEAR |
| | SQUEAK, *Ship's Corporal* . | ROBERT BOWMAN |
| | MR. REDBURN, *First Lieutenant* . | JOHN SHAW |
| | MR. RATCLIFFE, *Lieutenant* . | GWYNNE HOWELL |
| | CLAGGART, *Master-at-Arms* . | FORBES ROBINSON |
| | RED WHISKERS . . . | FRANCIS EGERTON |
| | ARTHUR JONES . . . | KEITH RAGGETT |
| | BILLY BUDD . . . . | PETER GLOSSOP |
| | NOVICE'S FRIEND . . | WILLIAM ELVIN |
| | DANSKER . . . . | DENNIS WICKS |
| | CABIN BOY . . . | DAVID McLOUGHLIN |

Programme for *Billy Budd* at Covent Garden, 10 December 1971

career the dynamic or developing force has been an interest in stage-craft and characterisation: certainly the sour-faced Beckmesser of Covent Garden's *Meistersinger* was something one would never have thought to see, and a triumph of art over nature.

Normally, the alliance of art and nature is what has made Tom Allen so liked and valued among the singers of his time. Indeed, if a word were to be chosen by consensus to describe him (his singing, acting, manner and personality) that word would most probably be 'natural'. The baritone is, after all, the most natural of male voices, and Allen is a most happily-suited exponent. As for the naturalness of his singing, notably absent from his book is any discussion of method or technique: it seems he 'just sang'. A school-teacher gave him lessons and he went through the course at the Royal College of Music, but none of the usual jargon or doctrinal insistence pesters these pages. Yet here is the 'true singer', and method of some sort there surely must be. Whatever it is, it has worked like a charm and has made the art of singing seem an act of nature: which is probably as high a compliment as could be paid to any method yet devised.

97

CHAPTER 20

# Janet Baker

I first knew of Janet Baker as a deed without a name. A friend had been singing in *The Dream of Gerontius* and had come home like one who has glimpsed the gleaming battlements. His wife told me about it. 'Tom says this girl who was singing the Angel ... she's going to have a marvellous future. I've never known him so carried away.' So who was she? What was her name? 'Oh dear,' she said, 'I've forgotten. It was Jean or Jane or Janet or something. Tom'll tell you.' So he did. And so I learned of Janet Baker.

But there can be much in a name. In Mannheim, or Milan, or Moscow, 'Janet Baker' may seem the most romantic of names, but in England's home counties it is decidedly plain. It may have occurred early on to somebody concerned with her career that she should change it. If it ever occurred to her herself, the idea would have been dismissed within ten seconds.

Subterfuge, pretence or show would be foreign to her nature, and for us, her public, she has been the soul of what is honest and principled in her profession. A record collector and, as they used to say, 'connoisseur' once suggested (privately) that her singing of the aria 'Dopo notte' from *Ariodante* in a Handel recital sounded so incredibly fluent and light that he was inclined, in fact, not to credit it and to wonder whether it might have been recorded at a lower pitch and speeded up. I made some enquiries in a quarter where the truth might have been known and met with an amused and amazed negative. 'Besides,' he said, 'Janet would die rather than have a hand in any such thing.'

'Janet would die.' The figure of speech seemed not altogether hyperbolic. We had seen her 'die' so many times and face death oftener still, so that an image formed, more challenging and embattled than Kathleen Ferrier's radiant but relatively passive warmth. Seeing the two of them in memory now on the concert platform, one senses the audience moving towards Ferrier while Baker comes forward towards them. She would often open her recitals with a dramatic monologue or concert aria, Monteverdi perhaps, or Haydn. In this, with eyes almost as expressive as the voice and with the whole body involved, she would commit herself to a passion of questioning, of defiance or repentance, of pleading or reproach,

transforming the classical formalities into urgencies of the flesh-and-blood present.

Of her stage appearances I wish her 'comic' characters – her Dorabella, Octavian, Ariadne's Composer – were in my book of memories. I never saw them, and have to rely on the written word. 'In a bottle-green velvet suit,' wrote Elizabeth Forbes of Baker's Composer (*Opera*, January 1976), 'she sang with fierce concentration and intensity of feeling.' The voice was 'warm and lustrous', the character marked by 'impetuous youthfulness'. 'Youthful, ardent and very, very moving,' wrote Harold Rosenthal of her Octavian (*Opera*, June 1971), and, of her first Dorabella, 'it was perfect as one could wish, displaying an unsuspected sense of fun and singing her arias and duets with a Mediterranean warmth' (July 1967). Eight years later Elizabeth Forbes (February 1976) found the characterisation 'vulnerable and impulsive, by turns hilariously funny and almost unbearably touching'. And (how grateful one is for the snapshot of a particular moment) she recalled the 'enormous relish with which she launched into 'Prenderò quel brunettino'.

Then, among the heroic or tragic characters, memory recalls a burnished Julius Caesar striding across the stage as across a map of Europe, Penelope lamenting motionless within her dark cloak, Vitellia confronting her ambition, Mary Stuart (with that unforgettable 'Royal bastard'!) her mighty rival. In another unexpected extension of the stage repertoire there was Charlotte, at both the Coliseum and Covent Garden, summoning all her will-power to send the luckless Werther off on his desperate final journey. The two Didos stand magnificently apart from each other, the Queen of Berlioz's *Trojans* reckless in the extremity of passion, Purcell's quietly absolute for death in a noble exercise of self-control. With the last *Orfeo* at Glyndebourne I did not realise till reading *Full Circle* (London, 1982) that she was suffering from a severe and unidentifiable allergy; the *Alceste* at Covent Garden I did not see, yet *Full Circle* renders the experience so vivid as almost to persuade me I was there.

*Full Circle* is perhaps the one piece of autobiographical writing by a singer that should be required reading for everyone who enters the profession. As a day-by-day account of life in the last year of her career in opera, it finds her at the top. No one could hope to go higher, with the love and respect of all who most deserve respect in the artistic world, and with years of solid achievement behind her. Yet even here it is a life in which this well-balanced, well-organised member of the artistic family would wake up after a night's sleep to the familiar chill of recognition that this was another performance-day.

She can speak of 'the terrible fear that has dogged me all my life'; and, in the life itself and the principles which guide it, she finds 'there is a terrible kind of ruthlessness'. The fulfilment, the rounding-off of the circle with the last performance of *Orfeo*, seems so fraught with emotion that it is a wonder the heart can bear it: 'The sense of exhilaration and joy I had felt all day rose to bursting-point as the love of everyone in the building surrounded me.' 'To Janet, with love and admiration from your chorus, Glyndebourne 1982' came with a touchingly well-chosen gift. 'My chorus.' This is all emotion on a high plane, a precious but perilous exaltation. Safer, perhaps, the satisfaction (better, she thought, than a rave notice in *The Times*) of hearing an orchestral player remark quietly: 'Bravo. Smashin'.'

Throughout the book, winding in and out, are two little monosyllables, simplicity itself and yet a mystery: 'the voice'. It is through 'the voice' that the soul's work is done, and it is also 'the voice' which dictates the 'terrible ruthlessness' of disciplines and priorities. 'Given to me by God, to be

100

**Wigmore Hall**
Manager: William Lyne
Lessees: The Arts Council of Great Britain

# Song Recital Series

Thursday 26 April 1984 at 7.30 pm

# *Dame Janet Baker*

*mezzo soprano*

# *Geoffrey Parsons*

*piano*

**Arts Council**
OF GREAT BRITAIN

shared with others': that, she says, is 'the sole reason for being a performer'. The singer is 'a vessel' – and 'I have reached a point where I feel myself to be an empty vessel'.

It was not that the voice had, as we say, 'gone'; nor did it ever 'go' while she was before the public. By a very little, in the last years, the vibrations loosened. Originally as closely-textured a voice as any, it very slightly began to show the threads. Yet this was on records: I cannot recall that the last time I heard her sing (which was in *Sea Pictures* at the University of Warwick in 1988) there was any perceptible deterioration. And how well one knew the music in that voice. The recording made with the London Symphony Orchestra under Barbirolli dates back to 1965 when she was just over 30 and entering the years of her prime. If, so many years later, there had been some falling-off of sheer beauty in the sound, no one should have been surprised; but to our ears that night there was none.

And now, listening back over the decades to the voice in memory, what do we hear? Let me try a little random association. Curiously (perhaps), first to rise are the words 'I love you! Fool. I love you', which return to their context in *Phaedra*, the dramatic cantata Britten wrote for her and of which she gave the first performance at Aldeburgh in 1976 – a marvellously accurate appreciation, on his part, of the vessel, with its provision for that 'fierce concentration', its emotional involvement which is also (one can picture it in imagination) an involvement of the body. Then, perhaps by classical linkage, a most tender, in-drawn and reminiscent voice sings Dido's 'Adieu, fière cité'; then (Berlioz again) it asks eager, real questions about travel (the Baltic? the Pacific? Java or Norway?) in *Les nuits d'été*. And this makes me realise that I 'hear' the voice in English and French rather than German and Italian. Yet no sooner is that said than out jumps 'Bereite dich, Zion' and 'Addio, Roma' – another farewell to a city, Ottavia's in *L'incoronazione di Poppea*. And then – another invitation – Dowland's 'Come again', such a genuine, practical proposition that one almost reaches for the diary to fix a date. Oh, and now that we are in English, the *Sea Pictures* ('And see the land where corals lie ... The new sight, the new wondrous sight! ... I would ride as never man has ridden ...') and we are back to *Gerontius* ('Softly and gently') and to the voice heard all those years ago by my friend whose wife reported a great future for the girl whose name she could not quite remember.

# CHAPTER 21

# Jennie Tourel

The late 1940s in post-war Britain were known as 'the age of austerity'. Bread was rationed out in units, chocolates were on 'points', and the best the Government could come up with was to import innumerable tins of a fish called 'snoek'. Record collectors, however, had their own supply of champagne, a veritable fountain which would play for rather less than two minutes at a time but could be renewed perpetually. 'Ah, what a dinner I've just had!' exclaimed the happy lady in song and in French. She had had a drop to drink – more than a drop perhaps – and it made her laugh. As the record spun giddily on the turntable, her laughter made us laugh too. The 'champagne' was, in fact, a fine and sprightly brew, expertly bottled by Offenbach in his operetta *La Périchole*. And it was all the more remarkable in that, up to that time, the general verdict on the singer's records had been that they were very good, but a trifle *dull*.

But that just goes to show, for it is doubtful whether anyone who heard Jennie Tourel in the flesh would have used that word about her. Her Rossini arias on record, most particularly the finale to *La Cenerentola*, enjoyed a wide circulation, and for those who, like myself, were devoted to the memory of Conchita Supervia they seemed ... respectable. A pleasant, well-trained voice sang 'Non più mesta' with impeccably good vocal manners; but where, we asked, was the sparkle, the challenge, the ever-changing expression? We missed them, and dearly longed for the Spanish spell-binder, rattle and all.

Somebody should have told us (perhaps somebody did) that Tourel herself was a great admirer of Supervia and counted her to have been among the favourite influences in her early career. At all events, it was Tourel who gave New York's opera-going public (as Supervia had done for Londoners) their first taste of the authentic Rossini mezzo. When (for a single performance) she sang Rosina at the Metropolitan in 1945 she took over from a long and illustrious line of light sopranos which led back from Lily Pons to the house premiere in the first season of all, when the great Marcella Sembrich had converted the lesson scene into a miniature concert, with Proch's *Variations* as its show-piece. Tourel interpolated the solo from *La Cenerentola*. She also won approval, and was of course in the

vanguard, for in this department it was with the mezzos that the future lay.

Tourel was then 45, though ten years were docked from that in the public prints, which also described her as Canadian. Her family name was Davidovich, and she was born in 1900 at Vitebsk in Belorussia. The story of her banker-father on a business trip to Montreal, where her mother gave

---

## ROYAL FESTIVAL HALL
(General Manager : T. E. BEAN)

### Friday, October 2nd at 8 p.m.

WILFRID VAN WYCK announces
(Under the auspices of Emperor Concerts Ltd.)

## THE WORLD - FAMOUS SOPRANO

# JENNIE
# TOUREL

*Unequalled Among Living Singers* (Virgil Thomson—N.Y. Herald Tribune)

## LONDON PHILHARMONIC ORCHESTRA
(Leader : JOSEPH SHADWICK)

### CONDUCTOR :

# ROYALTON
# KISCH

SYMPHONY No. 39 in E flat  -  - MOZART

KINDERTODENLEIDER  -   -  - MAHLER

SYMPHONY No. 9 in C major  -  SCHUBERT

---

**TICKETS :**  3/6,   5/-,   7/6,   10/-,   12/6,
*from Royal Festival Hall Box Office (WATerloo 3191),  Chappells (MAYfair 7600)  and all Ticket Agencies*

Royal Festival Hall, 1952

birth, was devised to gain entry into the States in wartime when the need
was dire. The family fled from Russia in 1918, living for a while in Danzig
and Switzerland, and settling in Paris. There Jennie was heard singing
self-accompanied Russian gipsy songs and was recommended to teacher
Anna El-Tour (hence 'Tourel'). She joined the Russian opera in Paris and
at about the same time accepted an engagement with the Chicago Opera
where she sang small parts in the company of some remarkable singers.
Substantially, her career began with a *Carmen* at the Opéra-Comique in
1933. This came about from one of those dreamlike developments at an
audition, when she was asked whether by any chance she knew the role.
Swallowing hard, she told a fib and prepared for some intensive learning.

105

In 1935 when Giacomo Lauri-Volpi appeared as guest artist at the Opéra-Comique, Tourel sang Charlotte to his Werther. Her other favourite role was that of Mignon in Thomas's opera, and in this she made her debut at the Metropolitan. One of the performances was broadcast and recorded. For an account see Paul Jackson's *Saturday Afternoons at the Old Met* (Amadeus/Duckworth, 1992): almost as good as having a transcript.

What Jackson hears there (and the recording, primitive as it is, should surely become more generally available) is an artist, not merely of evident distinction but one who is clearly capable of arousing an audience ('Miss Tourel must be very happy today for the fine ovation she's been given at her debut,' said the announcer. 'People are really standing in the aisles and boxes applauding.') She also sang a successful Carmen, yet after this promising if limited beginning (one performance of each opera) there was no follow-up, and when she reappeared in 1944, few remembered the fleeting debutante of 1937.

Of course one wonders why this was so; and one also follows, with renewed recognition of the horrors of that time, the critical point her career reached just when it should have blossomed. As a Jew in the Paris of 1940 she seems hardly to have realised the peril she was in, and left only two days before the invasion. From Portugal she sailed to America, where she found that her 500-odd appearances at the Opéra-Comique counted for little and that she had to start building a reputation over again. Her luck changed when Toscanini, auditioning for a Juliet in the New York Philharmonic's anniversary performance of Berlioz's dramatic symphony, accepted her instantly and eagerly. A recital-debut followed at the Town Hall in 1943 in which a capacity audience heard an unusually varied programme of songs along with arias from *La Cenerentola* and *La clemenza di Tito*. In the audience was the composer Gretchaninov who later dedicated a song to her, and among her encores was Leonard Bernstein's 'I hate music'.

Bernstein became a lifelong friend, so much so that nowadays it is very often the first thing ('Lennie and Jennie') that the name 'Tourel' conjures up – almost as though the singer has been reduced to a page-reference in the composer/conductor's biography. They gave many concerts together, including one at Carnegie Hall in 1969 when Harold Schonberg in the *New York Times* compared them with the legendary associations of Gerhardt and Nikisch, Lehmann and Walter. On her death in 1973, the *NYT* also carried an obituary tribute by Bernstein in which he wrote, movingly, not only of her great gifts but also of the paradoxes of her nature. She was, he said, 'So richly endowed, surrounded bv loving friends, gallant admirers, and adoring fans. Yet she was never free of the always shocking awareness of isolation – except in those few thousand minutes of her life when she was transported by the bliss of communication through her art.'

Some of those 'few thousands', of course, we have on records. Of the 'live' recordings, one of the best and happily newly available now on CD, is of the recital she gave with James Levine at the Lincoln Centre on 19 January 1970. It was originally released as a commemorative issue not long after the singer's death, and I remember thinking how remarkable it was that a woman in her sixtieth year could subject herself to the test of such a strenuous programme and emerge unscathed – but of course that was based on an acceptance of the official date of birth (even the *NYT* obituary gave her age as 63), when in fact she was nearly 70. With that in mind, it is not 'remarkable' but astonishing. She sings sixteen songs followed by five encores. Her phrasing is broad, her intonation almost entirely secure, her registers well equalised, her movement from softest to loudest tones flexible and assured. And in the whole of the evening's singing you hear no wobble or intimation of wobble. The tone has lost the richness that we know from her early records (though even these were made when she was in her mid-forties), but there are still notes of great beauty, not least the high Gs and thereabouts.

Nor does she spare herself in the choice of songs. Beethoven's 'An die Hoffnung', for instance, is a formidable undertaking for a singer of whatever age: a short cantata rather than a Lied. The cry of hope here is worthy of an inspired Leonore, and each changing expression, from the tender call ('Dann nahe dich') to the contralto depths of 'sunken urns', is faithfully reflected in the voice. Finest of all is the Liszt group which follows, with the beautifully clean intervals and yearning spirit of 'Kennst du das Land?' and the bold attack of 'Vergiftet sind meine Lieder' contrasting with the stillness of singer and audience in the 'Wanderers Nachtlied'. For Debussy's Bilitis songs she somehow takes years off her voice to be a girl again (causing us incidentally to remember how cross Maggie Teyte was when she thought the accompanist George Reeves had given Tourel her 'secrets'). The Russian songs remind us of her origins, and, among the encores, the *Périchole*'s laughing song reminds us of our champagne fountain in the age of austerity.

Tourel's was a long, busy, rewarding career. She travelled widely, singing in Africa and South America, teaching in Jerusalem as well as at the Juilliard in New York. She gave a full share of her time to living composers. Most famous perhaps is her creation in 1951 of Baba the Turk in *The Rake's Progress*. Lord Harewood (*Opera*, November 1951) thought her badly miscast but added, 'What it [the role] got was a delicate miniature in appearance and sound, something in its way so perfect and pretty that no gentleman would have been disinclined to overlook the matter of the beard in consideration of the other attractions.'

Perhaps that was the kind of thing Bernstein meant when he referred to her 'gallant admirers'. Whatever he had in mind, there were surely tears in his eyes as he wrote the final tribute: 'Wherever she started to sing, that stage was the Holy of Holies. And she opened her mouth in praise of music, she was a High Priestess, and each phrase was the name of God, and that moment was the Sabbath of Sabbaths.'

107

CHAPTER 22

# Brigitte Fassbaender

Just as one sometimes thinks it is worth the agony of losing a train ticket, a house key, a wrist watch or whatever for the pleasure of finding it again, so it may happen that a bad night at the opera will have a redemptive pleasure in store by revealing all the more clearly the star-quality of a singer who shone among the general drabness. So it was with a dim *Fledermaus* suddenly lit up with the arrival of its Prince Orlofsky. Fassbaender's voice brings a thrill in itself, which with the eyes (big, black and looking out of a boyish face), the high cheek-bones and cavalier curl of the lip, commands immediate attention. That was it: when Fassbaender arrived, you paid attention. Not since the retirement of Elisabeth Schwarzkopf has there been a singer with such a sense of presence, both in appearance and voice.

It is also true that in concert-work she would allow herself a certain licence that Schwarzkopf would not have permitted at any price. She would lean across the piano towards her accompanist throughout an introduction or postlude, perhaps to show involvement, asserting that pianist and singer are as one, the piano's commentary felt as part of the singer's own expression. At first it was disconcerting, even suggesting a sort of supervisory function; later it gained acceptance as a collaborative gesture, or as arising out of the impulse to find some less formal stance than the held position which a singer normally adopts at the beginning and end of a song. At any rate it was an independent spirit that held sway up there on the platform, one not too narrowly bound by the conventions it still respected, or, for that matter, by the literal notation of a still-respected score.

A boldness of approach, then, stamped the Fassbaender evening; but it was the voice itself that really generated and sustained the excitement. London audiences had a recent opportunity of hearing it again in the course of masterclasses given in the Wigmore Hall. In these she would illustrate points readily, singing in any range from soprano to baritone. The upper notes were still there (we had, I think, a B-flat or two) and it was interesting to note how in the exchange of phrases it was often the younger voice that sounded frayed or surface-scratched. Always a special thrill lay in the lower register. Tough and steely, it has remained abso-

lutely pure and firm, a boldly affirmative sound, penetrative without harshness, a gleaming metal, like a suit of dark armour. Remembering the excitement of their part in her best days as a singer, one recalled also how these chest-tones were integrated within the full scale of her voice: she must, at one stage, have had to work hard at the 'bridge', which could so easily have given way with an audible and damaging weakness in the lower-middle area. In fact, memory (supported by records) tells of a sturdy voice from top to bottom, rather marvellously managing to get the best of both worlds by combining a variety of coloration with an essential unity of timbre and production.

Perhaps that is one of the advantages of growing up as a singer's daughter. If from the cradle onwards, the voices of leading opera singers are part of the air one breathes, then, for better or worse, something of their ways and means must be assimilated. Willi Domgraf-Fassbaender was 42 years old at the time of Brigitte's birth in 1939. He must then have been in his prime, securely placed as principal lyric-baritone at the Berlin Staatsoper, his reputation at home fortified by repeated successes at Glyndebourne and Salzburg. The house was a regular visiting place for friends and colleagues such as Maria Cebotari, Erna Berger, Peter Anders and Hans Hotter. The mother had been an actress, and Brigitte went to school with Anders' children, so that everything pointed in one direction. The initiative seems nevertheless (and characteristically) to have come from herself, the power and quality of her developing voice coming as a surprise to all concerned. She studied with her father at the Nuremberg Conservatory, and made her debut with the Bavarian State Opera in 1961. Again the circumstances were auspicious.

Central to Fassbaender's thinking in later years has been the value of an apprenticeship such as she herself served as a member of the company in Munich. Like most older singers – and, it must be said, like most older singers of whatever generation – she takes a generally disenchanted view of present and future conditions. The points are familiar enough: that young singers spend too little time on technique, that management and media will seize upon a talent and exploit it prematurely, that the pressure to become an international singer exacts a penalty which threatens the whole profession. The equivalent of her years in Munich is, she feels, something every opera singer should have. You learn the trade, develop the art, enjoying the stability of a base as well as the fellowship of a community. Given wise direction from the top, the singer will grow naturally according to talent. The opinion is, as I say, pretty general among senior artists, but it carries more weight when, as here, it comes from one whose temperament is so positive and active, so little likely to join in the commonplace chorus.

Of her own talents and their nurture in those early years, recordings allow us a more than usually vivid glimpse. Allotted a due succession of anonymous page-boy and ladies-maid roles, she was also afforded some

enviable opportunities from the start. In her second year, 1962, she sang Olga to the accomplished Lensky of Fritz Wunderlich in a production of *Eugene Onegin* that has since appeared on compact disc. Even here, and even from the first phrases, she has a way of concentrating the tone so that the ear distinguishes it in ensembles, and then in her solo there is that forthright delivery, making the words work. By the end of the decade she had clearly become mistress of this particular art, and in the famous *Meistersinger* of 1969 under Kubelik, the Magdalene is for once a leading character. All that chatter which generally goes unnoticed, is so finely pointed that each new entry is a delight and the maid becomes a radiant presence matching the mistress, the Eva of Gundula Janowitz.

Fassbaender came to sing a great variety of major roles, many of which are not on records at all. Her Princess Eboli in *Don Carlos* would have been something to hear, as, in not too large a house, would her Amneris. As with some other strongly characterised voices (Callas, Supervia, Martinelli, Gobbi) it is possible to 'hear' inwardly the sound of her singing, even in parts she never took or never recorded. And of course much did get recorded – some of it in excerpts such as her Carmen, one who has no truck with the slinky seductive business, but whose 'Seguedille' suggests that she would be fun to be with. Of her travesto roles, Hansel is on record and Octavian on film, an ardent portrayal, impulsive and charismatic in a way that recalls Irmgard Seefried, but is more credibly masculine. In *Così fan tutte*, her full-bodied Dorabella plays off against the silver-lined Fiordiligi of Janowitz. In the Wagner repertoire, her Waltraute is one of the glories of the Solti *Ring* and her Brangäne in the Carlos Kleiber recording has a strongly edged vehemence complementary to the imperious velvet of Margaret Price's Isolde. Her Azucena too is preserved, passionate with steely resonance, doubly moving by contrast in the tender delusions of 'Ai nostri monti'.

Even so, it is probably with two song cycles that subsequent generations will come to identify the essential Fassbaender. She is one of the few women to have had a success with *Winterreise*. With 'sorrow etched into the very timbre' and its 'strong, often deliberately harsh chest tones', her singing corresponds to Desmond Shawe-Taylor's description of Elena Gerhardt, in some ways more completely than do Gerhardt's own records. Yet the abiding memory of this *Winterreise* is not so much of sorrow as of stoicism. The strength of the more defiant songs almost promises to carry this embattled soul through; at the end of Fassbaender's performance (in the concert hall even more than on records) one was by no means convinced that this singer is meeting the organ-grinder in death. Perhaps the strength of such a performance goes against the grain of the work (and maybe that of itself heightens tension and the sense of tragedy). And perhaps it is not, after all, in the Schubert cycle but in Brahms's *Die schöne Magelone* that she is most completely in her element. Here she speaks a narration as well as singing the songs, their contrasts thrown into relief, their story-book adventures intensified.

The voice which with such eagerness and relish tells of the lovely Magelone is the same as that which, as a teacher's, quickens life in her pupils. 'Enjoy and laugh and dance,' she will say. 'Throw it over your shoulder' about one phrase; 'a feeling of dancing on your diaphragm' of another. 'Make fun with the words,' she urges, then, summarising: 'Control and discipline are something you can't do without ... and perhaps slowly, slowly, it grows within the heart.' Wise words no doubt; but more personal are two others: 'Dare it!' That's Fassbaender in a nutshell. And her voice, its peculiar gift and character among all the singers evoked in these brief chronicles, is the voice of adventure.

# CHAPTER 23

# Hans Hotter

'Auf wolkigen Höh'n wohnen die Götter' (*Siegfried*, Act 1 scene ii).

'On the cloudy heights dwell the Gods.' And in the lovely, irresponsible days of opera-going way back in the past, where the Gods dwelt there dwelt I. From a lofty perch in the gallery, the deplorable practice was then, in the first minute of an interval, to clatter down those stone stairs, out into the street and across the way to the Nag's Head, which was not then as it is now. It must have been while on some such errand that, after the second act of Covent Garden's *Walküre* or the first of *Siegfried*, I found myself standing next to the Scottish bass David Ward, a sturdy partaker and no mean Wotan himself. And now follows the confession to which all this is preamble. 'How's Hotter doing?' he asked, seeing that I had come over from the opera house. And I: 'He's got the wobbles,' I replied. The big man paused and put down his glass. 'Ay,' he said, 'and you'd have the wobbles if you'd sung the Ring as many times as that man has.'

There being little likelihood of that, we let the matter drop and changed the subject. But the exchange has remained vivid for forty years or more, and the rebuke was well deserved. The disrespectfulness of my reply had been gross, and its use of English unforgivable.

But this matter of 'the wobbles', delineated with nervous facetiousness as though it were some unmentionable medical disorder, persists. In Jürgen Kesting's *Die grossen Sänger* (Düsseldorf, 1986) the section on Hotter opens with a discussion of this very point. Two texts stand as chapter-headings, one (broadly) on the undesirability of the 'wobble', the other on the excellence of the rest. Kesting agrees that steadiness of voice-production is not merely desirable but an essential feature of good singing. As against that he quotes John Culshaw, producer of the first studio recording of Wagner's Ring cycle, acknowledging that some listeners found Hotter's unsteadiness more 'distressing' than he himself did, but warmly stating the grounds of his admiration which in his view far outweighed the objections.

What, anyway, is this 'wobble'? It is not a technical term, and though some scientific system of measurement might be possible the chances of establishing a tight and secure definition as a starting-point are probably small. Yet it is a quality in singing that listeners generally recognise and condemn. I do not doubt, for instance, that on that particular night at Covent Garden Hotter, as Wotan, had sung with what I perceived to be a 'wobble': that is (now attempting a definition) a recurrently obtrusive vibration of the voice, the vibrations being slower and wider than is normal, aggravated by the irregularity of their occurrence (not therefore the same as a 'beat'). But the remarkable discovery then is that the degree of looseness or irregularity needed to produce this impression can be very small. Take for example Hotter's singing of that phrase ('Auf wolkigen Höh'n wohnen die Götter') as heard in the Culshaw recording. No charge of 'wobble' would be likely to arise out of that; only with the high D-flat of 'Götter' is there a loosening, and even then it has to be by the standards set by a singer such as Friedrich Schorr, Hotter's predecessor in the interwar years. Yet the ear makes its adjustments perhaps too readily and is not initially deceived. Very often the experience is that when one starts to listen, as at some random point in that second scene, the immediate impression is of an unsteady voice. Wotan's second word for instance ('dir' in 'Heil dir') or the entrance of the voice at 'Gastlich ruht' ich', or the end of the phrase 'wer unhold ist': individually these are mild examples, not really justifying that horrible word, yet collectively they incur it.

Here is the paradox: viewed in one light, such tiny details (we are talking about the irregularity of a second's or a split-second's duration) are at most flecks of dust on the God's cloak; in another light they are woven fatally into the very fabric, or, rather, the very being, because the godhead lies in the voice.

It is perhaps at this point that a further thought should interpose as arbiter. As with so many dilemmas, we assume that a choice has to be made, whereas both views reveal a truth and we simply have to live with both of them.

'Wobble' apart then, let me give some further personal memories of Hotter on stage; and these, it must be said, are every bit as potent so many years later. The voice heard now in memory is broad, ample and enveloping. Still in this second scene of *Siegfried* (the one which in Anna Russell's sketch has Wotan coming down to Earth to play with Mime at Twenty Questions): its depth has majesty, its power ease; it travels, in Shakespeare's phrase if with a different meaning, 'up to the hearing of the Gods' and is located not so much at a place on stage as in space. But when we look at the stage, what we see is the God himself, a massive and noble being whose stillness is part of the power.

In other scenes, other operas, the power may lie in humanity and even weakness. In some ways, Hotter's masterpiece was the reduced (but extended!) Wotan of *Walküre* Act 2. The mute wretchedness of expression when under the lash of Fricka's tongue (especially if Fricka was the superb Rita Gorr) was like a great wolf-hound chided for a wrong-doing it thought to have hidden. Then came the long tale of shame in which the voice ranges

from passionate avowal to whispered confession. Most poignant then were the final moments of the act when Wotan looks down on the body of his son whose death has been fated with his connivance. These of course are features of the part, the creation of Wagner; but the part was never at once so human and so awesome as when embodied by Hotter's tall figure, his capacious voice, and his stillness.

115

If, as I believe, the year in which I clattered down the gallery steps to that encounter in the pub was sometime around 1960, Hotter would have been already something like 50 years of age. He was born on 19 January 1909, and had been singing leading roles since 1930. Even in his first year, with the small company at Troppau in the Sudetenland, he was cast as Wotan the Wanderer in *Siegfried*. Yet it was not entirely a matter of too-much-too-soon. He had wise and watchful friends who saw to it that at Prague and, from 1934 onwards, Hamburg he had work sufficient to give experience and not too much of it at any one time. Still, it may come as a surprise that one of his regular roles was that of Tonio in *Pagliacci*, and that he was also a Basilio, an Escamillo and a Scarpia. His roles in the Verdi repertoire included Macbeth, Iago, Boccanegra and (hard to imagine) Falstaff. In *Don Carlos* he played King Philip or, more often, the Grand Inquisitor (which it is said he sang more frequently than any other except Wotan). Handel's Julius Caesar, Mozart's Don Giovanni, Gounod's Méphistophélès, Mussorgsky's Boris and Puccini's Schicchi were all at one time or another under his belt. He took his share of 'modern' roles and premieres, most notably in association with Strauss. The Kommendant in *Friedenstag* (1938), Olivier in *Capriccio* (1942), and Jupiter in *Der Liebe der Danaë* (1944) were all his 'creations'. There were also oratorios (the Bach Passions for instance) and the very different and increasingly important world of the song-recital.

It was in Lieder that he was first heard in Britain. This came about, like so many of the most influential developments for European artists in the postwar years, through the perceptive agency of Walter Legge. He had been aware of Hotter since before the war, and had Sir Thomas Beecham thought him right for the role Hotter might have sung Sarastro in the famous recording of *Die Zauberflöte*. He might also have appeared at Glyndebourne, but John Christie thought it inadvisable, because 'if you spread out your arms on our stage, we won't be able to see your hands'. (Those hands, incidentally, were worth seeing – it is part of the Fassbaender family lore that he would hold baby Brigitte in the palm of one of them.) The Lieder recital (*Winterreise* for the BBC in 1947) led to his engagement at Covent Garden, and from there the international career opened out. He made his New York debut as the Metropolitan's Dutchman in 1950, singing in Rudolf Bing's first season there; and it was on account of Bing that he left the company three years later – the suggestion having been made that Hotter's strength lay in 'supporting' character-roles and as a bass, Pogner rather than Hans Sachs for instance.

His career on the operatic stage, 'wobble' and all, has spanned the decades as broadly as his voice encompassed the long Wagnerian phrases. He gave his official farewell appearance at the Vienna State Opera as the Grand Inquisitor in 1978, but was reported to have sung *Winterreise* as late as 1985. He also had a second career, as producer, his work including a *Ring* production at both Covent Garden and Bayreuth. For many years

116

Hotter as the Speaker in *Die Zauberflöte*

he has been a devoted teacher, and has served selflessly on adjudicating committees. Until recently he could still be heard and seen as the Speaker in performances of Schoenberg's *Gurrelieder*: the last occasion, in England, in 1994, was indeed unforgettable, his enunciation so fired by the spirit of the poetry, and his presence so instinct with unostentatious dignity. He was then 85. At the time of writing he is in his ninetieth year. In the fullness of time the musical world will sing his epitaph to the long notes of Brünnhilde's 'Ruhe, ruhe, du Gott'. In the meanwhile one (semi-) penitent critic will not flatter himself into supposing that there will be any special joy in Valhalla over this sinner that repenteth, but at least he feels better for having confessed.*

---

* It should be added (as pointed out in a letter to *Opera Now* by Noelle Barker who studied with him) that Hotter suffered, sometimes acutely, from asthma and various allergies.

CHAPTER 24

# Marcel Journet

References to 'in-depth casting' may look like a bad pun when they are made with the allocation of the bass roles principally in mind. But so it is: for a performance of *Il trovatore* or *Rigoletto* to meet the standards of a gala occasion, the company must call upon its leading bass or pay for one of the few international top-liners. If the tones which rouse the troops with that opening 'All'erta' lack the thrill of sonorous authority, *Il trovatore* gets off to a bad start. If the assassin's voice in *Rigoletto* is not dark as his trade and dangerous as the Mantuan alleyway at midnight, then an essential flavour goes missing.

The old record catalogues showed due appreciation of this when for their star of stars, Enrico Caruso, they chose as his invariable companion-bass Marcel Journet. In trios from *I Lombardi, Faust* and *Samson et Dalila*, quartets from *Faust* and *Martha*, and the sextet from *Lucia di Lammermoor,* the words at the end of the impressive list of singers were always 'and Journet'. In those famous recordings of the Sextet, the soprano (Sembrich, Galli-Curci or Tetrazzini), baritone (Scotti, De Luca, Amato) and the make-weights, would change, but two remained constant: Caruso himself and the bass.

Journet also recorded duets with Caruso, as he did in this period with Geraldine Farrar, Giovanni Martinelli, Pasquale Amato and others. His solo records embraced a wide repertoire, French, Italian and German, including some notable Wagnerian selections. And curiously it was in a Wagnerian excerpt that he made the one mistake of his career as a recording artist. In 1908 a pioneering attempt was made to record the quintet from *Die Meistersinger*. Johanna Gadski was the soprano, and her difficult solo went well as indeed did the ensemble until about halfway through when a false entry was made by Journet, who stuck to it with disastrous results up to the final chords. A second 'take' put all right – and the first was issued! It is said that the single-sided disc appeared with a photograph of the five singers listening with every sign of delight to what was presumably a playback of their efforts. If a copy of that original envelope survives it must be something of a collector's piece.

As a rule, reliability was Journet's trademark. It is the lot of basses to sing night after night, often in secondary roles that pass without comment

118

Journet as Méphistophélès in *Faust*

– as long as the artist puts not a foot wrong or a phrase out of place – and
Journet took his full share of these. After training in Paris and making his
debut in 1891 at Béziers in *La favorite*, he served his apprenticeship at La
Monnaie in Brussels. He came to Covent Garden first in 1897, reappearing
with a single year's absence in every summer season till 1909. In 1900 he
became a stalwart of the Metropolitan in New York, singing with the
company in a total of 416 performances over an eight-year period. Seasons
at Chicago, Buenos Aires, Rio de Janeiro and Monte Carlo all brought
success but were incidental to the great reputation he enjoyed at the Paris
Opéra where he sang almost to the time of his death at the age of 66 in
1933. There was also a remarkable St. Martin's Summer when, from 1922
to 1929, Toscanini engaged him for some of the most important produc-

119

tions mounted during his second reign as Musical Director at La Scala, Milan.

It is often said that Journet spent much of his career under the shadow of one colleague or another. P.G. Hurst in *The Golden Age Recorded* writes that his 'undeserved part in the early days of his great career was to serve as a sort of understudy to Plançon'. That most accomplished of singers was also principal lyric bass at the Metropolitan, and it would have been with him and Edouard de Reszke in mind that the New York critic W.J. Henderson, recalling what in his view were the debased *Huguenots* performances of the post-De Reszke era, described Journet as 'a lamentably weak and colourless defender of the faith' (*New York Sun*, 28 December 1912). Later it was pretty certainly the arrival of Chaliapin, and his commandeering of the best roles, that made Journet leave the company.

And yet he was not altogether undervalued in these years. His first two seasons at Covent Garden, for instance, gave him enviable opportunities with the *Faust* Méphistophélès, the Landgrave in *Tannhäuser*, the King in *Hamlet*, and old Marcel ('defender of the faith') in *Les Huguenots*. With the Metropolitan company he was tried out very thoroughly, and with evident success, on tour as their regular Colline, Ferrando and Sparafucile, Pharaoh to Plançon's Ramphis, Chaplain to Melba's Lucia, and so forth. By his second year he was sufficiently well established to take part in the jealously observed opening night of the New York season as Capulet in *Roméo et Juliette*. This was, after all, 'the Golden Age of Opera', and the top jobs were as hard to get as ... as I daresay they are nowadays.

Journet's international reputation was made in New York and London, but the likelihood is that the best years of his career were spent in Paris. His debut at the Opéra occurred on 2 October 1908 when he sang as the King in *Lohengrin*. From then till the time of his absence during the First World War he must have been in his absolute prime as a singer. Records testify to that, also making it clear that this prime was truly magnificent. He returned in 1919, and among the total of 29 roles which he sang there at the Garnier were eight house or world creations. He also returned to Covent Garden, where he had last been heard in 1909. The role announced for the occasion had been that of Leporello in *Don Giovanni* which would have further distinguished the famous revival of 1926. This failed to materialise but the following year he appeared as Escamillo in *Carmen*, a role he repeated in 1928 with the addition of a more consistently praised performance as the Father in *Louise*. In Milan his roles were the Father again, Golaud, Méphistophélès, Hans Sachs, the Wanderer (*Siegfried*), Dosifei (*Khovanshchina*) and Simon Mago in the long-awaited world premiere of Boito's *Nerone*: the plums, in fact.

It was an illustrious career, yet, in all truth, what keeps it alive, and its exponent alive as a 'singer of the century', are the recordings he made principally in this prime period, from roughly 1908 to 1916. These of

course include the associations with Caruso and other luminous contemporaries, but there is also a rich legacy of solos in which, no doubt, the most immediately impressive feature is the voice itself. A solidly comprehensive instrument, it serves in many capacities. Its main category, as *basso cantante*, brings to mind the finely even, well-nourished cello legato exemplified in his French arias, Dapertutto's Mirror song in *Les contes d'Hoffmann* or Solomon's lyrical avowal of love for the Queen of Sheba in the opera by Gounod. His softening of the voice for Mark Antony's reading aloud of the love-letter from Cleopatra makes newly attractive that piece of rare late Massenet. By contrast, the sectarian relish ('Piff, paff, pouf, slay them all!') of the old Huguenot and the 'valse infernale' sung by the sire of *Robert le Diable* testify still more powerfully to the singer's versatility. Best of all may well be the solo from Adam's *Le chalet* with Journet

121

most persuasively groomed as the sonorous and accomplished successor to Pol Plançon, most stylish and immaculate of basses on record.

The Wagnerian excerpts add another dimension. Later, when the electrical process of recording had come in, the 50-year-old Journet would sing Wotan's farewell and Sachs's 'Wahn' monologue with distinction but they have not the glory of the records he made under the old process. There the voice is kingly and he presents in turn a Wolfram for whom the low notes of the Evening Star solo give no trouble, a Wotan who could rejoice in the high Fs so embarrassing to many, and a Hagen with confidence in ever more weighty resources at command. An unexpected treat to set alongside those is the Catalogue song of Leporello, an exemplary combination of lively characterisation and scrupulous vocal style. Don Basilio's recipe for slander in *Il barbiere di Siviglia*, and the sardonic nihilism of Boito's Mefistofele also impress as being both effective and uncheapened. A disappointment among the Italian arias may be King Philip's in *Don Carlos*, even in its incomplete form too outgoing and taken too fast. Fine, though, is the memento of his part in the *Nerone* premiere from 1924, showing the voice scarcely changed from what it had been ten, twenty years earlier. It did eventually change, as the later records make clear. Though the low notes themselves are still there, the timbre has lost depth. More regrettably, the once impregnable firmness has begun to loosen, and the style to become less polished. A loss of focus and a tendency to aspirate were noted by English critics writing of his Escamillo in 1928. His part in the complete recording of *Faust* should have been a model of golden-age standards borne aloft to inspire the 1930s, but this late Méphistophélès is a grand *routinier* rather than a prince of devils.

Even so, these were the years in which Journet won from fellow singers tributes that stand by him in the hall of fame. Ezio Pinza, looking back in his autobiography from a position as the leading lyric bass of his time (and probably, as we see it, of the whole century), recalled his young days at La Scala where two professional giants showed him the way. One was Chaliapin, the other Journet. 'I have never heard anyone (he wrote) go from high notes to low ones with the ease and sonority of the middle-aged Journet'. He was an artist, said Pinza, who never stopped growing, and in those years was 'crowned with glory'. The other tribute comes from the tenor Giacomo Lauri-Volpi, implacable foe to mediocrity and jealous guardian of his country's status as the land of song. In his *Voci parallele*, first published in 1955, he remembers singing the role of Arnoldo at the Metropolitan to the Guglielmo Tell of Giuseppe Danise, then, at La Scala, with Benvenuto Franci and in Buenos Aires with Carlo Galeffi. None of these eminent compatriots impressed him as did the veteran Frenchman: 'Heroism, plasticity, magnanimity, power: behold in them the voice, the art and the soul, of Marcel Journet.'

CHAPTER 25

# Lucien Fugère

In the Parliament of Singers, Fugère would be Father of the House. He was born in 1848 and lived to bestride the centuries, dying in 1935 and making his last records at the age of 82. His voice was still in fine trim, the style immaculate.

Fugère was the complete Parisian. The year of his birth is remembered as the Year of Revolutions and in Paris it saw the fall of King Louis-Philippe. The Second Empire, the Franco-Prussian War, the Commune, the Third Republic, the Dreyfus Case, the Entente and the 1914 war, Fugère was there for them all. The Paris of *La vie de bohème* and *Les enfants du Paradis* was the city of his inheritance; the Paris of Hugo and Proust, Garnier and Haussman, Saint-Saëns and Debussy, the Impressionists and the Cubists, Diaghilev and the *Sacre du printemps*, was his also. Through this extraordinary panoply of change, Fugère was a Parisian constant. Noticed first as a bright lad, with a voice and a powerhouse of energy, he became a mainstay of the Opéra-Comique, learning character-parts as fast as they were fed to him, accumulating altogether nearly a hundred roles and taking part in more than thirty world premieres. He sang elsewhere in France but only once abroad, a 'capital' Leporello in Covent Garden's Jubilee *Don Giovanni* of 1897. In Paris itself he was an institution, as a character ('Fu-Fu' to his friends), a teacher (the only one Mary Garden would ever acknowledge), and almost to the end of his life, as a singer-actor of unique skill and charm. Sacha Guitry, another local institution, wrote of him in 1929 as 'laden with years and with glory'. The audience, he says, still applauds with a full heart. They remember the great evenings, and they understand the singer's own emotions as he stands before them now, and if he gets (say) a little frog in the throat when he sings, they will understand that too and applaud just the same.

In that year, 1929, a book was published in which Fugère told his story to Raoul Duhamel, and since a nice signed copy has come into my hands I will read and report.

Fugère was left fatherless at the age of six, and his good schoolmaster, recognising ability, thought to make him a monitor. But even then he had just one thing in view: the theatre. Of course as soon as he was twelve he had to pay his way, and as his brothers were sculptors he was apprenticed

to the trade and set about repairing the statues and gargoyles of Notre Dame. And as he worked, he sang, picking up the words and tunes of popular songs and whatever he remembered from wherever he managed to scrape an entrance in the evenings.

From time to time in the course of the book Fugère intervenes. 'The Parisians of today,' he says, 'have no idea of the love of music and theatre there was then.' It appears that young people formed themselves into groups, 'singing societies', who met, with a president and rules, and, if you were a member, when it came to your turn you'd have to sing. Fugère would oblige with 'The Calf of Gold', Méphistophélès' song in *Faust,* and eventually someone took notice. Asked what he most wanted, he said 'Oh, to go to the Conservatoire of course', but in fact his destination was the

Ba-Ta-Clan, a Chinese-style *café-concert*. 'Ma voix était jolie et je chantais de tout mon coeur', Fugère explains. Anyway, he was a success; and he began acquiring a repertoire, starting with the role of Kif-Kif, servant of the ring in *Aladdin*. In the next three-and-a-half years he learnt much, including the singer's first law of survival: don't shout and don't force your voice. Even so, a few lessons with a reputable old-timer did not come amiss, and at one point Fugère was able to retrieve an almost lost voice by the regular use of exercises bequeathed him by one Raguenot, 'ancien ténor de l'Opéra'. On the strength of this, and with a growing repertoire, he was engaged in 1874 by the Bouffes-Parisiens, where the *operettes* lined a pathway leading to the Opéra-Comique. 1877 was the year of his transfer

Fugère as the Father in *Louise*

125

and the beginning of an association which lasted for half a century. At his debut, in *Les noces de Jeannette*, he was told that he sang his part differently from the way they were used to hearing it, but to carry on all the same. He was also told – and the pledge was honoured – that he had a job for life.

The house-repertoire was of course enormous in those days, with new pieces being added constantly, though most of those mean little to us now. Of the roles we know well, his three in Mozart (Figaro, Papageno and Leporello) head the list. In *Le barbier de Séville* (everything was sung in French) his role was first Figaro then Bartolo, in *La bohème* Schaunard, and in *Louise* the Father – but those last two operas had still to be written. Of the 30 world-premieres, the Massenet operas, *Chérubin* (in which he played the tutor-philosopher), *Grisélidis* (the Devil), *Le jongleur de Notre Dame* (Boniface) and *Don Quichotte* (Sancho Panza) are revived every now and again, and *La Basoche* is at least a name. Chabrier's *Le roi malgré lui* and Messager's *Fortunio* deserve to be much more of a name than they are; and of the others who can say, since (by and large) we have no opportunity of hearing them.

A particular kind of role became his after a while. As Capulet in *Roméo et Juliette* he played perhaps the first of the father-parts that were to become proverbial in French operatic parlance as 'les Fugères'. One greater than these came his way when in 1893 *Falstaff* was given at the Opéra-Comique for the first time – and the famous song of a minute, 'Quand' ero paggio' (or 'Quand j'étais page') was awarded three encores, sung four times in all. At the re-opening of the badly burnt Salle Favart in 1898 Fugère was selected as the most worthy representative of the theatre's tradition and was presented to President Faure from whom he received the Cross of Chevalier de la Légion d'Honneur. Then in 1900 came the role which was the cumulation of all 'les Fugères', the Father in *Louise*. Duhamel writes that the vividness of his emotions on stage in that role, even before opening his mouth to sing a note, were deeply moving. The composer himself thought so well of Fugère's performance that he inscribed his score of the opera with a greeting to the 'très haut et puissant artiste' who in effect decided the fate of the whole opera. A photograph and a single record of the lullaby are all we have to remember it by: enough, nevertheless, to conserve the flavour of this famous portrayal and provide a precious sample of its quality.

In 1907 he was involved as a passenger in a car accident, but not too badly hurt. In 1910 he loosened his ties with the Opéra-Comique though there was never any question of a severance. In 1920, aged 71, he celebrated his fiftieth anniversary there with a performance of *La Basoche*. Three years later he reappeared in *Le jongleur*, and the music critic of *La liberté* wrote that if by any chance Fugère's voice was thought to be played out, his singing of Boniface's 'Legend of the Sage Bush' would show just how little it had changed since the premiere some twenty years earlier. In

1927 he made a brief tour, again singing in some of his most admired roles, ending with his Bartolo in *Le barbier* back in Paris. There were more honours, another *Basoche*, and the Columbia recordings, by which we know him best.

Remarkably, the best of all these are the very last, made in 1930. That year's sessions brought the 'Grand Air' from Paër's *Le maître de Chapelle*, which is Fugère's masterpiece. The solo enacts in brief a miniature opera on the subject of Cleopatra, and vocally it uses every trick in the book: an exercise of brilliant resource, performed with wit, elegance, technical skill and a provision of 'infinite variety' worthy of the great Queen herself. Splendid also are the two songs of the absurd Fritelli in *Le roi malgré lui*. In the first he compares the French with the Poles (Henri of Anjou had been elected King of Poland), and Fugère achieves to perfection the change of expression, grave for the Poles, frisky for the French. Then in the second song the subject is Fritelli's native Italy; and again Fugère's panache, the cleanness of some very broad intervals, the nimbleness of movement, all are a marvellous tribute to sound practice and a tireless spirit.

The secret was no doubt the message confided in a song which he made particularly his own. In *Le vieux ruban* ('The old ribbon') he would gently murmur the refrain:

> Car le coeur,
> Par bonheur,
> Le coeur, mes petits enfants,
> N'est pas comme les rubans.
> Non! Non! je vous le promets,
> Le coeur ne vieillit jamais.

*Le coeur ne vieillit jamais*: 'The heart never grows old.'

# CHAPTER 26

# Edmond Clément

Fond of identifying certain types of voice with individual singers (the 'Dugazon', for instance, the 'Falcon' and 'baryton Martin'), the French might well have added a further category, a type of tenor called 'the Clément'. It would have been more use to us than the others, for he lived within the age of the gramophone record, so later generations would have had a better chance of understanding what was meant. More importantly, he is a useful archetype, perhaps the most purely and unmistakably French of all. With no admixture of the baritone or the heroic, he provides the perfect definition-by-example of the *ténor lyrique*, the *ténor d'élégance*.

Clément was born on 28 March 1867. Baptised Frédéric-Jean Edmond, he went to school at Chartres where he sang in the cathedral choir. A love of music and singing must have prevailed over more cautious plans, for he left the polytechnic where he had been studying civil engineering to enter the Paris Conservatoire. Here he became a pupil of Victor Warot, formerly a leading tenor at the Monnaie in Brussels where he had sung the title-role in the Belgian premiere of *Tannhäuser*. Clément won the *premier prix* and was promptly engaged by the Opéra-Comique. He made his debut as Vincent in Gounod's *Mireille* on 29 November 1889 and remained with the company till 1910, returning from time to time as late as 1916 when he again sang the role that launched his career as a young man of 22. Throughout this time he was careful not to stray far beyond the essentially lyric repertoire. Perhaps the most strenuous role he undertook was that of Offenbach's Hoffmann which despite its association with light opera is in fact exceptionally demanding. He was also a noted Don José in *Carmen*, a role with a strong dramatic element which, according to contemporary accounts, Clément by no means underplayed. In the modern Italian repertoire he sang Rodolfo and Pinkerton (both in French), and his roles in Mozart were Tamino and Don Ottavio. He was Paris's first Fenton in *Falstaff* (1894) and repeated this at the Metropolitan, New York, under Toscanini in 1910. He specialised, naturally enough, in French opera, developing a large repertory and singing in many premieres including those of Bruneau's *L'attaque du moulin* and Saint-Saëns' *Phryné*, both at the Opéra-Comique in 1893.

Internationally, Clément's career flourished most in the United States.

Although he appeared for only one season at the Metropolitan, he earned his place in the company's history. In addition to his part in two American premieres, *L'attaque du moulin* and Charles Lecocq's *La fille de Madame Angot*, he sang the title role in rare revivals of *Werther* and *Fra Diavolo*. And his greatest success, providing a reference-point for future generations, was as Des Grieux in *Manon* where according to the formidable W.J. Henderson of the *New York Sun* he 'ravished the ear with the infinite variety of his nuances in the *Rêve*'. In fact he remained in the critic's mind

129

as the singer who, among the select company who had distinguished themselves in this role, was supreme in the expression of tenderness. Years later in her autobiography. Geraldine Farrar recalled her role as 'the placid Charlotte to the romantic Werther of Edmond Clément' whom she described as 'an artist of the most exquisite taste and dramatic elegance'.

Werther, Des Grieux and Don José were also roles Clément sang with the Boston Opera Company. Accounts of him during this period suggest that while his singing was duly admired it was his stage appearance, or rather the totality of his performances, that most impressed. As Werther he 'stirred the gentle emotions ... with curly blond locks, a full, melancholy face, a sorrowful and sentimental glance; ruffles at his wrists, his flowing tie and sugarloaf hat the very essence of poetic dress'. Again quoting from Quaintance Eaton's history of the company, his Hoffmann was marked by 'grace and elegance, a masculinity yet a dreaminess that accorded well with the poet's sudden changes from introspective melancholy to flaring action'. In *Carmen* he found the Spaniard Maria Gay too rough and refused to sing with her again, whereupon he was presented with the ageing Emma Calvé, still a terror to conductors though perhaps a little more gentle with her tenors.

That brings Clément's career up to 1913, a year in which he toured the United States and Canada, opening, in New York (8 January) with a programme of French songs in which Henderson observed 'clever management of head tones, nicety in enunciation and subtlety in the placing of accent and colour'. He reappeared at the end of the month at the Aeolian Hall in New York singing with a colleague from Paris and Monte Carlo, none other than Maggie Teyte, in a costumed performance, with trellis, plants and foliage, of an operetta set in the Trianon at Versailles and revealing another side of Clément's art, an 'extraordinary finesse in the high art of comedy'.

With the outbreak of war he returned to France and, though aged 47, volunteered for service and was wounded. Afterwards he sang in concerts for the troops and devoted himself increasingly to teaching. Late in 1921 he returned to the Aeolian, where it seems that any decline in vocal resources found compensation in the undiminished finesse of his style. He continued to sing in Paris, from where Max de Schauensee, revered authority on singing, reported a voice not greatly touched by time even at the age of sixty and on a reception which was touchingly enthusiastic. Clément died three months later on 23 February 1928.

A little puzzle arises out of one of his appearances in London. On 25 May 1894, George Bernard Shaw was in high spirits celebrating 'the crowd of concerts and recitals which have been devastating my afternoons for weeks past' (he was music critic for an evening paper called *The World*). One of these occasions took place in a newly opened hall in Great Marlborough Street. The excessive resonance of the acoustics was one cause of

Clément as Don José in *Carmen*

vexation; another, the windows which Shaw hoped Clément might break 'with one of those strident tones of which he is so proud'. The frustrated critic then concentrated on the singer, whom he had heard previously that season at St James's. He asks if 'the English people have built up their nation through the centuries only to sit down now and hear a young man yell at the top of his voice'. It might do for the Opéra-Comique, he said, or for Australians, but it was not acceptable 'in the true artistic centre of London'. He had no doubt that 'Clément could sing very nicely if he wanted to; but, like most tenors, he doesn't want to. That is why great tenors are so rare, although good voices are so plentiful.'

The last sentence is of interest as it was written in what is so often represented as the Golden Age of Opera and particularly of operatic singing. But it is still extraordinary to read this about Clément of all people. Shaw was an acute observer and there must have been something in what he said – the other singers in that afternoon concert were Melba and Plançon but it was about the young Clément that he decided to complain. We, listening to his records, find any accusation of yelling and of not singing 'very nicely' a complete anomaly. For instance, we have among his earliest a most sensitive and accomplished performance of Count Almaviva's first aria in *Il barbiere di Siviglia*. Exquisitely embellished, in the tradition documented by Garcia, it has scales of unblemished clarity and fluency as well as the grace of some finely turned trills. Later recordings show no coarsening of this finesse, and indeed the later performance of Des Grieux's Dream song in *Manon* is still better than the first, more poetic in feeling and closer to the 'infinite variety' described by Henderson.

At that concert in 1894 Shaw found another cause for complaint, in the large, and in his view disproportionate, part of the programme devoted to songs by Herman Bemberg, who was also the accompanist. Clément recorded some of these, as did his illustrious colleagues. If at that concert he sang ('yelled') 'La neige' as he sings it on the record he made in 1911, then far from threatening to break windows and devastate the gentle critic's afternoon peace, he would simply have demonstrated the phenomenon which Shaw described as being so rare – that of a singer with a good voice who is also a tenor and an artist.

# CHAPTER 27

# Georges Thill and Ninon Vallin

Vallin and Thill – I hope their shades will forgive this posthumous coupling. They go together like Grisi and Mario, Melba and Caruso, Flagstad and Melchior and whatever more recent association may suggest itself. Viewed from our position late in the century, these two were the voice of France. That is, in opera and song, and in the interwar years at least, they come to mind most readily as the representatives of their national school, a school which certainly flourished before them, though more remotely as far as recordings are concerned, and which has appeared to be in decline ever since.

Yet they rarely sang together. They met on stage for a performance of *Faust* at Deauville in 1926, then for the 1931 season in South America where they were paired in *Faust*, *Manon* and *Pagliacci*, and then finally at Orange in a single performance of *La damnation de Faust*. Fond visions of legendary nights at the Opéra in Paris have to be abandoned, for the capital never heard its most internationally renowned soprano and tenor singing together till 1937, and then it was not at the Opéra but the Théâtre des Champs-Elysées in Berlioz's 'légende dramatique', strictly speaking not an opera at all.

They had a large area of repertoire in common, and their voices were in many ways ideally matched. In tone-quality they were not exactly rich, in an Italianate way, yet in their prime certainly there was great beauty of sheer sound. They produced freely, without a suspicion of throatiness, and were well trained to hold a scrupulously firm and even line. Though resonant, their voices had no vibrato, whether of the quick, fluttery or reiterative kind or of the wider and wobblier. As to style and dramatic expressiveness they probably fail to rank among the most imaginative or intense of singers, but they studied carefully and with respect, and their performances bore an individual stamp. They exercised their art in a wholesome way, taking no shortcuts and trusting to good taste rather than the easy appeal of emotional exaggeration and vocal exhibitionism.

The posthumous coupling, then, is very natural. Even so, another jolt comes with the observation that there was an eleven-year difference in their ages. Vallin was the senior, born in September 1886. From her convent school where she sang her first solo in the Christmas Mass a year

133

before Thill was born, she came to the Lyon Conservatoire, and from there went on to Paris, making her debut in 1911. She sang in the April of that year in Debussy's *La damoiselle élue* and came to prominence the following month as a last-minute substitute in the premiere of *Le martyr de S. Sébastien*. The amply built soprano appointed for the Voice from Heaven refused to ascend, and Vallin, in addition to singing her own role of La Vierge Erigone, climbed to the catwalk in her place. Debussy evidently approved, sent her an inscribed score, invited her to his studio and eventually played for her at the first performance of his Mallarmé songs in 1914. Thill was by then seventeen, an office boy in the Bank, with his singing limited to imitations of the voice of Enrico Caruso as heard in the *Voix de son Maître* shop on the Boulevard des Italiens. When Vallin had become the rising star of the Opéra-Comique and had even launched an international career in Spain and South America, he was drafted to the Front. He later joined the Air Force and, if his retrospective comments are to be believed, had the time of his life.

Thill survived the war and Vallin survived (but only narrowly) the Spanish flu. While he began on his student days, she came into her kingdom at the Opéra. She became the honoured associate of composers such as Fauré, Hahn, Poulenc and Falla. He in the meantime studied with the great Fernando De Lucia in Naples. There, his path, still at an incipient stage, touched momentarily that of his hero of the record-shop. On 4 August 1921 he attended Caruso's funeral. His teacher sang the solo, and he himself stood next to Titta Ruffo, the mighty baritone, who was too deeply moved to sing. Four years earlier, Vallin had heard the famous voice from a privileged place: she had been Caruso's partner on stage, first as Manon, then in *L'elisir d'amore*, *Pagliacci* and (as Micaëla) in *Carmen*, taking a full share of the evening's glory in Buenos Aires, Montevideo and Rio de Janeiro.

De Lucia, an ailing man, gave his last lesson to the pupil he called 'beau représentant de mon école de bel canto' in 1922, and Thill returned to Paris the following year. In 1924, he joined the Opéra as a principal tenor, and it is from this time that the two careers converge, though crossing so rarely. His first roles at the Salle Garnier were Nicias in *Thaïs* and Faust in the opera by Gounod, both of them works prominent in the repertoire of Ninon Vallin. Later it was so with *Manon*, *Werther*, *Roméo et Juliette*, *Alceste*, *Marouf*; and even when heavier roles came his way (Aenée in *Les Troyens*, for instance, or Samson, Parsifal and Radamès) he still maintained the lyric repertoire of his, and Vallin's, youth. But then, of course, both singers, far more than most of their compatriots, were on call as international artists and so spent an increasing amount of time going their separate ways abroad.

Both were among the very few French singers to be engaged for La Scala, Milan. Vallin was there, under her married name of Vallin-Pardo, in 1917 when she sang as Mignon and Louise, taking part also in the

Ninon Vallin

premieres of Rabaud's *Marouf* and Xavier Leroux's *Les cadeaux de Noël*. Thill's achievement was to take a coveted Italian role, as Calaf in *Turandot*, and be invited back the following year (1930) to repeat his performance and appear, still more surprisingly, in *La fanciulla del West*. Both singers returned many times to Buenos Aires, where Vallin sang in their first *Pelléas et Mélisande* and *Les contes d'Hoffmann* – in all three soprano parts. Both of them travelled widely, with postwar tours of Australia and

Canada; and both lived to a good age, Vallin 75 at her death in 1961, Thill, 87, in 1984.

A curious feature of their careers is the absence, to any very important extent, of London and New York. Vallin appeared at the San Francisco Opera in 1924 but had no North American career to speak of and never appeared at either the Metropolitan or London's Covent Garden. Thill was heard in both houses but without the success one might have anticipated. Indeed his second (and last) season at Covent Garden proved unlucky in the extreme. He was badly out of voice in his opening *Carmen*, and sent a letter from the Waldorf to say he could not guarantee the scheduled *Tosca* or the repeat of *Carmen*, and the veteran Martinelli stepped in and sang both. After the war he returned on a concert tour but like many foreign celebrities at the time found himself singing to a tiny audience. Yet he had been received originally with interest in 1928, the year in which Vallin, making a rare concert appearance in London, was noted by Ernest New-man as being past her best.

That is not what her records tell. Both of these singers had long and prolific careers as recording artists, and the duration of Vallin's speaks for itself. It began in 1913 and ended in 1956 when she gave a recorded talk called *Ma carrière*, illustrated not only by past recordings but also by her 70-year-old self there and then. The young Marguerite passes before us – 'Non, Monsieur. Je ne suis demoiselle ...' – with artful Norina and sinful Thaïs following up, and even a well-preserved fragment of the doll Olym-pia. The voice is worn, but true, firm and unshakeably on pitch.

In her prime the records show her to have been a soprano with an almost Mozartean capacity for rightness. Hear her in the famous solo from *La bohème* and wait for the usual faults – a pinched high note in the narrative, a scooped interval in the farewell, an excess of portamento (or no portamento at all), an insipid manner, a timbre out of character. She gives the fault-finder no satisfaction. It is marvellous too to find how she can pass from the airy delicacy of a song such as 'Le bonheur est chose légère' from Saint-Saëns' *Le timbre d'argent* to the steely mezzo of the solos from Falla's *El amor brujo* – and then not surprising to find the composer himself marvelling at this same ability to move in the course of one evening from the low tessitura of that work to the full soprano of *La vida breve*.

Thill's records are comparably resourceful. They show him, for one thing, as the kind of Wagnerian tenor (in *Lohengrin* and *Die Meistersinger*) we would welcome incredulously today. But then he is also a charming Rodolfo, his 'Che gelida manina' (or 'Que cette main est froide') a prize song among the hundreds. He sings Gluck and even Bach, with no pushing or hammering, crooning or aspirating, his vocal manners ever reliable. There are limits: he is he is rarely creative in style or incandescent with tragic intensity. Perhaps this too suggests an affinity with Vallin: at any rate,

Georges Thill

they seem now two of a kind, belonging essentially to the same period, and they go together.

They are linked further for posterity by their association in two 'classic' recordings, a complete *Werther* and an abridged *Louise*. Neither of these is mentioned in Thill's biography or in Vallin's, both of them more or less 'official'. An important essay by Victor Girard accompanying the recent edition on compact disc of Vallin's 1927-29 recordings on Pathé may suggest why. Thill, she told M. Girard, was 'a big baby and a bad colleague'. Whatever the offence, it was such that their relationship went from bad to worse during those recording sessions of 1935 till she walked out and left them to find another Louise for the finale. So that may be a further reason why France's first soprano sang so rarely with France's first tenor: she couldn't stand him.

137

CHAPTER 28

# Placido Domingo

In a mid-morning break that seems recent enough but must, I realise, have been in December 1971, a colleague drew his chair alongside mine, with a cup of coffee in his hand and the look of a man about to confess.

It was indeed a grave matter that he had in mind. 'D'you know,' he said, 'I don't think I've ever really *believed* in those tenors of yours. Caruso, you know. And all those Giovannis. Aureliano Pertile and that lot.' He went on to admit that he hadn't totally managed to believe in Jussi Björling either, whom he regarded as 'his' rather than mine.

The point being, of course, that they sounded so thrilling on records but corresponded to no experience encountered 'live' in the course of a fair trial-period of visits to Covent Garden and the Coliseum. But now, on this December morning, the case was altered. 'Last night,' he said. 'You should have heard. This was it. Young chap; first time here; I must show you the programme. But he was it alright, and do you know: for the first time I heard it with my own ears. I think I can believe in Caruso now.' If a miracle is, as the Archbishop in Shaw's *St Joan* says, an event that creates faith, young Placido Domingo was already something of a miracle.

Over the twenty years and more following his debut at Covent Garden* in *Tosca*, the miracle has been manifest in several different ways, and with a consistency that has perhaps robbed it of some of the startled attention that regularly rewards a more showy or short-lived brilliance. Domingo's story has been one of steady growth, successful adaptation, of gifts neither squandered nor withheld. Few if any of the century's leading tenors have passed the age of 50 with a voice so well preserved after unsparing use in such a wide and demanding repertoire; and within the tradition of the 'star' operatic tenor, only Richard Tauber comes to mind as having had an all-round musicianship comparable to Domingo's.

Yet curiously, this kind of description, appreciative and accurate as it is, effectively undervalues and even slightly undermines him. Inevitably in the present climate, commentary on the work of one of our two pre-eminent operatic tenors brings the other to mind. Though nobody with any

---

* The article was published first in *Opera Now*, March 1992: comments on Domingo's voice and art at that time still hold good in 1998.

sense would be prepared to run up a slogan such as 'Domingo for musical satisfaction, Pavarotti for a thrill', there does, I would say, persist a general notion that such may be the case. The formula is unfair to both singers, not so much for the positives stated as for the negatives implied; and on Domingo's behalf we should go back once more to that December morning of 1971, for what had so moved and in a sense converted my colleague was not, primarily, 'musical satisfaction' or evidence of all-round musicianship, but the thrill of a great tenor voice.

When Domingo first sang at Covent Garden (which was eleven years after his debut in opera) his voice was more richly beautiful than any other tenor's I had previously heard in the theatre or have heard there since. It was firm and steady, it had depth, and it shone. The shine was also utterly untarnished, and the quality of sound absolutely pure. That is to say, it had no surface-scratch, none of that upper layer of extraneous material that voices seem so quickly to acquire in the wear-and-tear of a professional singer's life. There was also a thickness or breadth to the sound which made it no surprise to learn that he had started as a baritone.

In the absurd exchange of metaphors that often constitutes the main part of a discussion on voice-quality, if one participant throws in 'gold', another might risk 'chocolate'. Both would be justified: the one in an effort to suggest the gleam of strong, valuable metal, the other supplementing this with a word for the smooth and sweet elements of the voice, its tendency to darkness, and, in the general array of tenors, to range with the thick, broad-bodied ones in the tonal spectrum, rather than with the thin. Upon such devices are we thrown when we want to talk about the sound of a singer's voice rather than the style of his art or his powers of expression.

In *Tosca* and *Carmen*, *Aida* and *Bohème* over the next three years, this great beauty of sound seemed to remain constant. Perhaps with *Un ballo in maschera* in 1975 and the double-bill of *Cav* and *Pag* in which he sang both Turiddu and Canio, we sensed the growth of power that brought *Otello* into view. *La fanciulla del West* found him in glorious form, his Otellos in Hamburg, Paris, Madrid, Milan and Barcelona having occasioned no loss of quality but only the addition of a more exciting thrust to his declamation. More *Aidas*, some inspired singing in *L'Africaine* and *Luisa Miller* followed and took us up to the first Covent Garden *Otello* in 1980. Hearing it, one could well understand how his voice came through apparently so unscathed, for he sang always well within his natural capabilities, taking the part on his own terms, without forcing either the baritonal or the penetrative components of his voice.

Even so, I would say that with the *Contes d'Hoffmann* at the end of that year and still more the *Toscas* of 1981 a difference did become noticeable. Hoffmann of course is itself an extremely strenuous role and it is not altogether easy to see what kind of tenor the part was written for: it seems to be one with the lyric grace of a Faust or Alfredo and the stamina of a Siegfried. Domingo, one felt, armed his voice with the steel which he must have forged and held in reserve for *Otello*. Then in the *Tosca*, one became aware that it was only in certain moments (parts of the Love Duet, or 'Io lascio al mondo' in the last act, for instance) that the absolute beauty of that first *Tosca* was heard again. With these combative roles, the Otellos, Samsons, Canios (not to mention the one which he himself holds most in

*Tosca*

*Characters in order of appearance*

| | |
|---|---|
| *CESARE ANGELOTTI, an escaped political prisoner* . . . | . GWYNNE HOWELL |
| *A SACRISTAN* . . . | . RICHARD VAN ALLAN |
| *MARIO CAVARADOSSI, a famous painter and republican* . . | . PLACIDO DOMINGO |
| *FLORIA TOSCA, a famous singer* | . GWYNETH JONES |
| *BARON SCARPIA, Chief of Police* | . KOSTAS PASKALIS |
| *SPOLETTA, a Police Agent* . | . JOHN DOBSON |
| *SCIARRONE, a Police Officer* . | . PAUL HUDSON |
| *A SHEPHERD BOY* . . | . DAVID PEARL |
| *A GAOLER* . . . . | . PAUL STATHAM |

Programme for *Tosca* at Covent Garden, 15 December 1971

awe for its demands upon the tenor voice, Arrigo in *I vespri siciliani*), it was as though the voice had grown its own carapace, a protective armour which strengthened the definition in among a great mass of orchestral sound, and which at the same time preserved the true tenor tone, obviating any need to rely on more baritonal weight or to open the sound dangerously in the *passaggio*, the area of the voice between middle and upper registers so vulnerable and tempting to exploitation in this increasingly heroic repertoire. If that has indeed been the process, then it has succeeded admirably. The voice is still whole and indivisible; there is no hint of spreading tone, and the quality, if harder, retains much of its characteristic beauty; to some ears, it has in this last decade become finer than ever.

These factors, the voice and its enduring splendour, should take prece-

141

dence in any review of Domingo and his work. Everything else – the acting, the musicality, capacity for hard effort and devotion to the cause – are attributes he shares with many other singers. The marvel is that they go with the voice.

His musicianship, for instance, surely is exceptional, not among singers in general but in his own particular class of 'star' tenor. Perhaps there are or have been other great tenors who could be put in front of an orchestra and could lead them through entire operas with a completeness of know-ledge and technique that they will respect. Domingo has done so, and others do not readily come to mind. Possibly others may have been useful pianists; though I doubt whether there have been many whom a conductor would care to entrust with the organ behind scenes in *Tosca*, or even with the bells, and Domingo has obliged with both. As for the hard work, his repertoire testifies to that (and with the recent addition of Parsifal he has made sizeable inroads into Wagner), the total list comprising about one hundred operas, with zarzuelas, oratorios and songs, many of the items surprising to find there, as for instance *Così fan tutte*, *Hippolyte et Aricie*, *Messiah* and the *Missa Solemnis*. His schedule has often been a punishing one, and always he is going on to something new.

Acting was mentioned. In opera there are two kinds, and ideally they go together: the staged, visual performance and acting with the voice. In the first category there have been certain moments that come to mind: a well-judged keenness of attention and then the sad acknowledgment of a half-foreseen inevitability as Cavaradossi shows us (but not Tosca) that he knows just what the simulated execution means; or the dangerous, pro-phetic flick of temper as Canio forces himself to take the villager's joke ('Un tal gioco') lightly; or the harrowing sense of isolation as the orchestra leads down into the depths of Otello's 'Dio, mi potevi scagliar tutti mali'. As for the acting done with the voice, that is a subtler art, and its mastery is part of a process that no true artist will regard as being ever completed. Domingo's earlier records were sometimes faulted in this respect, that they failed to go beyond a generalised expressiveness, not personal enough to be very memorable. I doubt whether anyone would say that after having followed through his recording of Dick Johnson's role in *La fanciulla del West* or Radamès in the *Aida* under Abbado; or who has listened to his inspired Faust in a generally uninspired recording of Boito's *Mefistofele*; or indeed who has come across his recent comic cameo of Don Basilio's solo in *Le nozze di Figaro*.

And anyway: these things are not now for niggling assessment as though we were settling a sort of vocal Income Tax claim. They are for celebration.

# CHAPTER 29

# Luciano Pavarotti

There are two kinds of Pavarotti-irritant: one is the person who assumes that any reference to a tenor must signify Pavarotti, and the other is the one who holds that in the great ages of operatic singing, Pavarotti (and for that matter Domingo) would be nowhere. The former is usually a cheerful type and quite willing to learn that there might be other tenors. The latter has often a deep fund of contempt and does not particularly want to be told anything.

I find it much easier to sympathise with the view that here is The Italian Tenor embodied, the very image of the species in voice and person, universally acknowledged (by people who would never go near an opera house if they could help it) as 'having something'. Pressed, they might say, 'Yes, you have to admit it, it did send a bit of a shiver through you when he sang that "Nessun dorma" thing at the World Cup.' They might even, if pressed further, acknowledge that quite probably no other sound on earth could have been there and then, at that moment, so right and so thrilling. They like the look of him too: the generous size, the comfortable shape, the beard, the teeth, the feeling that he gets a kick out of it. In turn it gives them the feeling that there may be 'something in it', a feeling they have probably never entertained before.

The others, the disdainful ones, are likely to have knowledge on their side, though, when it comes to argument, their knowledge is so inter-twined with taste, opinion and hearsay that it may not be quite so handy a weapon as it first appeared. But the argument which seeks to reduce Pavarotti to size goes something like this: 'He is outstanding today, no doubt about it. But where are today's tenors? Where are the rivals? Now, in Caruso's time there were Bonci and Zenatello, Anselmi and ... Well, De Lucia was still singing, and there were McCormack and the Russians. Then you had the Frenchmen, Clément and Franz, and there was the mighty Slezak. Or take the next generation: Gigli, Martinelli, Pertile, Lauri-Volpi, Schipa ... to name only the most obvious of the Italians. Even after 1945 you had Björling, Tagliavini, Di Stefano, Del Monaco, with Bergonzi, Corelli, Gedda and Kraus on the way up. They were big fish in a big pool; now half the pool has dried up and a minnow feels like a lord of Creation.'

From the programme of a recital at the Royal Opera House, 4 June 1978

Pavarotti as Tonio in *La fille du régiment*

It is, of course, far more incantation than logic, more incense than argument. The names of the dead always ring more sonorously than those who are still engaged in the humdrum business of living. If one consults the newspapers and musical journals of the time when these great ones were earning their daily bread one finds them all brought down to size by some disdainful person or other. One also finds the same moan about their scarcity. In what year, for example, might this quotation from a British

145

musical paper have been written? The subject is the limitations of the new tenor in relation to his predecessors, and the writer concludes: 'Still, we ought to be glad that we have at last a singer who continues the traditions of the great tenors of the past. Until he came, it almost looked as if the race of tenors, particularly of heroic tenors, had died out.' That was *Musical Opinion*, August 1904. The tenor in question was Enrico Caruso.

So, we may ask, how, in this royal line of scarcities, does Pavarotti stand? Let us report in two phases, rather as in the assessment tests where (I believe) they have a general survey common to all, and then an individual 'portrait' where the personal qualities can emerge, for better or for worse. In Phase A we look to the records and raid the shelves.

We have also to choose a piece of music, an aria, let's say, that exhibits Pavarotti on home-ground and which is also familiar to an array of comparable singers about to be brought alongside. I open the score of *Il trovatore* at 'Ah, sì, ben mio'. This is Manrico's aria to Leonora before their marriage: 'Ah, yes, beloved,' he sings, 'When we are each other's I shall have a braver soul and a stronger arm. But if in the pages of my destiny it is written that I should be among the victims, struck down by the enemy's sword, then in those last moments my thoughts will go to you and I shall regard death only in the light of my preceding you to heaven.' The aria is marked *cantabile, con espressione*, that is 'expressively, but in a smooth singing-style'. Directions for volume range from 'quiet' (*piano*) to 'very loud' (*fortissimo*) and, for tone, from 'sweet' (*dolce*) to 'forcefully' (*con forza*). The highest written note is A-flat, but a high B-flat is commonly inserted, with sometimes another placed three notes from the end.

We take Pavarotti first (1990, Zubin Mehta conducting). At the age of 55 he is still in fine, resonant voice, but the tempo is very fast: *adagio* is the marking, but this is more like *andante con moto* or even *allegretto*. His style catches the buoyancy of rhythm but forfeits something of the smooth legato suggested by the composer's *cantabile* marking. There is no crudity of emphasis (unless in the cadenza's additional high notes), but equally very little variety of volume or expression. Turn to his most eminent contemporary, Placido Domingo (1991, Levine) and we find a slower tempo, a softer tone at the start, a better *cantabile* style, a slightly more thoughtful approach. He also sings something that may pass for a trill in the two places marked, where Pavarotti (in common with the other Italians) does not. Franco Corelli (1964, Schippers) provides the first revelation. Not only has the voice a more lustrous vibrancy, but he addresses the aria with more affection, takes the 'destiny' passage seriously, introduces much more expression and variety. We also recognise with him the importance of the held note on the last syllable of 'trafitto' (G-flat), structurally placed as a kind of bridge to the second half. Corelli takes this softly, making a far finer effect than the other two, though he roughs up the cadenza with aspirates towards the end. Mario del Monaco (1959, Erede) has no notion of style at all, is careless over note-values and varied only in

146

the degree of his loudness: the best to be said is that he is firm and has a solid high B-flat. Giuseppe di Stefano (1956, Karajan) brings a surprise, for this is easily the most *intelligent* performance so far: he sees the argumentative form of the aria, almost presents it as a syllogism. His limitation is that he lacks needful reserves of power.

At this point, the standards being more secure, it would be well to return to Pavarotti, and (since the association is so close) to Domingo too. Both recordings used in that first round were later ones, and we may wonder how the singers compare with their younger selves. Domingo (1983, Giulini) now has a more expansive conductor and makes a more impressive effect of strength and nobility; the style is remarkably smooth, and the trills provide an added grace. Even so, the expression does not strike deep; there is a kind of emotional formality. Pavarotti, too (1976, Bonynge), benefits from a slower tempo and suggests more heroic determination ('braccio più forte'). At the first important modulation ('Ma pur, se nella pagina') where the score marks *con dolore* ('with grief) his voice remains unresponsive, and the 'bridge-note' 'trafitto' is a straight *forte*. He does sing *dolce* when marked, and even makes a slight gesture towards a trill; the high notes of the 1990 cadenza do not appear, and their absence is not regretted. Both tenors, we reflect, are better in their earlier versions, yet neither Pavarotti nor his rival has distinguished himself quite as we may have hoped.

And how do they compare with the great ones of old? Charles Dalmorès (*c*. 1908) immediately introduces a refinement not encountered so far: depth of feeling, 'trafitto' beautifully held, his single trill the most finely spun of all. Hermann Jadlowker (*c*. 1908) also has fine, genuine trills but lacks Italian vibrancy. Antonio Paoli (1911) is simply crude, careless and unsteady. But Caruso (1908) is a marvel: his expression that of a deeply concerned human being, his tone both sweet and noble, his phrasing in some ways best of all (the soft 'trafitto' leading down and literally 'bridging over' into the second half). From a little later the two famous tenors of Montagnana – Aureliano Pertile and Giovanni Martinelli – prove memorable, Pertile (three versions from the 1920s) a potent sculptor in sound, Martinelli (1915) the great linear artist. Pertile's emotion threatens to spill over and Martinelli begins with too much nasal concentration, yet in the Vitaphone film versions (1926) he is almost ideal, as in his Covent Garden debut (1939) is the young Jussi Björling.

The array of tenors here, like the aria itself, is fairly representative, and I would say that Pavarotti holds his own among them without emerging in any very great glory. If we then (as Phase B) look into his own special identity as a tenor, the count begins to add up. Here the first witness is found not among records but memories. I heard him first, at Covent Garden, in 1965 when he appeared with Sutherland in *La sonnambula*. It remains very vivid to me, for in the intervals the people I met wanted to talk about Sutherland and I wanted to talk about 'the tenor'. 'Yes, he's very good,' they said, and then went back to Sutherland. But he was much more than 'very good'. He was, for one thing, uncommonly graceful. In those duets, where the lovers imitate each other or nestle up together in thirds and sixths, he was as elegant as the Tito Schipa whose ways in such music we knew so well from records. There was fire in him too, and a good passionate ring to the voice. That was the first time. The second came a year later in *La fille du régiment*, and here of course, was the triumph, plain and unmistakable. We had no Schipa to set standards in this, for he and the rest of them kept well clear of those nine high Cs in 'Ah, mes amis'. Pavarotti sang them (like everything else) as if for joy, and we had heard nobody like him.

Since then there have been many occasions, of which I'll recall three. One is of a recital in which he included the Petrarch sonnets of Liszt. More beautiful lyric singing can rarely have been heard, and that in an unexpected part of the repertoire. Pavarotti is rightly thought of as a relatively restrictive artist in this respect, yet he will spring a surprise or two even so (as he did with his *Idomeneo*). The Liszt, as I remember it, was sensitive in expression, lovely in the Italianate sweetness and passion brought to the texts and to their quite formidable settings. Then there was his performance in *Luisa Miller*, of which the abiding memory may seem a strange one, for it is of the purity of his sound. I remember listening to the sheer quality of the voice and finding never a scratch and never a false vibration. Then, last, in *L'elisir d'amore*, where I understood he had been known to make an exhibition of himself: on this occasion, by contrast, he was quite modestly and tastefully a company-man, stealing no limelight, trying no tricks; a Nemorino of simple good nature and unostentatiously deployed talents.

He has never, I dare say, been much of an actor, yet several of his characters (think of the *Bohème* Rodolfo, for instance) remain vivid as genuine creations. He is not a great stylist, and yet he has sometimes been able to cultivate refinements (as in his 'Celeste Aida') which the more renowned stylists have not achieved. He has been a marvellous survivor, the range, ring, quality and firmness of his voice scarcely impaired. But to write (or to read) those words is to evoke the sound, and with that comes instant recognition of its uniqueness. Partly it is the phenomenal wholeness of the voice: the fact that such a freely ringing upper range can co-exist with such a solid body of resonant sound throughout. Partly it is a matter of personality, the face within the voice, the character within the face. Finally it is the fulfilment of a need. The Italian Tenor cuts a curious figure in the world's eyes: part romantic, part ridiculous; idol of the gallery, bête noire of the highbrows; the voice of passion, the voice of the ice-cream man. But he is needed, and for this generation Pavarotti has embodied him. He has played the part, like an operatic role, on the world stage, and nobody could have played it better.

CHAPTER 30

# Victor Maurel and
# Francesco Tamagno

Like Adelina Patti in our first volume, Maurel and Tamagno are 'Singers of the Century' by special arrangement. Their visiting cards are their records, but essentially they are guests of honour. Living and singing for the extra few years that nominally place them within our period, they are in reality outside it as far as the performances which made them famous are concerned. Their names live, principally to be mentioned when Verdi's last operas are discussed, but they are here at the party now because we want them, honoured old grandfathers on a night out, still able to set their voices ringing in a way that stills the chatter and opens a door into the past.

The records are indeed amazingly vivid, especially Tamagno's. These used to be poorly regarded, with the assumption more or less everywhere accepted that the recording processes of the early 1900s could not begin to cope with such a voice. In fact, it was to a much greater extent the reproduction systems that could not cope, and modern methods, now available to all through the best transfers to compact disc, bring Tamagno's voice into our times with stunning power and clarity. Maurel had less of a voice to offer, and the records are correspondingly less impressive in terms of sheer sound. Even so, here too is something precious: a style, a way of singing that is as much of its period as are the faded album-songs he sang and the clothes he wore while singing them. One of his records remains uniquely prized, and that is the memento of his Falstaff: 'Quand' ero paggio' sung three times, last time in French, with a small but deliriously encouraging audience, one of them still calling 'bis' at closing-time. And thus we have the voice of the first Falstaff of all, who was also the first Iago matching his voice with the first Otello, the mighty Tamagno, the sound of whose top B-flat would rattle the chandeliers and alarm Queen Victoria.

If these two great men, the grandfathers of our party, were indeed to accept an invitation, they would probably arrive separately for they were of very different nature and origin. Maurel was a Frenchman, from Marseilles, born in 1848, the same year as Lucien Fugère (who, come to

149

think about it, makes a third grandfather), and was a man of diverse interests, literary, architectural and even surgical. Tamagno was an innkeeper's son, and was refused entrance to the Turin Conservatory because of insufficient education. Two years younger than Maurel, he was at the same age of twenty when starting his career. That, however, was by way of promotion from the chorus to stand in for the second tenor singing the confidant Nearco in *Poliuto* (he interpolated one of those famous high B-flats and became the hero of the evening), while Maurel was already at the Paris Opéra singing leading roles such as Nevers in *Les Huguenots* and di Luna in *Il trovatore*. After that he made the statutory appearances in Russia, sang in some important Italian houses and made his debut at La Scala in 1870. Tamagno meanwhile relapsed into comparative obscurity, emerging at a Gala performance in Venice in 1871 and arriving at La Scala in 1878. The following season saw him sharing the stage with Maurel on two grand occasions, a revival of *Ernani* and the premiere of the re-written *Simon Boccanegra*. For this, Verdi added substantially to the role of Gabriele Adorno, introducing his aria with a passage that tempestuously prefigures *Otello*. He also expanded and deepened Boccanegra's own part, with the new Council Scene established as the centre of the opera and one of the great pieces for baritone in the whole of Verdi's work. Maurel's success in the role so pleased the composer that he is supposed to have said during rehearsals, 'If God gives me health, I shall write *Iago* for you', and *Iago*, not *Otello*, was what the opera was originally to have been called. Tamagno's career now flourished in South America as well as Spain and Italy (and he very quickly graduated from Nearco to Poliuto himself which became the longest-running role of his career, with his first performance in 1874 and his last, divided up, two or three Acts at a time, at Rome, Naples, Turin and Milan, in 1904). London had to wait. It was not till *Otello* had made him virtually indispensable that he came to England, and then to sing in the smaller Lyceum Theatre in 1891, not reaching Covent Garden till four years later. Maurel had been a regular visitor in the summer seasons from 1873 to '79 and then again, but with less regularity, till 1895. In that year, in addition to Iago, he sang his other great Verdi 'creation', Falstaff. Both singers reappeared at Covent Garden, Maurel finally in 1905, in which year Tamagno died at the age of 54. Maurel lived on, giving concerts in his sixties, teaching in London and then in New York, where he lived long enough to play a small but possibly decisive part in the career of Rosa Ponselle and, in the year of his death, 1923, to congratulate and advise Giacomo Lauri-Volpi in his first season at the Metropolitan.

Lauri-Volpi had interesting and characteristically contentious things to say about both Maurel and Tamagno. In his book, *Voci parallele*, he tells of the tall but decrepit and somewhat pitiful visitor to his dressing-room in the first interval of *La bohème*. Maurel had said, sadly, that he would like to be starting all over again but this time with the spontaneity

Victor Maurel                    Francesco Tamagno

exhibited by the young tenor. For himself, he believed that he had analysed too much and lost the 'santa semplicità' of the true artist. Lauri-Volpi
seems to think this very probable and reflects that the intellectual approach served him as Iago but not as Falstaff. Tamagno, by contrast, was
an instinctive artist, a 'physiological' singer, and (he believes) a dedicated
one. But the notion that Tamagno and Verdi's Otello were one and the
same thing is, he says, mistaken and dangerous. The part was not even
written for Tamagno, as is often thought: 'I have not written for any one
or any other particular artist', Verdi said in a letter to Ricordi, and of
Tamagno he said that he would be fine for much of the role but for a great
deal else in it he would not. Because Tamagno was eventually the tenor
chosen, and because he had such an abnormal type of voice, the role
seemed for a very long time to be out of bounds for all but the most
powerful of heroic tenors. Even Caruso, who had got so far with it as to
have costumes made, renounced the part and sold the costumes, because
(says Lauri-Volpi) 'the shade of Otello-Tamagno had terrorised him'.

Lauri-Volpi (born 1892) does not claim to have heard either of these
singers 'in the flesh', so it may be worth turning to some who did. Maurel,
despite a self-importance that made Verdi say at one stage that of course
he could if necessary put his opera in the waste-paper basket, seems
everywhere to have gained respect and admiration. To the most intelligent
of London's music critics in the 1890s he was something quite special, a
kind of oxymoron called actor-singer. George Bernard Shaw followed
Maurel in his course of lectures, which asked for opera to be taken
seriously, the individual performance being part of an organic whole.

151

'Restless cerebration' is the characteristic that impressed Shaw in Maurel's performance of Don Carlos in *Ernani* (and of how many can that be said?). His Méphistophélès in *Faust* was 'a distinct individual character, exhaustively premeditated, and put upon the stage with the utmost precision of execution', while as Iago 'he inaugurated a new era in operatic acting'. In other respects Shaw was more critical, partly of the voice which (in *Rigoletto*) 'will get him through the music only by an occasionally almost painful exercise of vocal ingenuity', partly of solecisms in *Don Giovanni*, and even of a falsification in his super-subtle Iago 'which is to be admired rather as a powerfully executed fantasy of his own than as either the Iago of Verdi or Shakespeare'.

Shaw made it clear that when he criticised Maurel it was by the standards of a serious critic, which he could not possibly apply in the general run of operatic reviews. He was indeed tempted to apply those standards as a compliment to the failed Otello of Jean de Reszke, and in doing so he passed comment on the famous original:

> His Otello will never be like Tamagno's; but he need not regret that, as the same thing might have been said of Salvini [the Italian actor who had so distinguished himself in the role]. The Italian tenor's shrill screaming voice and fierce temper were tremendously effective here and there; but the nobler side of the Moor ... was left untouched by Tamagno, who on this and other accounts is the very last man a wise tenor would attempt to imitate. (22 July 1891)

Others said much the same though *The Times* found an improvement on Tamagno's return to London in 1895: 'There is now some proportion and gradation between his extremes of tone. His rendering of the second Act was even more artistic than before, and his singing of the famous "Addio" was most expressive' (14 May 1895). In a later performance he was 'at his very best'.

That I would like to have heard. I have a feeling that the London critics had one great underlying objection: Tamagno was loved by the gallery. When he sang in *Le prophète, The Times* found the public 'aroused to an excessive and, in fact, rather absurd pitch of enthusiasm'. In *Il trovatore* the call to arms was 'answered by vociferous applause and of course encored'. Oh deary deary me. A much more favourable assessment was made in New York by a no less critical critic, W.J. Henderson. Of the *Otello* presented on 24 March 1890, he wrote concerning Tamagno that 'Everything he does betrays the presence of a fine and wide intelligence.' In his singing he found a nasal quality marring the middle notes, but: 'The upper register is full, round and rich, made mellow and sweet when the singer wishes ... He reaches the A-flat and A with such ease that he introduces on those notes the most delicious *smorzando* effects, and his B and C are immensely powerful. He phrases with the elegance of the true Italian

7ª Rappresentazione.

# TEATRO ALLA SCALA

Questa sera, Sabato 5 Febbraio 1887 alle 8 ¼ precise

## PRIMA RAPPRESENTAZIONE

del Dramma lirico in 4 atti, versi di A. Boito:

# OTELLO

### Musica di GIUSEPPE VERDI.

(Proprietà Casa Ricordi)

| | |
|---|---|
| OTELLO, moro, generale dell'Armata Veneta | TAMAGNO FRANCESCO |
| JAGO, alfiere | MAUREL VITTORIO |
| CASSIO, capo di squadra | PAROLI GIOVANNI |
| RODERIGO, gentiluomo veneziano | FORNARI VINCENZO |
| LODOVICO, ambasciatore della Repubblica Veneta | NAVARRINI FRANCESCO |
| MONTANO, predecessore d'Otello nel governo dell'isola di Cipro | LIMONTA NAPOLEONE |
| Un ARALDO | LACCHIARSINO ANGELO |
| DESDEMONA, moglie d'Otello | PANTALEONI ROMILDA |
| EMILIA, moglie di Jago | PETROVICH GINEVRA |

Dopo l'opera si daranno i primi due quadri del ballo di L. Manzotti:

# ROLLA

Le Sedie e le Poltrone sono esaurite. - Nella Platea non vi sono posti in piedi ed il piccolo atrio è chiuso al Pubblico.

## PREZZI PER QUESTA SERA

| | | | |
|---|---|---|---|
| Biglietto d'ingresso | alle Sedie ed ai Palchi | Lire | 5 |
| » | » al Loggione | » | 5 |
| » | » pei sig. Militari in uniforme | » | 2,50 |

Il Teatro si apre alle ore 7 1/4          Il Loggione alle ore artist and his enunciation of the text is simply delightful.' In *Trovatore* on March 27, 'He sang "Ah, sì, ben mio" with rare expression' and ' "Di quella pira" was delivered with intense power, and the high C was peeled forth and sustained in a manner that was startling. He was obliged to repeat it; and then he finished the Act with another C which rang out above the chorus and orchestra, and which he carried off the stage with him.' That sounds like another night to remember – unless, of course, like *The Times*, you find it all 'rather absurd'.

It is fascinating now to summon up these voices on their old records. Maurel, given that he was not far off 60 and was never (except in very early years) considered to be remarkable on account of his voice, sings pleasingly in some sentimental trifles by Massenet and D'Hardelot, but nothing (not even his 'dream' solo from *Otello*) suggests the subtle, intellectual singer of reputation. Tamagno, on the other hand, can be infinitely tender, heartfelt, subtle, by comparison. His 'O muto asil' from *Guglielmo Tell* is amazingly sensitive in expression and apparently limitless in vocal resource. His *Otello* solos are great in both voice and spirit. A letter to *The Times* on 6 July 1926, recalled vividly from all those years ago the ascending phrase in 'Ora e per sempre addio', describing in detail the accumulative power behind that climactic B-flat. It is there for us now, a miracle still, as it was when Tamagno heard the first play-back of the record and, overcome with amazement and emotion, embraced the machine which was to preserve his voice for posterity.

CHAPTER 31

# Emma Eames and
# Marcella Sembrich

We don't hear so much these days about the 'Golden Age'. Perhaps that is because the old folks who told of it are no longer at home. Maybe the younger generation has already a golden age of its own; or possibly, everyone, with the passing of the years, has become a little more cynical or sceptical or realistic.

A similar gradation of terms may apply to the Golden Age's chief chronicler and evangelist, one P.G. Hurst. As a writer he could be called forthright, combative or cantankerous; as a critic, selective or narrow, a man of conviction or a musical bigot: all according to taste. But nobody could deny that he was authoritative, and if he did not own the Golden Age himself that was because he had to share proprietorship with Herman Klein, at least until the time of the latter's death in 1934. Klein wrote *The Golden Age of Opera* (Routledge, 1933), Hurst *The Golden Age Recorded* (Oakwood, 1963). Klein was the author of *The Reign of Patti* (Fisher Unwin, 1920), Hurst of *The Age of Jean de Reszke* (Johnson, 1958). A veteran first-nighter (he could recall the English premieres of *Carmen* and *Aida*), Klein had been a friend of Sullivan, Saint-Saëns and Patti herself. Hurst may not have scraped up acquaintance with the de Reszke brothers, but he did know Zélie de Lussan, who had sung with them. Klein's nearest counterpart in length of experience at the opera in New York was W.J. Henderson, who was a confidant of one of the subjects of this chapter, Marcella Sembrich. The critical inheritor of their views on singers and singing then in Britain was Desmond Shawe-Taylor, and he, while a young man, made a friend of the other, Emma Eames.

That was something of an achievement, for, in the mid-1930s, when Shawe-Taylor met her, Eames was a *grande dame* of 70, even more of a Golden Ager in her tastes than Klein, Hurst or Henderson, having been herself an illustrious part of it. She had retired from opera at the age of 40, partly because that was the dignified and sensible thing to do, partly because when she looked ahead to the future the prospect did not please her. Once out of the business she made no secret of her poor opinion of the new generation (a kind friend repeated to Frances Alda, one of the current

155

prima donnas at the Met, that Eames had pronounced her 'all right for the chorus'), though from time to time she did find somebody she could admire (Conchita Supervia was one, Kirsten Flagstad another). She had been married to the baritone Emilio de Gogorza whose name was not now to be mentioned in her house, an establishment which was run along such Conservative (or Republican) lines that a Roosevelt dime was on no account to be seen there. In later years she mellowed somewhat, went to see *Kiss me, Kate* on Broadway and was even known to speak well of her loathed and mighty rival, Nellie Melba. Sembrich was a friend. They were twin pillars of the Golden Age in New York (both put out by the incursions of Melba, who of course enhanced the carat-valuation and could not be excluded). Seven years Eames's senior, Sembrich had a lighter voice and no designs on key-roles such as Tosca or Aida.

Those two passionate and modern roles would seem a surprising choice for a singer so repeatedly described as 'classic' and 'cold'. The coldness at any rate fuelled the most famous *bon mot* on the subject of Eames and Aida, James Huneker's 'last night there was skating on the Nile'. As Tosca, her calmness in the face of disagreeable possibilities was much criticised, and if she did indeed study the role with Sardou its creator and Bernhardt its great exponent, it was felt that their teaching must have inculcated principally the virtues of the well-known saying 'toujours la modération'. She also told Puccini that he was wrong about the climax of 'Vissi d'arte', but that is another matter.

*Tosca* was a relatively late addition to her repertoire, and indeed the opera had yet to be written in the years during which Eames was a regular visitor to Covent Garden. Her debut role there had been Marguerite in *Faust*, her Juliette following later in the season. Juliette was the part in which, two years earlier, in 1889, she had made her operatic debut, chosen and coached by Gounod himself. 'Twenty years old, tall, svelte, the figure and profile of Diana, the nose fine and the nostrils quivering, the carmine mouth exhaling the breath of life, the face a pure oval lit by big eyes full of independence and candour at the same time, the expression astonishingly mobile, the forehead high and crowned by a mass of blonde fleece, the arms superb attached to the charming shoulders – such is Mlle. Emma Hayden Eames. Such is the new Juliette.' And such, allowing for a certain amount of Hercule Poirot in the translation, was the account of her physical charms as they appeared to the critic of *Le Figaro*. In the glow of which we will leave her for a while and turn to the second, or perhaps more properly the first, of these great ladies.

Sembrich (originally Praxede Marcelline Kochanska of Wiesnivczyk in Galicia) also sang in Paris in the 1890s, and *Le Figaro* waxed lyrical on her account too, though now paying more attention to the musical side of the business: 'God be praised. I am thirty years younger since Saturday night. Mme. Marcella Sembrich sang to me; it seemed as though she sang to me alone, so intently did I listen to her Rosina in *Il barbiere di Siviglia*.

Emma Eames

Marcella Sembrich as Lakmé

She was incomparable – recalling the glorious time of our Theatre when the greatest stars were shining.' (Note that even in the Golden Age the stars seemed to have shone more brightly in the past.) Sembrich had appeared at Covent Garden, singing 'with dazzling brilliance', as early as 1880, but after 1883 her career centred on the Metropolitan, New York, in which she sang Lucia di Lammermoor on the second night of the new theatre's history. With Eames, she remained the leading resident lyric soprano of the company during the years when Jean de Reszke was their tenor, continuing in the early part of Caruso's time, and then retiring, both of them the same year, in 1909.

A lovely voice, a superb technique and a charming presence were among Sembrich's assets, but they were not her only ones. Her distinction among the prima donnas of her time (and perhaps of any other) is that she was a highly accomplished musician who, according to report, could have made an equally successful career as a pianist or violinist. While a girl still in her teens she played both instruments to Liszt, and at a concert in Paris was heard by James ('skating on the Nile') Huneker, who penned a lively description:

> Conceive my amazement when this modest-looking woman with the spiri-
> tuelle face sat down before the piano, and with a finger agility and a grace

and delicacy that Joseffy would envy, played Chopin's E flat Polonaise. Then she tuned her violin, which was handed her by her husband, and dashed off Weniawski's Polonaise in G, and in response to an overwhelming demand for an encore gave the same composer's touching *Légende*. Then to further mystify us, Sembrich, with that enchanting smile of hers, sat once more at the piano and sang – ah, so divinely, Mme. Viardot-Garcia's transcription of Chopin's D major piano mazurka. When I got out in the open air I felt like throwing my hat up and crying aloud, 'A miracle, a miracle.'

Sembrich's musicianship also extended to her song-repertoire. From 1900 onwards, but more especially after her retirement from opera, she gave concerts in the Carnegie Hall that were counted among the brightest regular musical events of the year. 'The cream of the music lovers, teachers, singers and students' was there, wrote Henderson of a recital in January 1913, and he too was moved to unwonted lyricism: 'Tears lie under the roseate surface of her humour; sweet sympathy dwells beside her darkest tragedy; love wells out through all.'

No adverse review of Sembrich on stage or in the concert hall has ever come my way. Henderson, though a friend, was not one to keep any serious dissatisfaction to himself, and he did note on that occasion tones that were at first 'a little cloudy'; but such comments are set in an almost reverential context. Eames met with a much more critical press. Klein appears to have disliked her personally, and in *The Golden Age of Opera* contented himself with a description of her as 'an American soprano of queer disposition but unquestionable talent'. George Bernard Shaw had a great time at the expense of her bread-and-butter-cutting Charlotte in *Werther*, and, professing not to understand why *Mireille* was performed at all, wrote:

> Still more insoluble is the casting of Miss Eames for the title part, the requirements of which are great range and great flexibility, enabling the singer to shake on high D at her ease. Miss Eames, even with her chief numbers transposed and cut to pieces, only got through, and that in a sufficiently commonplace manner, by the skin of her teeth – if she will pardon the expression. As to any attempt she made to place before us the ideal Mireille, I can only say that she never in her life was more emphatically that very attractive and ladylike person, Miss Eames of the Royal Italian Opera – well educated and with no nonsense about her. As it is on Mireille that the whole play depends, it is hardly necessary to add that every attempt to give the scenes an air of conviction soon broke down (*Music in London*, Constable, 1960).

The most frequently aired complaint about Eames concerned her 'coldness'. This is the point at which gramophone records play a part in the argument, for on the whole these are not cold. Her two last records, made in 1911, were of songs, Schubert's 'Gretchen am Spinnrade' and Tosti's 'Dopo': both are remarkable precisely for the warmth of voice and feeling. We even have a few moments of her performance on stage at the Metro-

Concert-Direction: Hermann Wolff.

# PHILHARMONIE.

## Freitag, den 16. November 1888, Abends 7½ Uhr:

# CONCERT

von

# Marcella Sembrich

mit dem

Berliner Philharmonischen Orchester unter Leitung des Herrn Kapellmeisters

## GUSTAV F. KOGEL.

## PROGRAMM.

1. Ouverture zu „Egmont" . . . . . . . . . . *L. v. Beethoven.*
2. Arie „Casta Diva" aus „Norma" . . . . . *B. Bellini.*
   *Frau Marcella Sembrich.*
3. Vorspiel zu „Die Königin von Saba" . . . . . *C. Goldmark.*
4. Arie aus „Mignon" . . . . . . . . . . *A. Thomas.*
   *Frau Marcella Sembrich.*

5. Lieder: a) Lied der Braut No. I ⎫
   b) Lied der Braut No. II ⎭ aus dem Myrthen-Cyklus . *R. Schumann.*
   c) Veilchen . . . . . . . . . . *W. A. Mozart.*
   *Frau Marcella Sembrich.*
6. a) Prélude; Andante religioso für Streichorchester . . *C. Massenet.*
   b) Canzonetta . . . . . . . . . . . . *F. Mendelssohn.*
7. Bolero (neu) . . . . . . . . . . . *Cesar Cui.*
   *Frau Marcella Sembrich.*

Die Klavierbegleitung hat Herr Kapellmeister KOGEL übernommen.

Concertflügel: C. BECHSTEIN.

politan in 1903, in which, from the dim distance, comes quite clearly the voice of a passionate Tosca. The anomaly is striking. There could be many reasons for the impression she gave to those who saw her – the manners of her puritanical upbringing, her training in a statuesque Delsartian style of deportment on stage, and her own habitual hauteur. But the London critics returned always to one particular observation: 'an immobile face' (*Musical Times* on her debut at Covent Garden in 1891). This

159

contradicts the French critic present at her Paris debut, but the *Musical Times* is perfectly clear and remarks of her Juliette: 'It is a thousand pities that she seems unable to be eloquent in face and impassioned in manner.'

Sembrich's recordings present an anomaly of a different kind. Often of great brilliance and beauty, they can also be disconcertingly uneven. Sometimes an irregular quiver in the vibrations, sometimes a still stranger inattention to detail: these are unexpected features in the work of this skilled musician among singers. Similarly we can look in vain for special insights in her recorded songs – and in Schubert's 'Wohin' she even sounds guilty of what amateurs know as 'slowing down for the hard bits'.

Between them, the gramophone and the press provide equivocal commentary on the Golden Age. Both of our sopranos were singers of great distinction, yet questions remain, coalescing to merge with the larger question-mark over the Age itself. Its great decade was reputedly the 1890s, with a kind of Silver Age to follow, the base metal of our own century taking over somewhere around 1920. My own scepticism has increased recently as I see the 1950s and early 60s with singers who at the time were disdained by connoisseurs now seeming to have names that dazzle in the incantation much as did those of the remoter past in the time of my youth. For Melba, Sembrich, Eames, and the de Reszkes read ...?

CHAPTER 32

# Renata Tebaldi

Tebaldi is central, and centrality is square. By general consent she is the acclaimed representative of her country's lyric art. Among all the Italian sopranos of her time and perhaps of the century she stands as the best known and most admired; but it is as a kind of enhanced norm. With a voice that was of exceptional beauty, a style which gave pleasure to people of taste, a warm and dignified stage presence and the good sense to stay within an appropriate repertoire, she won a position second to none in the postwar years when the thirst for great singing was so deep and expectations fed by gramophone records and legends of the past were so high. That this was also the age of Maria Callas may have been at once Tebaldi's misfortune and her most sure (though hardly most valid) passport to immortality. Rivalry between the two leading sopranos of the age is not unnatural, especially when they share a deal of common ground, such as the roles of Violetta and Tosca. However each individually may strive or appear to distance herself from such controversy, she must know it enhances publicity and reputation. The long-term danger for Tebaldi is that comparisons tend to polarise, in the general view bestowing the more exciting qualities upon Callas and leaving herself with the duller virtues. Callas was seen as the eccentric genius, Tebaldi the noble norm.

Such polarisation may be crude and objectionable, but it finds some validity in aural retrospect. There are still plenty alive in body and mind who heard both singers in their heyday and who can recount various details that have lodged in their memories. But most of us are gramophone-educated, record-haunted creatures for whom the singers have very nearly become their voices on tape or disc. We then assemble our Callas/Tebaldi mementoes, and find what we may have anticipated, namely that, however fond the Tebaldi memories, the vivid ones are of Callas. Callas smiles or weeps, goes on the warpath or licks her wounds, and we remember. Memories of Tebaldi are more generalised and draw upon a more narrow emotional range. Moreover, Callas's voice can be summoned at will; Tebaldi's arises only after the second call, and then somewhat doubtfully. She is being outshone.

The voice-character itself has much to do with this. Callas's voice had an element of conventional beauty; even so, the added appeal was that of

161

Tebaldi as Tosca

the *jolie laide*. The fascinations were undeniable but so were the blemishes. Tebaldi's had the perfection of regularity, properly equalised in its registers, pure in quality, even in texture, ample (but not exceptional) in volume. She did indeed embody in part a reaction against the past: in the one conversation I myself had with her she answered with quick interest a question about vibrato, saying that the rapid, reiterative type had been so prevalent ('it was about me everywhere') when she first took an interest in singing that almost her first objective in training had been to keep it out of her own singing. She was entirely successful in that, and her view of the matter coincided with the modern trend. The quick vibrato ('flutter' or 'bleat' as some will call it) never settled kindly in the typical Anglo-Saxon ear, and, most important, was kept at a wary distance by the recording industry. Tebaldi's tone was essentially 'straight', in unflecked, unspeckled conformity with conventional taste. It gained centrality; it forfeited idiosyncrasy.

To hear Tebaldi it is necessary to listen to her – which is not such a truism as it sounds, for there are many voices one can hear inwardly without needing to put on a gramophone record. The flick of a mental switch will not (I find) 'turn on' Tebaldi. So, going to the shelves and finding there three of the great Verdi roles, we settle down to listen. Leonora first, in *La forza del destino*: the solo at the opening of the Convent scene, with its nervous tension and broad dramatic sweep. The entrance is regal. 'Son giunta!' means more or less 'I've made it, I've got here!', but never were such words less colloquial in tone or more laden with fateful significance. For myself, I have been surprised so often by the initial impact of Tebaldi's voice that it ought to be a surprise no longer; but certainly this fullness and command impress doubly because they so exceed both memory and expectation. Then as one may be settling down to a conventional handling of the recitative, the ears' eyes are suddenly confronted by a woman fainting: it is there in the falling notes of Verdi's score, but Tebaldi makes it happen, acts it with her voice. This, we reflect, is Callas's preserve. 'Madre, pietosa vergine' lies in the most lovely part of her voice, and again a surprise may come with the realisation (for the umpteenth time) of just how lovely it is. The great B major melody ('Deh, non m'abbandonar') starts humbly and surges magnificently: that we did expect. But now comes a touch of insight, the kind of localised perception that is expected of Callas but not of Tebaldi, as the singing of the monks falls like a blessing on the troubled woman's ear and a new sweetness pervades the voice. With a corresponding relaxation of precise literalism she caresses the phrase 'A Dio sui firmamenti', and the world is transformed. Again the melody soars, intensifying its climax and this so very satisfying performance ends quietly, the last note beautifully rounded and sustained.

There, then, is Tebaldi heard. Back to her now for *Aida,* this time with two versions for comparison. Act 3 begins with the evoked memories of a homeland Aida knows she will not see again. Tebaldi recorded the opera in 1952 with Alberto Erede conducting and then in 1959 under Karajan. Seven years, or the difference between 30 and 37 in terms of age, mean more in an opera singer's life than in most. With Tebaldi little appears to have changed, but the climax with the top C is not to be lingered over, and the last note, the long-held pianissimo A natural, gives perhaps a second's unease before establishing itself. The voice has lost some of its freshness: not much. Similarly, the style and expression have gained something – but likewise, not much. The mood is a little softer, a little more responsive to the nostalgia; but essentially, in phrasing, emphasis, nuance and so forth, the performance is unchanged. It would be unfair to conclude from a single example that hers was not a developing or spontaneous art; still, there is no encouragement to think otherwise.

The third Verdi heroine, Desdemona in *Otello*, does however suggest that she did in some degree modify the voice according to the character. In the Willow song and Ave Maria, the grand-opera voice of *La forza del destino* and the mature-woman voice of Aida have been chastened, and though the singer is older (now in her fortieth year) the voice-character is younger. Not everything is ideal – the pianissimo 'prega' and the soft high note at the end of the prayer are not held for their full length – but it is still a most lovely performance. Tebaldi does not have the kind of voice (as did Tiana Lemnitz or Montserrat Caballé) that would 'float' an almost disembodied, ethereal top note, but, for compensation, her singing has a unity about it, and the absence of a 'special effects' department is among the conditions of her respected centrality in the operatic spectrum.

The general course of her career itself led very directly to that centre. For one thing, the moment was right. The new, postwar world needed new singers. In Italy the bombed La Scala was rebuilt and reopened. Toscanini, very nearly 80 years old, was called to conduct the inaugural concert; Tebaldi, then 25, was engaged to sing. As 'the Voice from Heaven' in Verdi's *Te Deum* she made a name for herself in two senses: the celestial quality of her young voice was manifest, and the 'voce d'angelo' tag remained with her, eventually to be the sub-title of her biography (by Carlamaria Casanova, English translation Baskerville, 1995). Three months later she made her stage debut in the house as Eva in *Die Meistersinger* (or *I maestri cantori* as the opera was sung in Italian), and this came exactly three years after her debut, playing Helen of Troy in *Mefistofele* at Rovigo in May 1944. By 1949, Lord Harewood who had heard her most recently at Florence in Rossini's *L'assedio di Corinto*, reported in *Ballet and Opera* 'she is probably the foremost lirico-dramatic soprano in the world'. And all of this in the first five years.

Covent Garden in 1950, the Paris Opéra and Rio de Janeiro in 1951, Buenos Aires in 1953, the Metropolitan, New York, in 1955: these were the step-by-step advances to international fame, their way prepared of course by numerous recordings. The USA rather than Italy now became the centre of her artistic life, and she remained a central figure on the Metropolitan stage for eighteen years. By around 1970 her schedule began to ease; 1971 was a year out; the rest was largely concert work. This took her to Russia and the Far East, and she bade her farewells, to New York at the Carnegie Hall, then to Milan at La Scala, in 1976.

It was not a career without troubles. Very early on, still in her twenties, it seemed to some observers that she was doing too much and putting a strain on the young voice. In 1963 she faced a vocal crisis that was also an

emotional one. Her return with a 'new voice' was welcomed sincerely, though well-disposed commentators tended discreetly to divert attention from the voice to the new acting, which was widely praised. The concert-tours also brought some rewarding latterday successes, their climax coming with a return to La Scala, after an absence of fourteen years, and an ovation which lasted fifty minutes.

Her final encore in that concert was the song 'Non ti scordar di me' (or 'Do not forget me'). The audience on that occasion wouldn't be likely to; nor would those who heard her repeatedly at the Met and elsewhere. But what of Posterity, the incalculable? New recordings replace old ones, new names become temporarily more potent than even the greatest of the past. Of the singers of this century, I suppose that the names of Caruso, Callas and Pavarotti will remain current for a while, and it may be then that Callas will come to her rival's aid. From time to time somebody reading about Callas will read too about Tebaldi, and may even go to the lengths of selecting a record (or whatever form 'records' take) from the shelves. 'Son giunta!' they will hear, and sitting up in their chairs (if they still have them) may even like, listen and learn. Some of the more enthusiastic may wonder at the vocal riches of a period that could boast two such sopranos at the same time. Someone might even think to look further at it and write a book called *The Golden Age Recorded*.

# CHAPTER 33

# Richard Tucker

'The role of Eléazar was sung by Mr Richard Tucker.' This was the last sentence of *The Times*'s review of the first London performance of *La Juive* within living memory, given at the Royal Festival Hall on 4 March 1973. Whether as an editorial cut-off or as critical put-down, it was cruel. As a puzzled member of the audience, one could see why the critic may have felt goaded into making such chillingly formal acknowledgement; even so, Eléazar is the principal character of the opera, and 'Mr Richard Tucker', on a rare visit to Britain, was one of the world's principal opera singers.

I can see him now, sitting very much at the centre of an event from which he seemed for most of the time curiously detached. When others sang he looked around as though in search of diversion. Occasionally (so it appeared) his glance would travel enquiringly towards a box on his left, at which he smiled privately but in public. Even when singing himself he appeared at first not to be personally involved, and, as I remember, he made no strong impression until it came to the famous aria. Then he was transformed. He sang with breadth and fervour, giving a fine performance in terms of sheer artistry. But it was the voice itself, its power of expansion, but most of all its timbre, darkly rich in sheen and texture, that held attention rapt and induced an almost pained awareness that the aria would soon be over and that we might hear nothing like it ever again. Indeed I myself never did: this strange event, in which wonder of two such different kinds prevailed, remained the one and only time I heard Richard Tucker. He left London the following day and never returned.

Fifteen years before, in 1958, he had sung here in some highly praised performances of *Tosca* with Zinka Milanov; otherwise he was known to us by records and reputation. Probably neither of these endeared him greatly. The records showed a fine voice, though they hardly prepared for its impact 'in the flesh'; as an artist, he seemed, on their evidence, capable equally of ardent, intelligent commitment and of a kind of thickness, whether of musical sensibility or of dramatic insight. As for the personal reputation, as it came to us in anecdotes and chance remarks, the character of the man seemed to be irredeemably spoiled by a comically obsessive egoism.

In his own country, and indeed half the world over, he was rated very differently. Those who heard him regularly in America knew the glory of his singing and probably learned too about the generosity of his character. In other countries, where he made guest appearances, he would sometimes draw applause and tears in a way that touched something deep in his audiences: maybe the age-old love of singing that suddenly recognised a legendary greatness, and maybe deeper sources of emotion than that. Certainly he was one of the most admired and loved singers of his time.

In his career he ended, and began, at the top. There were a few – a very few and very well-advised – try-outs in less conspicuous theatres, but essentially his operatic career began with his debut at the Metropolitan Opera House, New York as Enzo Grimaldo in *La Gioconda*. In some respects it might appear to have been the Rosa Ponselle story over again, but there were differences. Ponselle was 21 when she started with that most famous debut of all, as Leonora to Caruso's Alvaro in the first Metropolitan performance of *La forza del destino*. On 25 January 1945 Tucker was already 31, an experienced broadcaster with a certain following, so by no means a raw youngster. He had also sung for many years as cantor in the principal Brooklyn synagogue: when Rudolf Bing first heard him there he knew that the singer who could hold a two-thousand-strong congregation as securely as this man did would have no trouble with the 3,600 of the Metropolitan. All that Ponselle had behind her was the vaudeville, while what lay ahead was fraught with the agony of pre-performance nerves. The only kind of nerves Tucker knew took the form of impatience: he couldn't wait to get on stage and 'show them'. But then, Tucker had been particularly well-trained. He had, to start with, the traditional skills of the cantor, and then what seems to have been the exceptionally well-judged tuition of his teacher, Paul Althouse. A firm, impressive man who knew his own mind and who had been through the mill himself (a principal tenor at the Met from 1912 to 1940), Althouse won Tucker's confidence and channelled his impetuosity. When Tucker faced his Metropolitan debut, he had as much reason to feel sure of himself as Ponselle had to feel nervous; and from that time onwards the difference increased, for whereas her young career was inconsiderately handled by the management, Tucker's was nurtured carefully and with discretion. Theirs remain the supreme soprano and tenor voices to have come from America this century; and both could be taken for Italians.

The proof of wise procedure in Tucker's case lies in the fact that he was still singing superbly until the day he died, of a heart-attack at the age of 61. He was in his sixtieth year when I heard him in that concert performance of *La Juive* and his singing of the aria simply flew in the face of the fact. In the last ten years it seems he ran risks he would never have taken before: it was not merely that he added heavier roles to his repertoire but that he accepted almost literally a killing schedule. In his book on the tenor (Dutton, 1984), James Drake, who was also Ponselle's biographer,

167

Tucker as Rodolfo in *La bohème*

gives as an example his commitments for the first nine weeeks of 1966 – six different operas at the Met, three others in other major centres, and concerts, oratorio work and so forth over widely distanced States. He had had one serious heart-attack in 1962, and though he made light of it, the overtaxed organ no doubt had its reasons that the conscious mind would not admit. He felt a lot of singing still within him, and he wanted to waste as little of it as possible.

The quality of that singing we can at least partly estimate by means of written accounts, recordings and, when available, memories. My own single memory is potent, and if the genie of the lamp were to present himself it is probable that the five minutes of that aria from *La Juive* would be high on the list of times to relive. The recordings are as ever principal points of contact and means of preservation. Perhaps when there

168

Greater London Council

## 🔔 ROYAL FESTIVAL HALL
Director : John Denison C.B.E.

SUNDAY, 4th March at 7 p.m.

*Denny Dayviss*

presents

# LA JUIVE

an Opera in five Acts by
FROMENTAL HALÉVY
Libretto by Eugène Scribe
Premiere at the Paris Opéra February 23rd 1835

| | |
|---|---|
| ELÉAZAR, a Jewish goldsmith | RICHARD TUCKER<br>Tenor |
| RACHEL, his daughter | YASUKO HAYASHI<br>Soprano |
| PRINCE LÉOPOLD | JUAN SABATÉ<br>Tenor |
| PRINCESS EUDOXIE | MICHELLE LE BRIS<br>Soprano |
| CARDINAL BROGNI | DAVID GWYNNE<br>Bass |
| RUGGIERO | ROBERT BICKERSTAFF<br>Baritone |
| ALBERT | ANTHONY BALDWIN<br>Baritone |

NEW PHILHARMONIA ORCHESTRA
Leader: DESMOND BRADLEY
AMBROSIAN SINGERS
Repetiteuse: NINA WALKER
French Coach: PAMELA STIRLING
Conductor: ANTON GUADAGNO

is a film to go with the sound, that might bring us still closer, and the filmed *Firestone Hour* concerts are a likely source. What we see there is so ordinary that in a curious way it enhances the wonder of what we hear. The thickset, shortish body is the traditional tenor's; so is the breadth of face from the lobe of one ear to that of the other (rather like the shape Caruso gave to his own face in self-caricatures). But the whole physical appearance is neutral, neither attractive nor noble, but equally not weak or hard or arrogant. All distinction is in the voice. And that voice, however poor the quality of reproduction (let alone that of the programme), will instantly move anyone who loves singing. We can see he is no actor, most of all because when he does think to provide something by way of gesture it is so useless. Nor can it be said that he acts with the voice (a few little sobs in the Flower song from *Carmen*, many mightier ones in *Pagliacci* and a stage-laugh punctuating a poker-faced 'Questa o quella' do duty instead). He offers also little variation in volume: everything is sung out, good and loud. Then again, rather as in the face, there is an absence of offensiveness: no vulgarity, no aspirating, no hairpin legato but always the real thing and no gratuitous 'effects' beyond the almost statutory sobs. Clearly he is not the thinking-man's tenor; but the sound is magnificent. If I say

169

that it is brainless I am not meaning to imply that Tucker himself was unintelligent or that such singing does not involve a complexity of cerebral functions; but the 'brainlessness' in question is really a condition of its splendour as song. The brain concerns itself with meaning; words are a way of conveying meaning; so the more we think about the meaning of words in song the more inclined we are to utter them as we would in speech, where some syllables are weighted, others lightened. The Italian singer's practice has traditionally been to treat syllables according to their note-values but not their speech-values. Even their composers encouraged them to do so: no English composer would have set the words 'Celeste Aida, forma divina' as Verdi does, with the final 'a' of 'Aida' and 'divina' given such length and prominence (first beat of the bar, highest note of the phrase). Italian singing and writing for the voice are, in this sense, based on a principle of 'brainlessness'; and, paradoxically, it is this as much as anything else that makes the song sound so good as singing. Tucker was a singer entirely within the Italian tradition as far as this is concerned, whether (as in the *Firestone Hour*) he sang 'Celeste Aida, forma divina' or 'Song of songs, song of memories'.

There was, however, another element in his singing, and this is the Jewish inheritance, which was the prime formative influence and remained at the centre of his being. Tucker himself placed as the supreme moment of his career not a performance in the opera house but a Shabboz in the synagogue at Vienna. He was amidst a congregation which, in the biography, is described as being composed of the young and the old: the middle generation missing, victims of the Holocaust. His manager, John Giuliani, was there, and his account is movingly quoted in James Drake's book. Tucker sang without choir or accompaniment, and it seemed to Giuliani that 'that day he sang more powerfully than at any other time in my memory'. The emotion was indescribable. He sang the next night to a triumphant reception at the State Opera (a record sleeve-note of Viennese songs tells that the police riot-squad was called out to clear his way to the stage door), but the greater work had been done earlier in the Judenstrasse.

There were other times in his life – in Israel on the eve of the Six Days war, or with the American troops in Vietmam, or at home obdurately travelling to be at his father-in-law's funeral when he was a sick man himself – when a certain greatness of character reduces the brag-and-bounce of his egoism to triviality. In rather the same way, the solid gold of such a voice (it goes for Caruso too) and the simple goodness of such singing still have the power to halt the musical world in its sophisticated tracks while it fleetingly contemplates the oddness of its priorities, by which song and singer are valued for their affinities with painter, poet, actor, philosopher, scholar and critic: for almost everything in fact rather than for their essential selves, whether as singer or song.

CHAPTER 34

# Marilyn Horne

If the name of Ponselle arose in association with Richard Tucker, it does so still more insistently with Marilyn Horne. In her autobiography (Atheneum, 1983) she tells how Richard Bonynge heard her for the first time in rehearsal with his wife Joan Sutherland in *Beatrice di Tenda* and phoned immediately to the record company's director saying 'Get over here quick. We've got a girl who sounds like Rosa Ponselle!' This was early in 1961. In December 1963 I heard her myself for the first time at her debut in London. Her name was still unknown to me, and my attendance at the concert had more to do with the appearance of the Los Angeles Chamber Orchestra and the performance of a new work, *Silent Boughs* by William Kraft. This was for soprano and strings, and Marilyn Horne was then billed as a soprano. She sang first a Bach cantata and then gave an encore. This was an aria, I think by Mercadante, unknown probably to everyone in the hall; but it was this that impressed. I knew that I had never heard a voice like it, either in the flesh or (and here the certainty faltered) on records. But on records, and on second thoughts, yes, there was a memory stirring; and the voice that surfaced was Ponselle's. It was the low notes especially, but also the richness and splendour throughout.

'Rondure', a word out of Whitman, suggests itself. 'Grandeur' too. And (especially having read her book) 'humour'. And 'splendour' undoubtedly.

An aural rondure, one hastens to add, though of course the visual image is not one of angularity either. But the sound, if one tries now to summon it up, forms itself around the letter 'o'. Going up the scale the sound opens for a while, then shades in again; going down, it is the very essence of 'o'ness, of 'rondure'.

It was disorientating then to hear her next in *Wozzeck*. 'O' is simply not Marie's vowel: you don't feed this music of need with the voice of plenty (or vice-versa). Her performance was strong and, in the scene with the child, moving (it would be lovely to hear that again now); but the sound was not right for *Wozzeck*, and certainly *Wozzeck* was not what we wanted to hear her sing. Presumably by that time we had made the connection between *Wozzeck*'s Marie and Carmen Jones. The film of Hammerstein's 're-creation' had been made as long ago as 1954, but the dubbing was so good and Horne's gift for mimicry so expert that at the time I, like many others,

171

Marilyn Horne as Carmen (Metropolitan 1972)

assumed that Carmen's singing-voice was that of the actress, Dorothy Dandridge. It was of course a gorgeous sound and should have been noted in the little red book (or whatever) right from the start. But Carmen Jones was not mentioned in the biographical note of the Victoria and Albert Museum concert, and no reference to the sultry musical sullied the printed programme of Covent Garden's *Wozzeck*.

There was, in that programme, an advertisement for two recordings, one of music from Handel's *Julius Caesar* and the other of an album called *The Age of Bel Canto*. So already the signposts were pointing away from Berg and Kraft towards quite a different area of repertoire. Both recordings had Sutherland as their star attraction, but Horne contributed memorably and before long was a star herself. In the Handel opera she sang the aria of Cornelia, 'Priva son d'ogni conforto', and in notes made at the time I find: 'firm and rich, pre-eminently gentle, unfussy legato, sensitive inflexions' and then 'lovely Ponselle sound round the lower E'.

The full revelation came with a solo recital, made in 1964 and reviewed in *Gramophone* magazine the following May. Philip Hope-Wallace mentioned some previous associations (but not *Carmen Jones*) and continued: 'Now she fully comes into her own. Such an instinctive feeling for the dramatic and vocal problems posed by each item allied to so well based and well projected a voice must surely carry the singer far.' He went on to recommend for first playing the Page's cavatina from *Les Huguenots*: 'It is beautifully "sprung", caressingly phrased and ends with an audible smile.' Then, he suggests, the listener might complement this with the other Meyerbeer item 'the burden of which is Who'd be a prophet's mother?': 'Suitably darker in colouring, the singing of the aria is grave in exactly the right way.' For myself, most impressive of all, indeed stunning in its technical brilliance and richness of tone, was the cabaletta that followed. 'Comme un éclair' really did come like a flash of lightning, strong in spirit, definition and rhythmic energy. We knew marvellous records of this music by Ernestine Schumann-Heink and Sigrid Onegin, but if this was not their superior, or even their equal, it was not on account of voice or technique.

The record also included a fine account of another aria recorded long ago by Schumann-Heink, Sesto's 'Partò' in *La clemenza di Tito*. Here a fuller expressive capacity was revealed: a nobility of timbre that had much of tenderness and humanity within it. The more surprisingly encountered solo from *La figlia del reggimento* reminded us of the mezzo's soprano past. That too is interesting. The annals are full of mezzos who attempt the soprano roles and do themselves a mischief thereby; but there are not so many examples of sopranos taking the elevator on its journey down. Horne trained as a soprano and spent three years with the opera company in Gelsenkirche singing soprano roles such as Mimì and Minnie. Donizetti's vivandière was a role she learned for the San Francisco Opera as late as 1962, and no doubt that is how the aria came to be included among the mezzo parts represented in this recital. More interestingly, the singing provides an example of what in the book she calls 'moving the centre of the voice'. Even within the mezzo repertoire, it goes up for Adalgisa in *Norma*, down for Arsace in *Semiramide*. Here it is well up for the regiment's favourite 'daughter'. It doesn't sound 'right', but it involves a finely accomplished adjustment, and in the last part of the solo, when the troops arrive, it is splendid to hear a daughter with a touch of the sergeant-major about her.

173

No Verdi was included in this collection, nor in the subsequent operatic recital record: the Verdi roles have not been her happiest in the opera house (though Mistress Quickly was a peach of a part for her in riper years, leaving only a faint regret that she could not have added Falstaff to her list of *travesto* roles). What is significant in that programme is the prominence in it of Rossini. In the sequel to that first record she included Tancredi's 'Di tanti palpiti', and this, more specifically, pointed to the 'trouser roles' that were to become so closely associated with her. Arias such as that one and Graeme's 'Mura felici' in *La donna del lago* can hardly be heard by anyone of this generation without the sound of Horne's voice coming to mind with all its splendours and idiosyncrasies.

This is so where other and younger singers are concerned. In recent times so many of them – Kasarova, Podles, Larmore, Bartoli, Soffel – have entered the field, and so often, and involuntarily, they show that the Marilyn Horne sound is there in the memory-bank. What particularly fascinates them is the low register, and it is precisely there that the danger lies. As she herself developed in later years, the identity of this as a distinct 'department' of the voice became marked and eventually almost comical. A smile would spread through the audience affectionately and

174

gladly when she went down into the cellar; but it would not be something to copy.

I remember too that there seemed to me to come a time, perhaps around 1974, when records showed a voice that had changed and not for the better: the vibrations were less even, the sheen appeared less sumptuous. In the book, that year is shown to have been a critical one in her private life, with the death of her dearly loved mother and the separation from her husband, Henry Lewis. It was the year too of the Bernstein *Carmen* recording, which to my mind struck an all-time low in thick and raunchy tastelessness. After that it came to seem that whatever good might be found in a new Marilyn Horne recording it would probably not take the form of a notable artistic refinement.

Still, you do not go to (say) Dickens for refinement, and among singers there is something very Dickensian about Marilyn Horne. Her characterisations became larger, and eventually larger than life. When we saw her last at Covent Garden she was a sunshade-swirling, spaghetti-ladling Isabella, the Italian girl in Algiers, ready to laugh and lever herself out of any tricky situation. Before that, she had made a massive, dare-you-to-laugh entry as the bonny young warrior Malcolm Graeme in *La donna del lago*, a picturesque variant in the portrait gallery known collectively as 'General Horne'. In life, as her autobiography shows, she has a robust style of dealing with trouble whether in the opera house or the parking lot. In recital, she was the supreme puller-out-of-stops. If her arrival on stage didn't get them, the mere sound of her voice in the opening number would; and if that didn't work there was a virtuoso blinder in store.

So it seems to have been at her La Scala recital of 1981. The Milanese applauded no more than politely after 'Chloris sighed', though the anonymous Purcellian piece had been sung with trills and runs in profusion and all with gorgeous, opulent and probably quite inappropriate high-seriousness. Handel followed, and then what on the recording sounds like an encore-song; and now the 'bravo's begin. Spanish songs, *Semiramide*, 'Simple gifts' bring in turn the individual shouts of encouragement, the communal swell of approval, and the still more eloquent scarce-breathing silence. 'At the River' makes an inspired conclusion, with 'Beautiful Dreamer' and 'Jeanie with the light brown hair' gracefully perfect for the last 'arrivederci'. We had something similar at Covent Garden in 1986. The voice rattled a bit at a forte but was still miraculous, the technique triumphant, and the strong humanity of her singing touched unexpectedly in Mahler as in Samuel Barber. She again ended the evening with 'Jeanie', and anything lovelier could not have been imagined. As it happened, this was not the last time I heard her, but I remember thinking that, were it to be so, then as the Generals say to each other in *Julius Caesar*, 'this parting was well made'.

175

# CHAPTER 35

# Joan Hammond and Marie Collier

Notes that go up to the Gallery. John McCormack used to recall one that made him want to leap up out of his seat: it was a certain tenor's high C (more probably a B) in 'Che gelida manina' at a performance of *La bohème* in the Covent Garden Summer Season of 1906. For myself there was a moment in the Fountain scene of *Lucia di Lammermoor* when the vocal spray rose higher, clearer and fuller than seemed possible. Another, a couple of years before that, had a less likely setting in the Wedding scene in *Jenufa* when a phrase from the Mayor's daughter sent a totally unexpected shiver down the spine. And the original, the first, long ago but vivid to this day, came as our poor little tenor, barely audible above the orchestra, took his high A towards the end of the Love duet in *Madama Butterfly* and the soprano a moment later joined him. But oh the thrill of that arrival! It is an inspired touch on Puccini's part, catching the girl's sudden exaltation; but the voice of the singer must catch it too, and this one did.

There must be something about the Australian voice, for the singers in all of my three examples had come to Britain from Australia (the Lucia, of course, being Joan Sutherland on her famous first night). McCormack's tenor was Caruso; my Madama Butterfly was Joan Hammond. Hers was the first genuinely thrilling operatic voice I heard. The year would have been 1943 or '44, and the Carl Rosa Company was on its welcome wartime rounds. We used to mock, but they worked valiantly against heavy odds, going from town to town with a different opera for each night and flying the flag. Their principals included old-timers like Helen Ogilvie, Gladys Parr and Tudor Davies, who had done the state some service; and they announced guest artists for special nights – Gwen Catley for *Rigoletto*, Heddle Nash for *Faust,* Norman Allin for *The Merry Wives of Windsor.* Joan Hammond was the guest Butterfly. Her voice was of international quality and then in its prime; she also carried a note of personal conviction in her singing, an Italianate emotional charge such as I missed later even when hearing so fine an artist as Joan Cross in the role.

There can be little doubt that had it not been for the war, Joan Hammond would by that time have been singing in much more exalted surroundings. She came to Europe from Australia in 1936 to study in Vienna, where two years later she sang at the Volksoper as Nedda in

176

Joan Hammond

*Pagliacci.* Offers from the State Opera House followed, and in 1940 a contract to sing Violetta and Mimì at La Scala with further performances in Madrid and Barcelona. It was, she said, 'the most exciting prospect of my career'. With the outbreak of war and then Italy's entry as an ally of Germany, these prospects came to nothing, and it was fortunate that she had established a basis in Britain. In London she became a pupil (and not an entirely satisfied one) of the tenor Dino Borgioli. She also came to the notice of Sir Thomas Beecham who engaged her for a *Messiah* at the Queen's Hall. Neville Cardus reported favourably on the voice and style, especially admirable in 'Rejoice greatly': 'I have seldom heard the runs executed with more than her liquid fluency.' Letting us know that he had heard the 70-year-old Santley, whose 'noble tossing of (the) head' in 'Behold, I tell you a mystery' apparently showed that 'he believed in what he was singing about', Cardus added: 'The classic manner of Handel singing is not known to vocalists of the present day; we must be grateful then to a new artist, who, like Miss Hammond, can bring to him a culture and appreciation of her own' (*Manchester Guardian*, 19 December 1938).

Even this base was threatened when the bombs began to fall. Yet it was in that period, when one of the minor casualties of war was the performance of Italian or German opera in its original language, that the breakthrough came. In her autobiography, *A Voice, a Life* (Gollancz, 1970), 'Breakthrough' is the title she gives to Part IV, which starts in 1946. It

177

really dates back to 26 September 1941, when she recorded two arias by Puccini in English: the famous 'Love and music' ('Vissi d'arte') from *Tosca* and the then almost unknown 'Oh, my beloved father' ('O mio babbino caro') from *Gianni Schicchi*. And it was this, the 'B' side, that caught the affection of all the housewives in England, who sent in requests to the BBC's *Housewives' Choice*, and, as she realised on her return to Australia after the war, of a much wider public than that. There she found herself unexpectedly famous and besieged by requests for this two-minute plea of a Florentine girl to her daddy who for his roguery was consigned by Dante to everlasting perdition.

Still, whether placed in 1941 or '46, the first 'breakthrough' for Joan Hammond is perhaps a suitable point at which to leave her for the time being and take up the story of Marie Collier, the other soprano whose voice rose to the Gallery and left a lasting impression a many years ago. This was a voice that thrilled, not, on this occasion, when taking some spectacular high note, but in the middle range and by virtue of its timbre; nor was it the special focus of attention on stage, but one among several and in a relatively minor role. All the more impressive, then, that it rose to such effect. When I next heard her it was probably as Musetta, and such a Musetta as would have carried all before her in any house throughout the world. Later she came to overdo it, but in these early performances she filled the part precisely to the brim in a way never equalled in my experience. When she entered the Café Momus it was as though everybody's glass was suddenly full; the champagne flowed and it came from a magnum of a voice. The high notes were full and fresh, and the ears fair rattled with her vibrancy. Over that particular aspect of her singing friends would agree to differ, for there were some to whom the rapid vibrato was a pain. I even remember two young programme-sellers arguing about it: 'I think it's marvellous,' said one, and 'I can't stand it,' the other. This was in 1962 before a performance of *The Queen of Spades*, in which Marie Collier's Lisa was, in my memory, for ever to be recalled when that music was heard or thought of. What she brought to it was not the bright clarity of the authentic Russian soprano but a darker tone, tense with tragic foreboding. Later she came to the big Italian roles – Elisabeth de Valois, Tosca, Butterfly, Manon Lescaut – and to others in Janáček, Prokoviev and Shostakovich that were to bring her the highest critical acclaim. I still see and hear her essentially in those two roles, so contrasting in character, the radiant extravert Musetta and the yearning inconsolable Lisa.

She committed suicide in 1971. The shock of it – even if, as at first said, the death had been accidental – profoundly affronted the notion that people with so much animation belong to life. A memoir by Tito Gobbi (*Opera*, February 1972) afforded some insight: 'Highly strung, restless, impulsive, she was always searching for something she could not find, feeling tormented, tired and uncertain.' They had sung together on many

Marie Collier as Christine in *Mourning Becomes Electra* (Metropolitan 1967)

occasions, most famously when she deputised for Callas in *Tosca*, and the last time he had met her in Pretoria 'alone and very much depressed'. Apparently she gave an excellent performance, had a great reception and was happy again for a while; but the depression must have returned. She loathed the empty feeling associated with arriving in a strange place, being alone in her hotel bedroom, having all the tension of rehearsals and then back to the room and so forth for as long as the career lasted. Reports of her singing in the last year of her life suggest that the voice may have begun to fail. If she suspected this herself it would have been rather as with other possessors of brilliant voices, Callas, Welitsch, and Tibbett, of whom only Welitsch managed to cope.

Joan Hammond also was a survivor. In the course of her life were perhaps six times – six that we know of – in which a less robustly constituted character might have cracked. In 1939 she lost everything she had built up thus far in her career in Vienna. In 1940 her great opportunity at La Scala was taken away in the midst of physically harrowing journeys from London to Milan and back. In wartime London her home was bombed and she lived always on the move, always just about making financial ends meet. Later, in 1946, she faced a vocal crisis and, as she said, relearnt her technique; this after an Australian tour that entailed every kind of strain. In 1964 she started having heart attacks, and retired from professional life. In 1967 she lost much in a fire at her home; sixteen years later a bush fire took the rest. Yet she lived to the age of 84, was made a Dame of the British Empire, and somehow or other remained cheerful and unselfishly preoccupied throughout. Perhaps it was the golf, for if the opera houses and concert halls of the world had not claimed her, the golf courses would have done.

If I think about both of these sopranos now, as they were in the full and lovely bloom of their voices and art, it is with a sense of Hammond as the *spinto* type, Collier as the lyric-dramatic. One sad difference is that while Hammond's recordings capture something of her true voice (but hardly its richer constituents), Collier's has hardly been caught properly at all. She sings Chrysothemis in the Nilsson-Solti *Elektra* and that is some memento. But nothing that I have heard is quite 'it'. Both of these singers had an intensely personal way with the music they sang. Hammond's recording of 'D'amor sul' ali rosee' from *Il trovatore* sung in English, seems tonally shallower than her voice really was, yet the emotional concentration and something buoyant in rhythm and creative in phrasing and nuance is genuinely representative of her art at its best. Of Collier we should have her Renata in *The Fiery Angel*, her superb Katerina Ismailova and Katya Kabanova, her Emilia Marty in *The Makropoulos Affair*. Better, perhaps, than trying to capture or recapture from the available recordings, is to reread the verdict of critics:

Huge, warm and pulsating in tone. This is a true Puccini voice ... that crackling vibrancy which makes for haunting emotionalism. Miss Collier lives her music dangerously, but she keeps her production under control, and the result is a maximum of excitement. (Arthur Bloomfield, *Opera* 1969, on *La fanciulla del West* in San Francisco)

Of all the Commonwealth voices which have come to our aid since the war, none (save that of Joan Sutherland and she doesn't compete in this sphere) have had more lustre and sheer beauty of tone. (Philip Hope-Wallace, *Opera* 1961, of her first Madama Butterfly at Covent Garden)

Miss Collier has been the revelation of the season as Santuzza ... a most musical, attractive performance, never strident, voiced in tones that were round and darkly gleaming, able to convey sorrow, bitterness and desperation. (Andrew Porter, *Opera* 1960)

And one other, Arthur Jacobs (*Opera* 1964) on a performance of *Katarina Ismailova*: 'It was as if she were prematurely enacting the tragedy which has eventually to happen.'

CHAPTER 36

# Kiri te Kanawa

There is another voice that comes up from down under. As with Joan Hammond, Joan Sutherland and Marie Collier, a first memory attaches itself to the voice of Kiri te Kanawa and remains vivid over the years. *Boris Godunov* is an opera with a long cast-list, in which the Tsar's daughter Xenia is not especially conspicuous. She appears in one scene only, in company with her clap-happy nurse and loquacious brother. Soon all are upstaged by Boris's unanticipated entry into the nursery, and before long he has the stage to himself for the Monologue and Clock scene which are so central to the opera. Perhaps by contrast, the shy unhappy girl with the burden of royalty already upon her should be seen as part of the pattern, and not the least important; even so, there cannot have been many performances in the opera's history where at the end people have left asking 'Who was that Xenia?' The fact that on this occasion the Tsar was Boris Christoff only makes it more remarkable. But then, the Xenia was Kiri te Kanawa.

We know it now, and of course, re-read at this date, the name leaps out of the cast-list. It was unfamiliar then, as to many it was still a little while later when the voice of the Priestess in *Aida* again caused one to consult the programme. The programme tells me now, what I had forgotten, namely that the Radamès was Carlo Bergonzi; all the same, I remember it as a not particularly good *Aida* of which the properly dismissive remark to make was: 'And the best singing came from the High Priestess.' With no more than a few phrases to chant from off-stage, hers is not a spectacular role, and quite often it happens that, in whatever enchantment is involved, distance has played a part. On this occasion one somehow knew that if the singer had been on-stage the voice would have been equally pure and still more lovely.

Other brief encounters of this kind may have followed, but there was no doubt that when the big chance came, as it did very soon with the Countess in *Le nozze di Figaro*, the house was already full of folk willing her to succeed and then being simply, but deeply, moved by the extent of that success. The ovation after 'Dove sono' was intensely appreciative; nobody wanted to bring the performance to a standstill (this, after all, was Mozart) but equally there was, as it seemed, a unanimous desire to mark the

181

occasion. My own mental note, mindful of recordings and tales from long ago, was that perhaps this had been something comparable to the experience of hearing Meta Seinemeyer in the years when she held Dresden in thrall. There was that kind of firm centre within a vibrant timbre and a dignity that combined with pathos to make the utterance quite personal. Te Kanawa's voice as heard then was, I imagine, larger and fuller then Seinemeyer's, and that too was part of the glory: that such a very ample, generously rounded voice could also command the classic style, with fine phrasing and long, evenly-drawn lines that were a joy in themselves. Over the next years, throughout the 1970s and into the '80s, we were treated to a succession of lovely performances – as Micaëla, Tatiana, Desdemona, Amelia Grimaldi, Mimì, Marguerite. We came, in fact, to adore this young woman who in addition to her gifts as a singer looked so beautiful, acted so touchingly and moved on stage with such grace.

'Bliss was it in that dawn to be alive', and certainly not to be a critic was very pleasant. One did not have to beware of being swept away, and I remember thinking highly of Bernard Levin for airing his exasperation with two miserable-looking critics who were sitting where he could observe them in a concert given with orchestra at Covent Garden for a good charitable cause in 1976. All of Te Kanawa's singing that night seemed to me to be virtual perfection, and it was in the 'storia di Doretta' from *La rondine* that the floodgates opened so that one marvelled, even in the midst of such emotion, at the chemistry or whatever it is that turns sound into water. The song is of course designed to bring out the best in the voice that will bring out the best in the song, but never can the mutual benefaction have been shared more gratefully than it was among the audience that night. Exceptions were the luckless critics who sat within view of Mr Levin and who, if they applauded at all, did so feebly and with indifference. Next morning his report for *The Times* turned the spotlight full upon them. These two, he commented, were the sort who, had they been present at the feeding of the five thousand, would have demanded lemon with their fish and butter for the bread.

The principal dilemma for Te Kanawa's admirers at Covent Garden was that they did not want to lose her but thought she ought to go. In those years there was high indignation when the record companies produced one of 'her' operas but without her participation, and with this went an evangelical zeal to spread the word and let the world know. We need not have worried. The world was already better informed than we thought, and soon enough we were sharing her with New York, Paris, Sydney, Milan, San Francisco; we also learned, rather earlier than expected, that she had come to rank with the high earners in the profession and soon with the highest. Even so, our own impoverished capital, which seemed to lurch from crisis to crisis, was not utterly deprived. We heard her as Violetta, Donna Elvira, Fiordiligi, and soon there were the Strauss operas, *Arabella*, *Der Rosenkavalier* and in 1991 *Capriccio*.

182

Of course, not all was well: that would never do. In particular, word got around that in the German repertoire she learned her texts parrot-fashion and this reinforced the comforting notion that a pretty woman cannot be expected to be clever as well. She herself has been frank about it, stating (as reported by Helena Matheopoulos in an information sheet circulated by her record company) that she did not speak German and that she learnt the words phonetically with the aid of a coach. That, to my mind, is information for the biographer but not for the music critic (professional or amateur) whose job it is to judge the performance on its merits. If native German speakers and thoroughly competent linguists find their pleasure spoilt by this aspect of the singer's work, then that is a statement of personal fact and no one can argue with it. But when the complaints come, as they frequently do, from less well-qualified sources, one may be forgiven for finding them less impressive. It always seems to me that if the allegation of parrot-fashion learning is true that only makes the achievement all the more remarkable. It is one thing, and formidable enough, to commit to memory the words and music of these Strauss operas, quite another to memorise a Babel of meaningless syllables and make them sound like sense, which she does. These days, moreover, it is not merely a matter of giving a performance on stage, about which people can argue confidently since there can be no certain evidence, nor even of performing with the knowledge that a sound-recording is being made, but of doing so in front of cameras, the evidence of which can be scrutinised in infinite detail on home-videos the world over. Te Kanawa's Countess in *Capriccio* at San Francisco is thus exposed to universal examination. I cannot claim to have been over it in the minute detail required, but have paid sufficient attention to suggest that if this is not indeed the work of an intelligent woman playing an intelligent woman it is the best imitation of an intelligent woman playing an intelligent woman the world has ever seen.

For most of her English-speaking audiences the limiting factor in the enjoyment of her Countess and Marschallin has had less to do with language and more to do with voice. The Countess came into her repertoire at a time when the vocal radiance had dimmed. In *Der Rosenkavalier* it was more a matter of unsuitable tessitura. The Marschallin's voice soars high in certain passages but for the most part works within the middle register, with heavy demands upon the lower half of that register, which is just the area of the voice in which least fullness and thrust of tone is available to this singer. The Marschallin, I believe, is the only role taken into her repertoire, in which Te Kanawa has been ill-fitted to deliver. Otherwise – and this has been one of the most gratifying features of her career – she has kept within the lyric soprano range, her one excursion beyond it, in *Tosca*, having been abandoned immediately after a first trial.

We have then to see what that entails. The lyric soprano's is the voice of youth. Te Kanawa was born in 1944, 45 therefore in 1989, which was about the time when her future began to look uncertain. An artist must develop. The usual resource for the lyric soprano at that age is to increase the proportion of concert-work in her schedule, and to extend and deepen her art in song. Te Kanawa has given some delightful recitals, but something would have to change for this to become her sphere. When she sang a group of Lieder she was not superficial; in Fauré and Duparc she was remarkably idiomatic. But this still did not seem to represent a likely point of growth. At the time of writing, her latest new venture in recording has been a collection of German operatic arias including some, such as Agathe's solos in *Der Freischütz*, which would have been welcome at any time and are welcome now. Yet this recital too seems (if the distinction will hold) to be less a matter of development than of diversification. The point at which growth does seem apparent is to my mind the last one might have wished for. 'I think Tina Turner is wonderful,' she said in an interview for the *Daily Telegraph*, and 'I'd love to do something by Andrew Lloyd Webber' (22 March 1991).

Back (from the brink) to the dates. Born 1944; and we came in at the *Boris Godunov* of 1971, *aetat* 27. If that was the start, it was a late one. But of course much had gone before. The adopted girl with parents of (respectively) European and Maori origin was a singer almost from the cradle. She made a local radio debut at the age of six, and won New Zealand's most prestigious singing competition at 21. By 1965 she was popular in her country on records and television, and was awarded New

General Administrator: John Tooley

in association with
Scott Concert
Promotions Ltd
presents

Sunday
3 December
1978

A Gala Recital in the presence of
Their Royal Highnesses
Prince and Princess Michael of Kent

# Kiri te Kanawa Soprano

**Richard Amner** Piano

in aid of the
British Kidney Patient Association

The Royal Opera House Covent Garden Limited receives financial assistance from The Arts Council of Great Britain

In accordance with the requirements of the Greater London Council persons shall not be permitted to stand or sit in any of the gangways intersecting the seating; or to sit in any of the other gangways ; smoking and the taking of photographs in the auditorium are not permitted.

Zealand's first Gold disc in 1968. Her years at the London Opera Centre were also eventful, and her singing of the title-role in Rossini's *La donna del lago* in the 1969 Camden Festival marked her clearly as a singer to watch. She was also a girl with a lot of living to do. Yet in an ideal world these dates should all perhaps have been moved back to about three years earlier, and the Xenia in *Boris Godunov* at which we 'came in' should have occurred at the age of 24. Then there would have been further room for development at the other end. Perhaps not. Perhaps a condition of that decisive and crucial success with the Countess in *Le nozze di Figaro* was the relative maturity of voice; and never to be forgotten is the way in which it came to us as a compound of promise and achievement, an instant satisfaction and an assurance of greatness in the making.

Since then the facts on paper would suggest that all the promise of that night has been fulfilled. We, who were there and have watched ever since, know that that is not quite so. We also know that some of the loveliest singing we have heard in our entire lives, both 'in the flesh' and on records, has been hers; that some of the most exultantly lit-up of nights in the opera house have owed their incandescence to her; and that this, in the long run is what matters.

CHAPTER 37

# Frederica von Stade

Deprivation is relative, and relatively speaking I don't suppose that in our part of our part of the world we have much right to complain about anything. But one protest must be lodged forthwith: we in Britain have not had our fair share of Frederica von Stade. We met her and duly fell in love in the Summer of 1973. Considering that Paris had already fallen earlier that year, and that half the critics, conductors and producers of Europe and America became suitors there and then, we did well to have her back to London, Edinburgh and Glyndebourne as promptly as we did. But soon it became clear that our days were numbered, the visits being ever more infrequent and now, at the time of writing, seemingly things of the past.

As with most misfortunes, this has its positive side, and to that we turn for consolation. It means that she has already acquired the magic of period. She is fixed now within perhaps a dozen years, the nearest point of which is distant by roughly another dozen. That also means that she is, like Arcady, for ever young. Perhaps if she were to come back to us, we ought in our own best interests to stay away. Of course there would be no chance of that, and, from all we hear, the spirit of youthfulness, and to a large extent the appearance and even the sound, remain constant.

One thing is for sure: we shall not see her Cherubino again. The pageboy of *Le nozze di Figaro*, who in Massenet's sequel, *Chérubin*, celebrates his seventeenth birthday, remains her most famous role, and she said goodbye to it ('Say goodbye now' as the old English translation of 'Non più andrai' had it) at the Metropolitan in 1995, on her own fiftieth birthday. When she first sang the part at Glyndebourne, 22 years earlier, it was in a vintage *Figaro* with Kiri te Kanawa following Elizabeth Harwood as the Countess and Ileana Cotrubas as Susanna. In his history of the festivals Spike Hughes wrote: 'The cast was exceptionally good, and I'm not certain that, in the tradition that "all Glyndebourne Cherubinos are good", the young American, Frederica von Stade, was not the best of them all.' She had come to that production from another, and brilliant one, in the Royal Opera at Versailles. *Opera* magazine's correspondent (May 1973), noting that 'all the cast loved their roles', said of von Stade: 'Never have I seen a Cherubino who looked so much the male adolescent in love with the whole world;

186

Von Stade as Rosina in *Il barbiere di Siviglia* (Covent Garden 1975)

the *travesto* instead of being the usual handicap, helped to create an equivalent charm which fitted perfectly with the period.' The other principals, incidentally, were Janowitz, Freni, Bacquier and Van Dam, a cast to match the jewel of an opera house.

1973 was the year of breakthrough. Up till then, having come to the Met virtually straight out of college, she had spent three years singing mostly small parts, starting as one of the three boys in *Die Zauberflöte*, the first of her many *travesto* roles. Her best chance in that season of 1970 came with another of them, that of Nicklausse in *Les contes d'Hoffmann*. 1971 brought Sièbel in *Faust*, 1972 Cherubino and Hänsel. At least the New York apprenticeship provided plenty of practice in the wearing of trousers. It must have been at the very least a relief from type-casting when the Met offered Rosina in *Il barbiere di Siviglia* and the Washington Opera Society enterprisingly came up with Penelope in *Il ritorno d'Ulisse in patria*. Those roles in fact charted two main lines of development in her career.

In both it must be said that time and place were auspicious. The Rossini revival was just then getting under way; the moment had also come up for Monteverdi's operas, *L'incoronazione di Poppea* being the other with which von Stade was involved. Her Rosina, praised in New York, had the

187

virtue of being found too refined when introduced at La Scala. Her Cenerentola more than compensated for any lack of brilliance by its touching humanity and naturalness. Elena in *La donna del lago* was one of her Covent Garden roles, and the effect of sincerity combined with the customary charm of voice and manner did much to offset the uneasy matching of soprano role and mezzo voice. Most lovely and suitable of her Rossini singing was very probably heard in the rarely revived *Otello*, beautifully sung on records both in excerpts and in the complete work with José Carreras in the title-role. That too was written for soprano, but the character's tenderness and the music's lyricism asked for just what she had to give.

As for Monteverdi's *Ritorno d'Ulisse*, this gave her the role which many who heard her in it will remember with warmest affection. At Glyndebourne she came to it at a time when Janet Baker's unforgettable performance stood as the inevitable point of reference, and the comparison was an interesting one. The role imposes upon its singer a discipline of restraint very like that of the character herself, the woman who waits with patience and fidelity, using her wits and fortitude to resist the sensible, self-serving advice so freely offered. Janet Baker was heroic in the intensity of resolution and controlled passion: for this Penelope we felt pity, certainly, but more especially a kind of awed wonder which confirmed our own role as spectators. With von Stade we were drawn in. On the face of it, we, like the unwanted suitors, were distanced by the isolation of her stillness and reserved, aristocratic presence; yet it was also a presence that evoked sympathy and fearfulness on her behalf. About her totally undemonstrative Penelope there was more that told of strain, the tension of perpetual watchfulness and the effort of maintaining hope. The moment everyone remembers is that of the return and recognition, with the movement at last of those rigidly controlled hands and the long-awaited fulfilment mirrored in the miracle of a smile.

The other roles most affectionately remembered by her British audiences are Charlotte in *Werther* and Mélisande. The Massenet roles in *Cendrillon* and *Chérubin* never came our way, but the delectable recordings leave an impression almost as vivid. Her success as Mélisande came as a surprise to some, partly because of the sturdy, outgoing 'image' created by her boy-roles, Cherubino and Octavian, and, once in skirts, by the scheming Rosina too. It is also questionable whether Mélisande, low in tessitura as it is for soprano, should be sung by a mezzo: the fragile, girlish quality tends to be compromised. In the event, von Stade used her voice with such discretion and gave such cool, delicate charm to the characterisation that any misgivings were soon appeased. Her Charlotte was simply one of the most touching performances of all. Singers have been known to find the part so exasperatingly passive that they vow never to sing it again. For von Stade it is intensely sympathetic, even to the extent of her wishing that it and not Cherubino had become her recognised 'visiting-card'.

188

Von Stade as Cherubino in *Le nozze di Figaro*

Dramatically it shares with Monteverdi's Penelope the imposition of restraint and patience, while the warmth of feeling so generously expressed
in the music heightens the emotional involvement to such a degree that
any mere passivity is purely external.

A tone of sadness, appropriate to Mélisande as to Charlotte, seems
native to the voice. The happy personality, as it is generally and no doubt
rightly perceived, may seem to disown this, but it too is part of the general
perception. It gives a special flavour to her singing of music that with
others can seem to wear a fixed smile, an invariably light, pretty dress.
The *Songs of the Auvergne*, with her, have more of yearning in them. Even
a gentle, simple, major-key composition such as 'Jenny Rebecca', the most
popular of her encore-songs and named after her daughter, elicits a tone
which even in the words 'what a lucky girl you are' seems to know that in
this world ('C'est au tour de la pauvre petite') every three-day-old is
eventually going to need all the luck it can get. And then in a work which
touches the depths as does *Les nuits d'été* her voice, like a painter's brush,

189

limns the desolate autumnal landscape of 'L'absence' ('Entre nos coeurs, quelle distance') and even imparts a kind of wistfulness to the enticingly sketched idyll of 'L'île inconnue'.

Von Stade is a singer who has made her resources work for her while aware of their limitations. She knows that the volume (the breadth and penetrative power) of her voice does not accommodate the big mezzo roles in Verdi. Karajan wanted her to sing Eboli in *Don Carlos* and she declined, just as she resisted the many invitations to sing Carmen. She has made mistakes, most notably in attempting Adalgisa while Rita Hunter attempted Norma at the Metropolitan in 1976. The most surprising of operas to find in her nineteenth-century repertoire is *La sonnambula*, which was given at San Francisco and Dallas in an adaptation of what is commonly known as 'the Malibran version'. Among the modern operas, some of them with roles written with her in mind, the most surprising is certainly Conrad Susa's *Les liaisons dangereuses*, in which she played the Marquise de Merteuil and, for the first time in her life, a thoroughly nasty piece of work. Reports tell of a deeply impressive last scene, where in front of a mirror the face changes in acknowledgement of what it sees there – which, Marschallin-like, is an ageing woman, but in this instance without the reserves of goodness to find comfort or grace.

As for the singer's own mirror, they say that if it reflects the face and form of a still beautiful woman it does not lie. For the voice I add a little personal prayer that since last heard it has not been too busily employed in the upper register, which seemed to be wearing thin; also that the ways and means of her light-music repertoire (*A Little Night Music*, *On the Town* and so forth) have not too noticeably infiltrated the system. I also hope that plans for concerts in the year 2000, including at least one in London, will come to rich and ripe fruition. And when they do, do I want to be there? Oh, I'll be there, all being well. But that wasn't quite the question.

CHAPTER 38

# Tiana Lemnitz and
# Meta Seinemeyer

There may be any number of reasons why one singer 'gets on' and another, equally well endowed, does not. But amid all the uncertainties and speculations one word stands fast and brooks no argument. Meta Seinemeyer was one of the loveliest singers of her generation. She came to the Dresden Opera in 1924 at an exciting moment in its history. For five years she sang to an adoring public. Reports of her success spread through Germany, and the unique timbre of her voice on records increased her fame further afield. She sang in Berlin and Vienna, briefly in North and South America, and finally at Covent Garden in 1929, the year in which at the age of 34 and on the 19th of August she died.

Tributes came in from many sources. The German press told of 'sweetness and womanly grace', 'ideal beauty of sound', 'impressive warmth' and a 'silver splendour' which 'reached everybody's heart'. In London, operagoers grieved sincerely, for fresh in their minds was the late opera season in which outstanding interest and hopes attached to this newcomer. Most gratefully remembered now must be the words of Fritz Busch, who in his memoirs wrote of the famous performances of *La forza del destino* produced in Dresden as part of the Verdi-revival by Franz Werfel and conducted by himself: 'We had as Leonora the unforgettable, sadly short-lived Meta Seinemeyer, outstanding in that part as she was in other emotional lyric-dramatic roles of Verdi and the lesser Italians. In Giordano's *Andrea Chénier* she was a deeply moving Maddalena. Her voice resembled Elisabeth Rethberg's, though she did not attain that singer's mastery; instead, there was the sense of an incomparable soulfulness that can be well described as "tears in the voice".' On her tomb, he said, should be inscribed the last words of *La forza del destino*, 'Salita a Dio' ('Risen to God') or in the German text 'Die Seele lebt': 'The soul lives'.

That summer season at Covent Garden had given her valuable opportunities, which would no doubt have led to the wider international career which was generally thought her due. Even so, they appear by today's standards to have been absurdly limited: she sang Eva, Elsa and Sieglinde, but in a single performance of each. Earlier, all three had been sung

191

by Lotte Lehmann, queen of hearts in that house since 1924. Seinemeyer arrived unheralded and unknown. The general reaction was no doubt much as reported in a book called *Among the Covent Garden Stars* by Josephine O'Donnell, secretary to the General Manager, Eustace Blois, and then to Sir Thomas Beecham:

> One evening a great favourite had to disappoint her huge circle of admirers, owing to a sudden feverish cold, and again we were fortunate in having a very good substitute. She was, however, quite unknown at Covent Garden, and as people clustered round the doors of boxes there were many expressions of discontent before *Die Walküre* started.
>
> At the first interval I passed two dowagers and heard one say to the other: 'But how very fortunate! I was in such a naughty temper when the Act began – but she sings delightfully!'
>
> 'And looks charming too!' said the friend. 'I hope she comes to sing something another year.'

What a picture of the period! The author goes on to say that there was no return, and to explain why; but there is no doubt that on the strength of her three appearances that year Seinemeyer would have been expected back and the house would have been eager to hear her.

Of her debut *The Times* reported: 'Her subtle acting, and charming presence combined with a voice of warm and sympathetic quality to make a most human figure of Sieglinde. Mme. Seinemeyer's voice is not quite strong enough, especially on the lower and middle notes, to come through some of the big orchestral climaxes ... Apart from this she took her place worthily beside a Brünnhilde [Frida Leider] and a Fricka [Maria Olczewska] whose excellence is now familiar to Covent Garden audiences.' The point about limited volume was common to most of the reviews, but references to freshness, clarity and 'the impression of a real person' balanced the criticism. Then, with her second role, the *Daily Telegraph*'s critic found that she had 'managed to take the measure of our opera house' and presented a 'charmingly girlish Eva' with the voice ringing 'delightfully fresh, clear and pure'. The *Saturday Review* cheered the absence of that 'kittenish archness which singers of the part so often substitute for real youth'. Particularly memorable, they found, were her duets with Friedrich Schorr as Hans Sachs: 'nothing could be lovelier than the soft notes of these two voices, which have remarkable carrying power even at piano.'

Whatever Covent Garden thought of her, she was not entirely delighted with it, telling friends that it hid 'shamefully between a vegetable market and the chief lock-up'. It was in London, too, that she was reckoned to have caught the influenza which precipitated her death, though the causes were more deeply rooted. She went briefly to Bad Kissingen for a cure, but returned, a dying woman, to Dresden. Only a few hours before her death she married Frieder Weissmann, her accompanist and the conductor in

The cover of an LP recital on the Helios label

many of her records. The State Opera's orchestra and chorus performed at her funeral in Berlin, and back in Britain Herman Klein found himself with an experience strange to him as he listened to the voice of the so recently and unexpectedly dead woman on records sent to him for review in *The Gramophone*: 'I need not dwell on the sensations that one experiences on hearing anew the voice of a singer who has just passed on. It is one of those strange phenomena that the gramophone alone can create – an impression far more touching in its realism than any that the camera can convey.'

Not long after Seinemeyer's brief, spring-scented track reaches its abrupt end, the longer, leafier path of Tiana Lemnitz comes into view. Born in 1897, only two years after Seinemeyer, Lemnitz outlived her by more than half a century, dying at the age of 96 in 1994. Both were among the most gifted of singers in the interwar years. They shared in repertoire the lyric roles of Wagner, and others such as Elisabeth de Valois, Aida and Desdemona in Verdi, Mimì, Manon and Cio-Cio-Sàn in Puccini. After that, contrasts: there was an emotional tension in Seinemeyer's singing, an almost ethereal serenity in Lemnitz's. If we summon up an aural picture of Seinemeyer's voice, it is in stressful music such as that of the *Forza del destino* Leonora or even of Schubert's Gretchen; with Lemnitz it is in the

193

long restful phrases of Agathe in *Der Freischütz* or the dreamy pianissimo of Wolf's 'Wiegenlied im Sommer'. In the profession she was called Madame Pianissimo, not because her voice lacked power but because (if the expression is permitted) the pianissimo was her forte.

She too appears in Josephine O'Donnell's book, again with a sign of the times. She chats with the author and tells her about her career, at the climax of which: 'It was actually the Prussian Minister Präsident, Hermann Göring, who had me appointed to the Staatsoper, Berlin, having heard me sing Eva as a guest-artist in *Meistersinger*.' The name is spoken with pride, and no embarrassment seems to arise in the way it is reported (earlier in the book but in this same summer of 1936 the bass-baritone Rudolf Bockelmann had shown her his prize possession, a cigarette-lighter inscribed to 'dem grossen Künstler' also by that appreciative opera-goer whose name now lives in infamy). Lemnitz by all accounts remained an unrepentant devotee of the Third Reich to the end of her days. I never think that we should judge a person, let alone an artist, by such abhorred but uprooted facts; but I do find it a paradox, and a painful one, that the woman with the angelic voice should have been, as seems all too likely, the taunter of the virtually exiled and vulnerable older Lehmann when they were thrown together in the intimacies of *Rosenkavalier*'s first Act in 1938.

In that year, nevertheless, Lemnitz confirmed the impression she had made in 1936, and that was already a strong one. Some of the terms were such as had greeted Seinemeyer ('natural womanly grace', 'purity of tone and lyrical feeling') but without any suggestion of insufficient volume. When she sang her Pamina to the Tamino of Richard Tauber, *The Times* told of a voice 'of beautiful quality to match, and perhaps more than match, his own. Indeed her singing of the great song with which she leaves him in the crypt of the Temple called forth the greatest applause of the evening.' In *Lohengrin* the same journal noted 'a restrained mezza voce of beautiful tone quality that suggested reserves of power'. Ernest Newman in *The Sunday Times* thought her Elsa 'finely sung, but the character was made a trifle too sophisticated by over-elaboration of points of detail'. In *Die Zauberflöte* he found, as most did, 'a rare sense of style', giving as his summary the view that she was 'one of the finest artists Germany has sent us in recent years'. And perhaps we need to remind ourselves that, for Newman, 'recent years' probably comprised the whole postwar period.

Perhaps her greatest admirer – in the sense that there was probably no one at once more ardent and more influential – was Walter Legge. Our two sopranos, Lemnitz and Seinemeyer, have this in common: he worshipped them both. Years later, their voices were foremost in the 'recorded examples' that were, as he said, 'nectar and ambrosia' for his wife Elisabeth Schwarzkopf's musical appetite. Curiously, in the passage from which those quotations are taken (*Opera News*, 1975, reprinted in *Elisabeth*

Tiana Lemnitz

*Schwarzkopf: A Career on Record*, 1995) he tells of 'large doses of Meta Seinemeyer to show how essentially Teutonic voices can produce brilliant Italianate sound', but does not mention Lemnitz who I know figured prominently in these sessions. He had an uncannily sure instinct about a special singer, and both Seinemeyer and Lemnitz were special. We know it, with an equally instinctive certainty, from their records. Certainly I myself shall not forget the first hearing of both, Lemnitz a miracle of purity, softness, breath-control and musical sensitivity in the arias from *Der Freischütz*, Seinemeyer in a song of Anton Rubinstein called 'Night', ennobled by the vibrant individuality of this intense, compact tone.

Lemnitz has become an archetype; Seinemeyer is in danger of being forgotten. I have met people who heard them both, though they are getting a little thin on the ground now. Of Lemnitz they will recall the power behind the pianissimo in her singing and the natural conviction of her acting. I also remember a very old man (as he seemed to me), a German, who had travelled the world and settled in Britain and who seemed to have heard every singer in the previous fifty years. And the greatest? 'Oh, the greatest. Well, there was Ponselle', he said, 'and there was Seinemeyer'. Then he shut his eyes and listened. 'And Seinemeyer', he repeated.

# CHAPTER 39

# Elisabeth Grümmer

Grümmer's is the name that slips the memory. Not everybody's memory of course, but I, if asked without due notice to recall by name that marvellous generation of sopranos who appeared out of Europe in the years immediately after the Second World War and who specialised in Mozart and Strauss, would say 'Schwarzkopf and Seefried, Ljuba Welitsch, Jurinac and Della Casa … Gueden … and …'. The pause might be embarrassingly prolonged before 'and Grümmer' happily surfaced to balance the account and complete the sentence. Why this should be so may have several explanations. Most decisive, very probably, is the pure accident that out of all these singers Elisabeth Grümmer is the only one I never heard 'in the flesh'. For five years (1951-56) she was a fairly frequent visitor to Britain, but later she came here rarely and always on occasions I missed. She is also slightly out of mental alignment in that in this connection one thinks first of Vienna as the centre, whereas she was based in Berlin. It might be urged then that a further reason, and perhaps a more potent one, lay in her relatively restricted place as a recording artist.

Relative (it then follows) to whom? It is here that something personal in a different sense comes into the picture. With Grümmer as with Sena Jurinac, or, rather, on their behalf, a finger is habitually pointed in a certain direction ('Ah, but I didn't marry the record industry,' Jurinac is reported as saying when the question arose). Then, while the fingers point, the tongues are busy with equally pointed pleasantries. 'So sincere!' they will say. 'So spontaneous!' And then, for good measure, 'so unaffected, so unmannered'. With this subtle interplay of stage winks and nudges is indicated the lone figure of Elisabeth Schwarzkopf, former favourite of the gods, now abandoned on Naxos and free to indulge her well-known mannerisms to the empty air and heart's content. The wrongness of this assessment of the one singer does not help the cause of the other, or of others who are used in the campaign of supposedly deft inconspicuous sniping.

In fact Grümmer was by no means neglected or under-represented on records. The three Wagnerian roles that stood at the centre of her operatic repertoire are all there, complete and in well-known recordings: the three Es, Elsa, Elisabeth and Eva. So is what in some ways is the loveliest of her

196

Grümmer as Agathe in *Der Freischütz*

portrayals, that of Agathe in *Der Freischütz*. Her recorded Mozart includes the 1954 Salzburg *Don Giovanni* and the 1961 *Idomeneo*. Her Freia and Gutrune in the *Ring* cycle are preserved, as are important excerpts from *Le nozze di Figaro*, *Così fan tutte* and *Die Zauberflöte*. In a famous recording, under Karajan, Walter Legge cast her as Hansel to Schwarzkopf's Gretel. She also sang in an abridged *Queen of Spades*, excerpts from *Otello*, various arias and lieder, not to mention the Bach Passions, Haydn's *Creation* and the Requiems of Mozart and Brahms. Missing are the two Strauss roles, the Marschallin in *Der Rosenkavalier* (though her Octavian can be sampled in excerpts) and the Countess in *Capriccio*. It is still a not inconsiderable discography that is outlined here.

If the record companies did not exactly neglect her, the critics for the most part wrote decidedly in her favour. She was, for instance, a special favourite of those in *Opera* magazine, who rarely, and then very gently, voiced any complaints. We can, in fact, follow her career through the annals of that magazine. In the very first volume, in July 1951, Christopher West reported on a performance of *Faust* in Berlin, which he had attended primarily in order to hear the Margarethe: 'such beautiful lyric singing was a joy to hear, and one completely forgave her limited acting range'. Making her Covent Garden debut later that year, she was welcomed as an Eva in *Die Meistersinger* worthy of comparison with Tiana

197

Lemnitz. In 1952 she took part in the Edinburgh Festival, singing with the Hamburg Opera as Pamina, Eva and (standing in for Marthe Mödl) Octavian. All accounts agree about the fine quality of her voice, and Lord Harewood reported that in *Der Rosenkavalier* she 'made a tall, shapely boy and did some ravishingly beautiful singing' (*Opera*, October 1952). Back in Berlin, her Euridice in Gluck's opera 'looked like a Botticelli madonna', and as Pamina in Vienna (1953), though some sharpness of intonation was detected in the first act, she was 'consistently good in the second'. At Salzburg in 1954 Andrew Porter struck what was probably the first (and wise) note of warning, saying that 'her voice had suffered from too many Donna Annas in past years'. Harold Rosenthal added that she had 'neither the weight of voice nor personality for the role', which nevertheless remained central to her repertoire for many years. As Desdemona in Berlin's *Otello* 'the nobility of her bearing was matched by the artistry of her singing' (Horst Koegler, *Opera*, July 1955), and as Ilia in *Idomeneo* the following year she was 'ideally suited'. This was also the debut-role of her single season at Glyndebourne: 'her soft high notes were a joy to hear' (Rosenthal, August 1956), and again came the comparison with Lemnitz. Comparisons with Jurinac followed her too, in this and as the Countess in *Le nozze di Figaro*: 'moving and sympathetic ... not eclipsing Sena Jurinac in the part but more than a mere substitute'. At Edinburgh that October for another *Zauberflöte* she was in 'most exquisite voice'. Then towards the end of the year came her triumph in Berlin's first *Capriccio*, Koegler's review of which suggests that here was perhaps the high-point of her career. She was, he said, a 'ravishing' Countess: 'she radiates such human warmth and such womanly charm, and she is so lovely to look at, that I for one prefer her to any other singer who has so far tackled this role', and he added that he had heard them all (*Opera*, January 1957).

With *Lohengrin* (sung also at Bayreuth) and *Tannhäuser* these operas continued to form the main body of her repertoire. In *Der Rosenkavalier* she graduated from Octavian to the Marschallin in 1960; and, perhaps less suitably, the Salzburg *Idomeneo* of 1961 and '62 saw her as Elektra rather than Ilia. According to André Tubeuf, her voice 'always was, and still is, an exquisite instrument' but this 'raging, jealous character ... is totally at odds with her luminous personality' (*Opera*, Festival Issue 1962) (it should be added that the recording made in 1961 calls the purely vocal side of the criticisms in question, and even the dramatic side too, for the Act 1 solo is hair-raising in its angry energy, the mad laughter of Act 3 is entirely convincing, and in between comes singing that matches the beauty of the music, which characterises a better-rounded, less one-dimensional figure than the 'raging, jealous' description suggests). Not long afterwards arrived the first report suggesting a more serious deterioration. A reviewer from Tokyo, where her *Figaro* Countess was heard late in 1964, noted that the voice had 'lost much of its bloom and quality in the upper register'. Later at Wuppertal for *Don Giovanni*, Koegler, devoted admirer as he was,

Grümmer as Majenka in *The Bartered Bride*

detected an 'unpleasant hardening of the timbre'. The year 1967 brought her belated American debut, with the New York City Opera in *Der Rosenkavalier* and then with the Metropolitan Company on tour when she made six appearances as Elsa in *Lohengrin*, the first in Boston where she told an interviewer 'Granny can still do it'. A seventh performance was given at the Met itself – her single performance in the house. In Germany her career continued for a few more years on familiar lines, and it was there, in Berlin, that she sang on stage for the last time, as the Marschallin in 1972. She taught in Lucerne and Paris after her retirement and died at Warendorf on 6 November 1986.

It had been a long, honourable and rewarding career. And of course it dated back further than this postwar survey suggests. Her debut was made, like so many others, as a Flower Maiden in *Parsifal*. This was at Aachen, where the young Karajan had been quick to recognise her talent. By 1940 she had graduated to leading roles such as Alice in *Falstaff* and Octavian. Her first move was to Duisberg but no sooner had she become established there than the theatre suffered a wartime closure. Her chance then came when the Berlin Opera began to reconstitute itself in 1945 and she was offered the role of Majenka in *The Bartered Bride*. Other early roles were Mimì and Micaëla. She also sang the soprano lead in Winfried Zillig's *Troilus and Cressida*, Marthe in Leo Blech's *Das war ich* (both 1951) and Berlin's first *Peter Grimes* in 1947. Abroad, in addition to the

199

British and American appearances, she was at La Scala, the Rome Opera and the Colón, Buenos Aires. All the same, she remained essentially a home-artist, and the glory of her career lay in that quarter of a century when she was principal lyric soprano at Berlin.

Questions arising are (maybe) incidental, but worth a thought all the same. One is the question of why her considerable legacy of recordings contains, proportionately, so few Lieder. She gave many song recitals in the course of her career, and one of the earliest of her records, 'Maria Wiegenlied' by Max Reger, is lovely in every respect. The pat answer is that Schwarzkopf was at EMI and happened to be Mrs Legge. But Legge was a man always searching for that something-more-than-talent, and the repertory could easily have been dovetailed (Schwarzkopf, for instance, sang no more than a little of Schumann and Brahms). Grümmer might have tried Deutsche Grammophon, but they, in the 1950s, had Seefried; or Decca, who had Della Casa. An alternative explanation could be that, as a recording artist in the studios, she was not really very good. EMI (or HMV in those days) did produce a Lieder recital in 1958 with Gerald Moore as pianist. The Brahms songs go well, but the Schubert group is strangely unresponsive. The inner yearnings of the girl Suleika, for instance, are hardly to be guessed at, and even in as uncomplicated a song as the lullaby ('Wie sich der Auglein') no coloration of tone or moulding by portamento suggests the caress of tender shading which others have brought to it.

The other question concerns her international career, which might have developed further. Here it seems likely that her own temperament was the determining factor. Grümmer was ambitious to do well, to sing beautifully and to give pleasure; but she does not appear, from all one gathers, to have been ambitious 'period'. With the unique position she enjoyed in Berlin she had no great reason to travel. The voice needs rest, the spirit needs security and there's no place like home.

I fancy too that her principal motivation was of a kind that drew her in towards a natural centre. As in so many instances, it touches what we call the private life, which with a famous artist is always likely at least to a certain degree to be public too. She had one husband, her one love, and he was killed in an air-raid. She married a violinist, Detlef Grümmer, leader of the orchestra at Bonn and later at Meiningen where Elisabeth Schilz was training to be an actress. It was the sound of his violin, the daily practice of the legato, *cantabile* style, that most influenced her concept of the singer's art. She was away, singing at Duisberg, when he died, holding his violins as he sheltered in the basement of their home at Aachen. It is said that she never fully and inwardly recovered from her husband's death; and when she returned to singing after the war it was perhaps more than anything else to preserve the memory and perpetuate the sound of that violin.

# CHAPTER 40

# Elena Gerhardt

Civilisation gently asserted itself in wartime London when the pianist Myra Hess inaugurated her lunchtime concerts at the National Gallery and particularly when for song recitals she co-opted the most renowned Lieder singer of the age. The very names of the two artists helped to proclaim sanity, for at that time 'Hess' signified primarily Hitler's deputy and 'Gerhardt' was as unmistakably German as an Erhardt or a Göring. They performed Beethoven and Schubert, Brahms and Wolf. Gerhardt sang in German, and a little bit of ground was reclaimed from barbarism. So it was natural that when Gerhardt came to write her autobiography, Myra Hess (now Dame) should contribute the Preface. In it she wrote: 'The name of Elena Gerhardt lives in the minds and hearts of countless men and women all over the world.' That was in 1953. Thirty years earlier another Englishwoman, Ursula Greville, had met Gerhardt in New York and, Gerhardt having said that she loved England and English audiences, reassured her 'that they would love her till she died' (*Sackbut*, June 1924). Happily, her death was at that time many years distant. She eventually made her home in London and lived there for the rest of her life, till 1961. Her memory, too, survived her. It was kept alive by older music lovers including a number of influential writers, such as Desmond Shawe-Taylor, who adored her. But now he is dead, and so is most of the generation that last heard her, not, primarily, on records, but 'in the flesh'. And, sad to write and almost incredible as it would be for them to read, she herself has become not so much forgotten as disowned. Amongst all the famous singers of the century Gerhardt appears to have become chief of the great unwanted.

Proof lies in the record catalogues. At the time of writing, there is no disc devoted to Gerhardt. Among her slightly younger contemporaries were Elisabeth Schumann and Lotte Lehmann, both admired singers of Lieder as well as opera, and of them and their song recordings plenty survives and is currently available. Other Lieder singers such as the baritones Hüsch and Schlusnus and the great bass Kipnis are plentifully represented. Gerhardt can indeed be heard: in 1931 she was invited to inaugurate the series of Hugo Wolf Society issues, and now that all six volumes have been republished in the new format her volume has appeared along with the rest. But that is more on account of Wolf, the Society and the other artists than her own. The fact is that by and large she has lost her public.

I personally find this more than merely sad, but then I am probably of the last generation to have been introduced to Lieder by Gerhardt's records. It now seems ridiculous that I never heard her 'live': she gave her last concert in 1947, and with a little initiative I could probably have been there. But in the earliest days of record-buying it was Gerhardt who provided the first Brahms and Schubert songs in my collection. The dark, tensely passionate tones of 'Vor dem Fenster' are vivid still, and also the memory of how wonderfully they contrasted with the lightness and buoyancy of 'Die Forelle', which was the coupling on that ten-inch record. Then it was to her that I owed my first taste of *Winterreise*. The dingy brown labels and gunge-laden surfaces of the records picked up in a junk-shop were no deterrent, and it is still her voice I hear in 'Der Wegweiser' as the note is held over ominously shifting harmonies telling of the road along which no traveller returns.

Still, there it is: no love like first love, and it is unlikely that Gerhardt will be many people's first love in, as they say, the foreseeable future. Important, then, if only in justice to her, are the words of Shawe-Taylor, who (also as a young man) heard Gerhardt in 1928 when she sang *Winterreise* at the Queen's Hall: 'Speaking for myself, I do not remember to have been more strongly affected by any other concert, nor can I recall another performance of Schubert's cycle which, in the controlled intensity of passionate grief, came within measurable distance of hers. It is in these songs, above all, that we remember the strong, often deliberately harsh, chest notes of her mature voice: it seemed as though sorrow and bitterness had etched themselves into the very timbre' (Gerhardt: *Recital*, London, 1953).

Now, while the impressions so strongly recorded in that memoir would have been confirmed by many who were present at that concert, including many of the best judges, they would certainly not have been unchallenged even in the heyday of Gerhardt's fame. Not everybody was happy with what they heard, or, at least, if they found much to admire they also had reservations. When she sang in New York in January 1915, W.J. Henderson wrote of 'a singular union of high accomplishment with shortcomings found among a much inferior rank'. He thought the voice beautiful but imperfect in its 'placing', and when she sang with vehemence he found that the tone quality became hard and cold. Ursula Greville, who was a great admirer, found not so much a coldness of tone as a certain placidity, even inhibition. Then, she said, she met Gerhardt on board ship and heard her sing in a ship's concert: 'It was the first time I had ever heard her without her little notebook in hand, and her singing, in spite of the extraordinary rolling of the boat, which made her use gestures she would never have

permitted herself to use under ordinary circumstances, seemed so much freer.'

It is perhaps worth resurrecting what might be called The Great Gerhardt Debate which took place in the columns of the *Musical Times* at the height of her career (and just about the time when she so impressed Shawe-Taylor) in 1929. In the March issue two performances in London of *Winterreise* were reviewed. One was by Gerhardt with Harold Craxton at the Queen's Hall, the other by the tenor John Coates with the young Gerald Moore. MT's critic preferred the latter. Of Gerhardt he wrote: 'Her art is not one of surprises, and having heard her sing half a dozen songs one knows exactly what to expect. Her careful, true enunciation and musical vowels induce one to sit on and hear her out. Naturally picturesqueness and youthful impetuosity were absent from this beautiful but rather monotonous performance.'

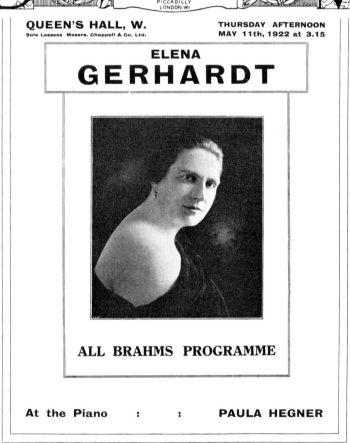

Six months later appeared 'A Tribute to Gerhardt' by Charles W. Orr. Without referring directly to the critic (H.O.C.), this writer attacked 'a selection of Lilliputian sharpshooters' whom he says he knows well: 'they belong to the army of unsuccessful professional vocalists and self-satisfied students of singing whose chief pleasure in life consists of snatching a fearful joy from pouring streams of verbal acidity upon any artist who is definitely among the elect.' He writes of Gerhardt's 'lovely voice' which 'is still capable of conveying the most varied emotions by means of the subtlest graduations of tone'.

There followed a more telling attack by one of the magazine's senior critics, H.J. Kimbell: 'We know precisely, after a little, what Madame Gerhardt will do with any song. We know her characteristic mood of noble placidity, and that once outside that she has little to say.' As to her *Winterreise*, he went so far as to declare that its limitations 'can be put down only to a narrowly limited mind'. He detailed various other faults and then, as though conscious of having been thoroughly beastly, added that if these faults had to be 'so bluntly indicated, the fault lies with the fatuous excess of her admirers'. In the November issue the paper was congratulated by Khaikosru Sorabji on its 'admirable exposure of the Gerhardt infallibility legend', and the Editor announced: 'This discussion is closed.'

It is unlikely that infallibility was ever claimed on her behalf, but if there was indeed a myth then at least it had its origins in fact. As a twenty-year-old at the Leipzig Conservatoire she had auditioned for Artur Nikisch, then conductor of the Gewandhaus Orchestra and soon to be widely regarded as the greatest conductor of the age. He was sufficiently impressed to do what he had not done before, and play the accompaniments for her first Lieder-Abend. Thus began a musical association that lasted till the time of the First World War. Their concerts did indeed become legendary, and on her reappearance, with art and voice matured, she gained a standing in the musical world not shared at that time with any other singer. When the current generation of critics and others wrote their memoirs they placed her, uniquely, with Pablo Casals, Bruno Walter and the handful of others they considered the greatest musicians of the era.

As for the recordings, which it seems nobody now wants to hear, they, like the Gerhardt debate, tell a mixed tale. I was recently listening to her record of Schubert's second Suleika song, following up a comparison of the recording by Elisabeth Grümmer (see p. 200) with the far more expressive one by Janet Baker, But now, with Gerhardt instead of Grümmer, the comparison took a different turn. At first Baker's record brought a kind of relief: it was more dependable both as performance and recording. But, on return to Gerhardt, there was a complementary relief in the subtler freedom of tempo, the variety of shading and emphasis, with (eventually) more to take home and remember, especially in the handling of the last lines.

All told there may be some twenty song recordings, no more than that and perhaps not so many, that remain a precious possession; and these are sufficient to explain why Gerhardt was 'Gerhardt'. A time must surely come when they are heard again and newly acknowledged: and then it should not be long before she is once more actually *wanted*.

CHAPTER 41

# Elly Ameling

The audience at a masterclass have come – of course they have – in order to learn. With serious brow and industrious fingers they attend to the printed programme as if the ascertaining of works to be studied were the sole aim of their existence. Then somebody says 'I last heard her ten years ago' and suddenly that becomes more interesting than 'Meine Liebe ist grün' or 'Mandoline' or whatever. But still something unspoken, some suppressed, almost furtive, excitement is in the air. It is of course that we are waiting to hear who first will say 'I wonder if she will sing'. The thought then arises that it might be as well if she did not. 'God forbid,' says someone a little too hastily, and we sit in some trepidation.

There was trepidation too, but only on my part, when, many years ago, about to hear Elly Ameling for the first time 'in the flesh', I wondered whether she would live up to the lovely sound of her voice on records. The fear then had been that, as with other light sopranos in my experience (Elisabeth Schumann among them), the voice would have worn thin and have acquired that tinkly metallic patina that compromises its purity unless engaged in singing something quiet and slow and exquisite like Schubert's 'Nacht und Träume'. Great joy had been the outcome on that occasion. She sang Bach's *Wedding Cantata*, and a purer, clearer bell of sound could hardly be imagined. And similarly at this masterclass, at the Wigmore Hall on 26 February 1998: perhaps consulting the programme while a soprano sang her Brahms, suddenly one looked up, for another voice had entered and briefly echoed the phrase just heard, except that 'echoed' is not quite the word, for this illustrated. It illustrated a point, certainly, but also, in the literal sense, it lit up, illuminated; and that same bell-like purity of tone, remembered from the first time of years ago, was heard once more.

Radiance, then, radiance of tone and of personality, that is Elly Ameling's gift: and as she smiles, sweetly, we hear the smile in the voice. Sweetness and light: not a bad combination, if that is all there is to it. But of course there is more. The idea of Ameling as a sweet little miss is as wide of the mark in terms of real character as a phrase such as 'light-soubrette charm' would be in reference to her singing.

She is – let's not say, for heaven's sake, 'a tough cookie', but strong, both

as a woman and an artist. Even up there on the platform at this master-class, the teacher has that best kind of strength which is a thoughtful awareness of complexity combined with a clear-sighted way through the difficulties. 'I find it slow. It almost stands still. Let's see what we can do.' The pupil-singer gets from the start a well-defined reaction, a particular point to concentrate on, and a bit of brisk, businesslike encouragement to believe that progress will be made. Then come the complexities. What is wanted, it seems, is a better legato and 'more on the words'. But 'Ah!' we think, 'both at once?' The good teacher knows our thoughts, however, and addresses the point directly. 'This sounds like a paradox,' she says, 'but like many apparent paradoxes it is not.' The song is Brahms's 'Unbewegte laue Luft' ('Motionless warm air'), and you can begin (we are told) by giving us more of the 'w' in that first word, but on the note, with full singing-tone. The German language may involve you in a congestion of consonants, as in 'Gartennacht plätschert die Fontäne', but at least you don't need to impede the flow of tone still further by articulating the 't' ('plätschert') and the succeeding 'd' ('die') separately. So, in such detailed matters we make progress over the apparent paradox of how to achieve a smoother singing-line and clearer enunciation of words at the same time. Yet such points are still incidental to the high and serious study of legato itself. She illustrated it by evoking the sound of the violin where all the notes are played with even tone. Words complicate the issue for a singer, but still the violin-playing ideal is to be kept in view, and a first principle in combining it with the intelligent singing of words is not to emphasise the important syllables but rather to lighten the unimportant. One thing you must *not* do – and oh how glad I was to hear this! – is to make a little growth or crescendo on each individual note. It had to be said to two later singers: 'Be on your guard all the time.'

Back home, we treat ourselves to a recital. So much to choose from, what is it to be? Some Bach for a start, and why not the *Wedding Cantata* in which the now so-familiar and beloved voice was heard for the first time. But first 'Bist du bei mir', as a kind of prelude, and, as it happens, another happy corrective. Just as the masterclasses correct any notion of the simple-soubrette mind, so this selection instantly dismisses any thought that what we are to hear will be merely dreamy, laidback loveliness. Lovely it is (the voice from 1966 having just that bell-like purity as remembered), but the tempo is sprightly, and the singer makes you think. 'Geh ich mit Freuden zum Sterben und zu meiner Ruh': 'I go with joy towards death and to my rest'. The song can be taken slowly and dreamily: the music will allow it (and it is one of the glories of Bach that he can be played at almost any tempo and will still sound like music). But for this singer, the key-words are 'mit Freuden', 'with joy'. When Elly Ameling sings 'zum Sterben und zu meiner Ruh' one can almost sense in brackets something like St Augustine's 'but not yet'. This is the voice of the living world, and the world in springtime.

So also in the cantata. We'll choose, for this highly selective programme, the middle section, with its recitative about breezes, and its aria 'Sich üben im Lieben' ('To practise loving, to dally and embrace'). The recitative, almost arioso, is sunny and serene, with a blissfully smooth run at the end, and the triple-time aria is so thankfully free of that deadly emphasis on the first beat of the bar which is sometimes reckoned to be evidence of rhythmic vitality. We can appreciate the legato here: it is no bland leveller but a rule that prevents pecking and aspirating while allowing within its judicious government a freedom for occasional staccati and tonal lighten-ing. The whole thing is charming.

But again an association with Elisabeth Schumann (who also recorded this) comes to mind. She was once described as 'a fair-weather singer', meaning that her range of colour and emotion was confined to brightness and pleasure. Might that be said of Elly Ameling? So, with this in mind, as we move on to Schubert we play (and it would not otherwise be first choice) 'Gretchen am Spinnrade'. And yes: 'meine Ruh' is not particularly

**Wigmore Hall**
Manager: William Lyne
Lessees: The Arts Council of Great Britain

Two Recitals by

# Elly Ameling
soprano

## Rudolf Jansen
piano

## French Series
Wednesday 30 November 1983 at 7.30pm

## Song Recital Series
Saturday 3 December 1983 at 7.30pm

## Arts Council
OF GREAT BRITAIN

'hin', nor is 'mein Herz' notably 'schwer' (the first lines of the poem go 'Meine Ruh ist hin, mein Herz ist schwer', 'My peace has gone, my heart is heavy'). The musical modulations evoke little response in the voice; the girl's recollections are placid, and only towards the very end of the song does the urgency mount to frank avowal. The voice is beautiful, its character maidenly, and to a surprising extent the song can look after itself when sung so well: it is expressive even if the singing is not. But then, one reflects, this after all was a recording made in 1965, which is early. Try it ten years later, and much has changed. The words ('schwer', 'nimmer', 'Grab') now have meaning, and each stage in the song's development gains its response. The climax now has not merely urgency but desperation, and the quiet ending is expressive of emotional exhaustion. No 'fair-weather singer' gets this far with her Gretchen.

We could try more Schubert (of whose songs Ameling has probably recorded more than any other woman), or more Lieder; but on, I think, to French song where again she has her own distinction. She sings Fauré probably better than anyone since Gérard Souzay. For reminders we take 'Soir' and 'Mandoline', coupled on her French recital called *Soirée* with Rudolf Jensen. In the first, with true French delicacy, she intimates the 'quelque chose' of death, and finally ('si doux') lets the sound die away with exquisite gentleness. But strength and warmth are characteristics too, as feeling rises and emotion deepens. Then in Poulenc's 'C'est ainsi que tu es' this chaste voice reveals its sensuality, its desire and intimacy most potent at pianissimo. More frank in 'Les chemins de l'amour', the sensuality is never, despite the 'chemins', expressed at street-level, nor does the style copy or compete with the song's dedicatee, Yvonne Printemps. Yet the portamenti, elisions and lingerings are in place, and the enchantment holds sway in unbroken line.

That song of Poulenc's is the first of our encores. Two more are allowed and both are drawn from the delightful and unexpected collection called *After Hours*. With the pianist Louis van Dijk, she gives a programme of songs by Gershwin and Porter, with one, sheer magic, by Vernon Duke called 'Autumn in New York'. We follow that with Gershwin's 'Someone to watch over me', with a dreamily improvised bit of sing-along easing back into the words for a last refrain. Both are sung with an entirely natural, unselfconscious grace, and I find them as moving (certainly at this point in the programme) as anything we have been playing.

Breadth rather than narrowness, character rather than blandness: these are the findings here. As for the lady herself, I understand that there may also be surprises for anyone who supposes that the artist who sings so sweetly could not have a head for business. The organisation of her tours is itself a triumph of clear thought, energy and determination, for they have taken her not merely all over the world but into parts of it where a song recital comes as from another planet. The travelling is part of an immense appetite for life, for knowledge and experience. These are strong positives. She once told Graham Johnson, to whose complete Schubert song edition she has contributed one of the most demanding volumes, that her idea of heaven on the day of a recital would be to go out for the day with a packed lunch, out into the Italian countryside, to walk and walk and come eventually to a town with a marvellous museum or art gallery; there to spend the afternoon, and then come back to the hotel and into the concert with a mind filled with the beauties of the day. Most singers, I believe, prefer to stay inside and rest.

CHAPTER 42

# Hugues Cuénod

Into the Ark at floodtime come tinker and tailor, physicist and physician, peasant and poet, composer and conductor, and singer: two of each. Singer, female, must be someone who gets things right first time, no messing about, and good company for the rest of the inmates: Dame Felicity Lott, I shouldn't be surprised. The male should have those qualities too, be adaptable, turn his voice to anything, and be a good long life in case the dove and olive-leaf are a long time coming. He should of course be Hugues Cuénod, 95 when last heard of and still going strong.

It was a name first known to most of us, I daresay, through the famous Monteverdi recordings of 1937 directed by Nadia Boulanger. These were a most unlikely addition to the catalogue in those days, a remote, totally uncommercial bit of window-dressing for the old curiosity shop, or so they must have seemed. But they travelled the world (remember Doc in *Cannery Row* recalling 'the infinitely sad and resigned mourning of Petrarch for Laura in the opening of "Hor ch'el ciel e la terra" ', which must have been from the Boulanger recordings as there was then no other). It was these which introduced Monteverdi to modern times. After three hundred years of silence, the madrigals were heard again and the brave new world of old music opened up for exploration. Cuénod's young tenor was heard mostly in duets with another, Paul Derenne, and so well-matched were they that it could be difficult to tell them apart. Yet Cuénod's was a most distinctive sound, a strange mixture of sweet and dry, with a little flicker or crackle of fast vibrato sparking in a voice that was also firm in definition and discreet in its blending with others. 'Ohimè, dov'è il mio ben' was one of those lovely, lyrical-declamatory pieces with agonised augmented intervals and rich Italian thirds; the elegant, imitative 'Zefiro, torna' with its ground-bass, and the nonchalant 'Chiome d'oro' were others, and all for ever, in our minds, who first knew them from these records, associated with the voice of Hugues Cuénod.

They were sung to piano accompaniment, and, though that would never do nowadays, the piano was part of their charm, as it told of the Paris salon, a place of high civilisation, of easy, graceful scholarship and young people with fresh voices singing together for the love of it. That is still how they sound; and now, on compact disc, we have also the same group in

Brahms's *Liebeslieder* waltzes, Boulanger sharing the piano-stool with the twenty-year-old Dinu Lipatti. Their performance contrasts with the equally delightful Viennese one of postwar years: theirs was a lilting, nostalgic indulgence for early evening recreation, while the Parisians are spry and witty, making lively music before cocktails and lunch-time.

It was his meeting with Nadia Boulanger that made Cuénod 'serious' about music. He was, he says, thoroughly committed already to the musical life, but in an easy-going, fun-loving way. It was a strange route he had taken, to arrive in Paris via Austria. Born in Vevey, Switzerland, in 1902 (of a family descended from the great Duke of Marlborough), he decided that the family banking business was not for him; something artistic, he thought, and something with music in it. But in those days nobody, it seems, went from Vevey to Paris, and after a time studying cello, organ and voice at the Basle Conservatoire he headed for Vienna. There he heard the operas and many of the great singers, but nothing French. He was 25 when eventually he arrived in the French capital, where he began singing professionally, making an operatic debut at the Théâtre des Champs-Elysées in the French premiere of Krenek's 'jazz opera', *Jonny spielt auf* in 1929. His voice had developed from baritone to tenor, though he has always demurred at any talk about his voice as such. His repertoire grew, but when he met the great Mary Garden, original Mélisande on a visit to the city in which she once reigned, he was assured by her that his repertoire of Bach and Schubert was very boring and that she would arrange an introduction to Noël Coward. In that same year he joined the Master's company who were exporting *Bitter Sweet* to New York. Cuénod played Aubrey Beardsley and sported the green carnation which he was able to produce 55 years later when he took part in the Carnation Quartet at the Wigmore Hall, aged 82.

In those early years he would sing in cabaret and operetta, though always eager to learn. The Boulanger *Ensemble Vocale*, with its exacting professional standards and stimulating repertoire, proved an ideal means of bringing him into the kind of musical life he needed. The war intervened ('I was an impossible soldier,' he says), but his name was made and he knew his way around. In the postwar world, with its eagerness to relearn the past, he was recruited to sing works by 'history-book composers' such as Schütz, Buxtehude and Couperin. At the same time, his intelligent musicianship and pragmatic vocal method made him attractive to modern composers. He came to know Poulenc and found in him a kindred spirit. Roussel, Milhaud, Ibert, Martin and many others also wrote for him. Jean Français wrote his *Diable boiteux* for Cuénod and his fellow member of the Boulanger Ensemble, Doda Conrad. His recording of Couperin's *Leçons de ténèbres* was heard by Stravinsky who wrote the tenor part of his Cantata, with its long and fiendishly difficult setting of 'Tomorrow shall be my dancing-day' with Cuénod's voice in mind. He and Jennie Tourel sang in

the 1952 premiere, as a year earlier they had done in the premiere at Venice of *The Rake's Progress*.

It was in that opera, as Sellem the auctioneer, that he made his Glyndebourne debut in 1954, and thus began an association that notched up at least 470 performances in fourteen roles. The last was that of the Cock in *The Cunning Little Vixen*, of which he has many stories, quite unrepeatable. He had first been recommended for the role of Monastatos in *Die Zauberflöte* in 1935, but his height was thought to be prohibitive. That spindly 6'5" came to seem almost part of the Glyndebourne furniture. Everyone will have their own favourites among his roles there: Don Basilio or Dr Caius, the tippling Lucano in *L'incoronazione di Poppea* or the *travesto* roles, Erice the nurse in *L'Ormindo* or Linfea the matronly nymph in *Lo Calisto*. He loved the summer seasons, 'a big party' he called them,

213

and was delighted to be given the cameo parts, as concentration on stage was, he said, one of his problems.

These character-roles continued to come his way, his last being the old Emperor in *Turandot*. He sang the part in London's first performance of the opera with the full Alfano completion in 1982. Three years later he made his debut at the Metropolitan, New York, to the Calaf of Placido Domingo. He was then 83, even older than Martinelli when he sang the part in Seattle; and surely making an all-time record as far as Met debuts are concerned.

But essentially this, so far, is notes and mementoes stuck in a picture-frame where what matters is what is within. Within, for our purposes, is Cuénod the singer. He has left some wonderful records, of which a generous selection has been published in an edition of six volumes, seven compact discs in all. The first, of baroque French music, includes the Couperin which so impressed Stravinsky. A stylistic point that is bound to strike us now is the human and affectionate nature of the singing. With a very slight element of quick vibrato and an absolutely even vocal line, it presents a notion concerning the singing of such 'period' music very different from that exemplified in current practice. He is faithful in his use of the voice as a solo organ-stop: for a whole section a softly-voiced woodwind-stop will be selected and kept to, then for a louder section perhaps one of the reeds. The classical idiom is respected and good singing-practice is maintained, without fussy inflexions, bulging notes, and without that abominable doctrinaire modernism, the dehumanised voice that has been ironed so as to flatten its healthy natural vibrations. There are long passages here of quite astonishing virtuosity and great spiritual beauty. In Volume Four, with Bach and his predecessors, there is something comparable, but here is another striking quality one might not have thought to find in Cuénod. Schütz's *Eile mich, Gott, zu erretten* opens with an almost fierce concentration of serious, dramatic fervour, still more impressive when contrasted with the softness of *O süsser, o freundlicher*, the third of these Sacred Concerti.

In another of these volumes Cuénod sings Dowland, Monteverdi and Poulenc. The sixth brings troubadour songs in French, German and Spanish. There are also lovely things outside this series, including a recital of French songs made for the English firm Nimbus in 1977. Chabrier's 'L'île heureuse' has all the elegant charm of the French school, resourcefully deployed, irresistibly youthful in spirit: and we have to remind ourselves yet again of his age, which in that year had reached 75.

I heard him last in 1984. Graham Johnson arranged two remarkable concerts at the Wigmore Hall under the inspired title of *Such the Tenor Man Told* (the audience had to supply the last line of Hardy's poem for themselves – 'When he had grown old'). The second 'tenor man' was Peter Pears, a mere septuagenarian, though no longer singing. Cuénod, once started, convinced us he could (as they say) have sung all night. At the end of the first half he joined the other singers for the Green Carnation Quartet

*Wigmore Hall*
Lessees: The Arts Council of Great Britain
Manager: William Lyne

*The Songmakers' Almanac*
Patrons: Gerald Moore, Eric Sams

*"Such the Tenor Man Told" I: Hugues Cuenod*
A song portrait of the life and times of a great singer of French song.
Mélodies by Fauré, Duparc, Debussy, Poulenc, etc.

Programme from the Wigmore Hall, 27 September 1984

in *Bitter Sweet*. After the interval he began with Machaut's 'Douce dame jolie'. I was sitting next to Desmond Shawe-Taylor whose memories went back a long way. He had heard, for instance, Ben Davies, born in 1858 and still singing in the early 1930s. But nothing that he could think of quite matched this, for the voice was supple and perfectly supported, and it seemed utterly unchanged. Cuénod would turn away such marvelling with a joke: 'Of course nothing could be changed,' he would say, 'since nothing was there in the first place.' That would be quite in the spirit of the man who has also said that he was in demand more 'for the strangeness of my repertoire than for any other reason'. But of course there were many other reasons, especially for wonderment that night. Some were personal – the age and the vitality, the dignity and subdued, self-deprecating levity. But most of the reasons had to do with singing. 'I have *no* technique whatsoever,' he said (now aged 95) in a broadcast discussion with Graham Johnson. 'I built on my own experiences little by little.' There are many much-vaunted techniques deriving from prestigious schools and teachers that fail to serve half so well. He also admitted to taking a physical pleasure in singing. In a way that was very French he added that he supposed this was a sin. In that case, we reflected, it must be the sin whose wages are eternal life.

215

# CHAPTER 43

# Tito Schipa

'And now, here is a tenor who never shouts, but whose singing is always delightful and sensitive to the ear.' That was the sentence which introduced the voice of Tito Schipa in a special 'sampler' record from the early 1930s. A mandoline accompaniment was eased-in, and then softly, almost insidiously, there entered this veiled, slightly misty voice that cleared as it rose, lingered in the upper regions just long enough to work its spell, and returned to ground level, there to be faded at a sign from the judicious producer bringing back the link-man to tell us more. 'There!' he exclaimed. 'Wasn't that delightful! Tito Schipa singing *Napulitanata* on DA 1054.' He went on to savour such period pleasures as those provided by Marek Weber and his Orchestra or by Vocal Gems from *Monsieur Beaucaire*. But that sample of the 'tenor who never shouts' did its job wonderfully well. The melody itself must take some of the credit, for to a boy listening to it in the no-holiday summer of 1940 it carried the faintly scented promise of a dusky Mediterranean evening, and the singer's descending phrases were like sandalled feet on a path winding downwards between whitened houses luxuriant with mimosa and oleander. But it would have done nothing without the voice. That voice, from the whitish mists of its lower notes up into the Elysian air and light of its high register, proved once-heard never-forgotten. Not only the voice of course, for that in turn was subject to a subtle, very personal refinement of usage. It was not merely the negative virtue of 'a tenor who never shouts' (he could shout, after a fashion, as the reverse side of DA 1054 delightfully showed). It was rather as though he sent out his tone on a thread fine as a spider's, perhaps to glow in the sunlight or glimmer in the shade, hang there wondrously poised or glide on to join another thread and reach a still more distant breathing-space.

So it was when you 'turned over' 'Napulitanata' and found, on the other side of that record made in America on 10 September 1928, a song called 'Chi se nne scorda 'chiu'. This was written by Richard Barthélemy, a good 'serious' musician and for a while accompanist to Caruso – but it sounds like a song picked up on the streets. After a verse telling of the delights of a certain evening, it takes up its refrain – 'Core, uh quante fantasie, n'una vene, n'auta va' ('one comes and another goes') – a nonchalant purveyor of

216

banality such as, in Housman's phrase, 'makes the rough road easy walking' and 'spins the heavy world around'. It was a song Schipa took with him everywhere, right to the end of his singing days among those tatty, disintegrating pieces of sheet-music that were the terror of accompanists who were supposed to make sense of the scrawled instructions, keep them in one piece and transpose them at sight. He would give

217

unashamed street-voice to some of the song's exclamations, and then, for the final refrain, would sing the second-half pianissimo on a single breath. I don't think I have ever heard anyone else sing that song: while Schipa was alive they wouldn't have dared and nowadays I don't suppose anybody wants to.

He was of course first and foremost an operatic artist, and though his repertoire was limited, as were the volume and range of his voice, he has left a sufficient number of recordings to assure us that at best his singing of Donizetti, the lighter Verdi roles and part of the French lyric repertoire was exquisite. He was not a virtuoso singer, and, although *Il barbiere di Siviglia* was a great stand-by of his, his graceful singing of the Count's solos in Act 1 (the fearsomely testing 'Cessa di più resistere' in Act 3 was never given in those days) lacked the brilliance of truly confident bravura. Ottavio in *Don Giovanni* was another of his most admired roles, yet his recording of 'Dalla sua pace' is undistinguished and 'Il mio tesoro' is remarkable principally as an exercise in the skills of the artful dodger. But in certain operas and certain passages – Ernesto's 'Sogno soave e casto', Alfredo's 'Parigi, o cara', Werther's 'Pourquoi me réveiller?' are examples – his records are the touchstone, the essential reference-point in comparisons and commentaries and in the eternal business of understanding and appreciating the art of song.

But it is here that the equally eternal 'but' intrudes. That description of Schipa as 'a tenor who never shouts' was typical, and it illustrates the way in which he was, and is, set apart from most of his fellows. Schipa was the 'sensitive' tenor, the tenor 'from the neck up', the one whose appeal is likely to be recognised by the finely discriminating listener rather than the collector of top Cs and thrilling decibels. It is at this point that reputation and reality part company. Schipa was *not* an intellectual singer and not, beyond the field already indicated, a musician's singer. In a broader context, music has not much to thank him for, and so far from being intellectual ('a tenor from the neck up' rather than 'down') he does not appear to have had any intellectual interests in his private life, but to have preferred jazz, cinemas and circuses to symphony concerts, poetry and painting.

That phrase ('Tito Schipa: Singer from the Neck Up'), not a very congenial one, stands as the chapter-heading of 'A Critical Appreciation' contributed by an Italian critic, Franco Serpa, to the biography written by Tito Schipa Jnr. (English edition, Baskerville, 1996). Following on afterwards come lists of Schipa's appearances and recordings. In the first we find an operatic repertoire that settled down, from roughly 1922 till 1954, after the first ten years or so, into the repetition of the same ten operas. Occasionally something else turns up, but from 1920 he performed no new opera till 1926 (*Don Giovanni*), then nothing till 1936 (*Il matrimonio segreto* and *L'arlesiana*), and lastly (and most enterprisingly) *The Magic Flute*, in Italian, for La Scala in 1937. Circumstances rather than choice

218

Schipa as Sir Edgar Ravenswood in *Lucia di Lammermoor* (La Scala, 1936)

may have played their part, but such are the facts. He also gave many
concerts, and these occupied an increasingly large proportion of his professional life. The programmes of these recitals, in as far as I have direct or
indirect acquaintance with their contents, divided into halves, the first
(broadly) 'serious', the second 'popular'. A notable feature was that the
'serious' half was severely limited in available repertoire, with the same
small handful of 'arie antiche', lieder and other 'art-songs' with 'M'apparì'
or 'Una furtiva lagrima' for encores, while the 'popular' half called on a

seemingly endless supply of songs of the 'Napulitanata' type but mostly not half so good. This is reflected in the discography which, once into the 1920s, is steadily taken over by these things. The years from 1935 to 1942 were his busiest in the recording studios, but everything other than these 'part-two' songs is an exception. This is not the discography of 'the thinking man's Italian tenor', and it is not much use to the musician.

Further than this, these 'popular' songs were increasingly of the sort associated with sentimental films and a tawdry dance idiom. Schipa appeared in thirteen sound-films, of which those known to me are not merely poor but puerile. Again the tenor 'from the neck up' does himself no kind of artistic service by taking part in them. It belongs, I'm afraid, to a process of sad decline. The biography, once past the peak of the mid-1920s in Chicago, makes painful reading. Even at this time the attractions of a Hollywood lifestyle, fashionable underworld connections (it was quite smart in those days to know 'Al') and his own jazz band are already at work. He seems to have been lamentably credulous and impetuous, open to exploitation so that though an astronomically high earner he was for ever on the verge of financial ruin. He also became a victim of politics; being an open supporter of the Fascist regime (or the government of his country) he met with protests abroad and became generally *persona non grata* after Mussolini's fall; he then, of all absurdities, got himself suspected of being a Soviet agent or fellow-traveller because of his success with audiences and the hierarchy in the USSR. His last years, always in search of new chances and renewed success, are sad to contemplate; and when he died, in wretched conditions, the New York doctor, an Italo-American, wrote on the certificate the description 'war veteran'.

I wish that an outline of the second half of his life could have gone something like this: 'In 1930 he met *x* and *y* who were preparing new and scholarly editions of seventeenth- and eighteenth-century Italian songs, which from that time occupied an increasingly prominent place in his recitals. Later he developed an interest in the work of young composers such as *z* whose song-cycle xxx, inspired by and dedicated to him, is now widely regarded as the highest achievement of Italian writers in this genre. During the war he explored some of the forgotten operas of the early nineteenth century, and throughout the remainder of his life used his considerable international influence to secure their production. In several of these productions singers trained by him testified, by their achievements, to the art of which he had been the acknowledged master.'

But sweet dreams can leave a bitter taste. Schipa is a singer as dear to my own heart as any. His voice – the very sound of it, but also his way with any number of single phrases – has been a prized inner possession for almost sixty years. But he has been placed on pedestals not made for him. On the right ones he still stands supreme.

220

# Aksel Schiøtz

Prize-givings are not always such just and jolly occasions as the smiling faces and applauding hands suggest; still, if there was ever a prize well-deserved and approved *nem con* it could be the one posthumously bestowed on Aksel Schiøtz and Danacord's ten-volume compact disc edition in the Historical Awards of *Gramophone's International Classical Record Collector* Quarterly in April 1998. Schiøtz was something more than a good singer: a thorough musician, a valued teacher and a man of courage. He had his share of misfortune in life, and since his death has been too often forgotten or underrated. Moreover, the records are splendid.

That is: they are fine in themselves, as specimens of recorded vocal art, and they are also excellent examples of technical skill and editorial thoroughness on the part of the producing company. In these competitive days, a record's presentation can often decide the issue, other things being equal, and it was good to see each disc given its own booklet, with information and photographs relevant to the particular contents. Even so, it may have been a sense of justice that was uppermost and that made the award so satisfying; and, indeed, moving, for present to accept it was the singer's widow, an indomitable old lady who spoke with noble restraint and a powerful warmth of feeling.

Schiøtz himself died in 1975, and in his seventieth year. His career as a singer ended, sadly and abruptly, when he was scarcely more than forty. As with many singers of his age, the Second World War broke out just about the time when his career was about to take off. In his early thirties he had become one of the most popular singers in Denmark, and his name had spread abroad at least as far as England. He now had to wait till 1945 to make any further progress on the international scene. The moment came; he recorded for HMV and was engaged to sing at Glyndebourne. Then, cruelly, disaster struck as a tumour developed on the acoustic nerve. The necessary operation was successful except in one crucial respect: it left the right hand side of his face partly paralysed and the doctors said that singing would be out of the question. With practice and persistence he worked to make it possible, though at best it meant renouncing the tenor repertoire (or pitch) and starting again as a baritone. He made a valiant attempt, but shortly after a return to the concert platform in 1948 it became clear that his singing days were over.

Before the release of the Schiøtz edition on CD, one could have written thus far with regret but (perhaps) no particularly acute sense of loss. Regret and sadness take on a more tragic aspect as one listens. He was so clearly one of the singers who should have gone on (like Jussi Björling, his contemporary) to lead the postwar generation. His was such a wholesome art, its loss something the world of singing just then could ill afford. His Bach and Handel, sampled first in these records, are exemplary in voice-usage, forthright in tone (not resorting to the pallid, slightly whining head-voice-mix that was coming increasingly into fashion) and scrupulously avoiding aspirates in runs. The style is very plain, without the use of *appoggiature* or other embellishments: such was the taste of the times, whereas (as with Kathleen Ferrier) we now rather long for the occasional decorative flourish which in those days would have been censured as operatic exhibitionism. But the fluency of passage-work in his solos from *Messiah* and the *Christmas Oratorio* shows a virtuoso's mastery. He achieves an ideal evenness, demonstrating that a genuine legato in such music is possible, much to be preferred, and fully compatible with precise articulation. It is just the sort of lesson that was wanted then, as it is now, and the only consolation for the loss of Schiøtz as a singer is the thought that he re-emerged after his illness to become a first-rate teacher.

An element of the prophet-in-his-own-country enters the story here. The Copenhagen Conservatory declined to appoint him to a teaching post, on the grounds that he had not graduated; and it was, typically, the USA that welcomed him and gained the reward. A link was provided by American visitors to Denmark who asked him for lessons. They were impressed and delighted, and urged him to take a professorship in the States or Canada. Arrangements were made, and in 1955 he emigrated. He had conducted his first masterclasses at the Stratford Festival in Ontario and enjoyed the experience. Masterclasses became a central part of his life as a teacher, and he made it a condition of any appointment that they should be incorporated. This was so in Vancouver, Boston, San Francisco and many other places, so that altogether he was in America for some fifteen years.

If his own country in some respects failed him in those years, it has made at least partial amends since. The annual award to a Danish singer given in his name has done well, and several of the winners, such as Auge Haagland, Paul Elming and, most recently, Inge Dam Jensen, have enjoyed international success. Still, a strange kind of rejection does seem to have beset him in his years of greatest need, and even when the School of Educational Studies gave him a chair in 1968 there was little satisfaction. This, it seems, was due to a lack of students which in turn derived from the kind of indifference or dull acceptance which the young often have towards what is native to them and familiar. Schiøtz had, after all, been

222

very familiar, a national figure throughout the war years, and to that extent part of the parents' generation, and hence 'establishment'.

It may be, too, that in some perverse way his popularity in those years became an artistic liability. In his prime, during the period of Occupation, he was heard continually in concerts and on radio, especially associated with the Danish songs which did much to maintain spirits in those dark times but which seemed dated and limited later. He was also a popular singer in the other sense, that he sang 'pops', or what would have gone under some such heading at that time. It was an open secret – or soon became so – that Aksel Schiøtz was 'The Masked Tenor', the anonymous vocalist in dance music or sentimental songs, some of them recorded with cinema Wurlitzer organ accompaniment. Under his own name, he was not above singing film-songs or Cole Porter's 'Night and Day' or Oscar Rasbach's 'Trees', and in 1942 he 'created' the title-role in an operetta by Emil Reesen called *Farinelli* (its subject restored, evidently, from castrato to tenor). Such ventures may not have improved his standing with the Conservatoire and academics. They are nevertheless included in the compact-disc edition, and show him singing in a mild, unselfconscious way, without any cheapness of appeal though also without any very evident flair.

Curiously, flair, vague term as it is, does manifest itself in the strangest, least typical of the items, recorded towards the start of Schiøtz's career. In 1934 and '36 he took part in two so-called jazz oratorios. The first is called *Geography*, the second *The School Upside Down*. In the second, the Headmaster is a treble from the Copenhagen Boys' Choir and as good as the young Michael Jackson or Jimmy Osmond any day. In *Geography* the Three Rhythm Girls answer the teacher's (Schiøtz's) questions ('Who is the greatest man in the United States?' 'Chaplin, yes Chaplin') in impeccable foxtrot, while a snazzy pianist, who looks well spaced-out in the sessions photograph, supplies a crisp and clever accompaniment. These are charming 'period' pieces, and it is good to find Schiøtz involved in them. On the label of the first, incidentally, he is named 'baritone', image of man's doom: 'Baritone thou art and unto baritone shalt thou return.'

By timbre, Schiøtz was certainly a true tenor, yet one fancies that despite his voice being so naturally placed and produced, he must have wondered, in those early years, exactly what to do with it. The voice was light, but light music was clearly not going to set its boundaries. Just how much he could have done in opera remains doubtful. He studied Gounod's *Faust* with John Forsell and sang it on stage at Copenhagen. His recording of the cavatina is most beautiful in feeling, tone and phrasing; it also has a high C cleanly taken and with a skilful *diminuendo*. Yet, despite the top C, the tessitura of 'Salut, demeure' lies comfortably within the middle register, and the impression made by his other relevant recordings is that such a tessitura is just about right for him, whereas the higher-lying 'Un' aura amorosa' from *Così fan tutte* suggests that in such a context the high As mark pretty well the upper limit of what was available. Nor is it a voice with an Italianate ring or dramatic passion in its apparent scope. It is interesting that the opera through which his name is most often recalled is Britten's *Rape of Lucretia*, in which, at Glyndebourne in 1946, he shared the role of Male Chorus with Peter Pears. Could he (I wonder) have sung Grimes?

There is something of a paradox here, for, despite the limitations of what he could do and the greater ones of what he actually did, one of the great merits of his recorded legacy is its breadth. Its most distinctive area

Glyndebourne, June 1946. *Left to right, seated*: Benjamin Britten, Eric Crozier, Nancy Evans, Ernest Ansermet; *standing*: Otakar Krauss, Kathleen Ferrier, Aksel Schiøtz, Rudolph Bing.

is Danish song, but also right at the heart are the great song-cycles, *Die schöne Müllerin* and *Dichterliebe*. The opera and oratorio excerpts provide further extensions and there are other, less predictable items such as songs by Dowland. To everything, he brought the well-produced beauty of his voice and the intelligent care of his musicianship. All of this – together with the sense of justice – is sufficient to account for the *Gramophone* Award. I like to think that it also may have had to do with the *type* of singer he was. The runner-up was a similar, slightly less well-presented, set of discs, devoted to the art of Hugues Cuénod. Both of these were artists first and tenors second. Among the many 'historical' singers whose recordings were eligible, these two made a broad yet very individual contribution to music. The prize-giving showed recognition of that, and, I suspect, had quite a bit to do with repertoire.

CHAPTER 45

# Oda Slobodskaya

As castaway Number 521, Slobodskaya was interviewed on the subject of her Desert Island Discs in the celebrated BBC radio programme in December 1960. Asked the ritual question of whether she would try to escape she replied that indeed she would. 'And how would you set about it?' asked the ever-inquisitive Mr Plomley. 'I would light a fire,' she said. 'Ah, but would you be able to light it?' was the next question. 'What would you light it with?' 'I would light it,' she said, 'with my *feu sacré*.'

That was the flame she carried with her throughout her life. In the last years, her own, appallingly real desert island of despair claimed her in a sea of devouring pain, but that too she transformed into a place where the spirit might flame. When the pain came, she said, she would speak or sing over to herself the words and music of her song-repertoire, and when she failed to remember some of Pushkin's words or Prokoviev's notes she would be so furious that physical pain was put in its place: grievous and terrible, but not absolute.

During those last months she found another consolation, in the reassurance that she could still be useful: a pupil had decided to teach herself Russian and would come to her bedside to learn the pronunciation. Nor would she acknowledge the possibility of defeat: only a few months before her death, Slobodskaya wrote to a friend saying that she hoped to attend his lecture and was 'even planning to sing a few little easy folk songs personally'. She died on 30 July 1970, aged 81, and although she had no family she was dearly loved and deeply mourned.

She had travelled widely during this long life, but London had become her home in the 1930s and there she stayed, cutting a familiar figure – albeit an exotic one – in the musical life of the metropolis. She was unalterably 'the Russian lady' as she walked to the shops or went from room to room in the College. Though she had left her native land as far back as 1921, she still spoke with an accent that told of long Russian nights and stories round the samovar. The black hair, furs, laughter and melancholia all proclaimed her origins. But those origins themselves were swathed in mystery. The year of her birth was for long officially 1895 till it unwound to 1888. After that, details are few till they present us with a debut at St Petersburg in 1919. This was in *The Queen of Spades* and led

to a two-year spell at the Mariinsky where she sang, in addition to the Russian lyric repertoire, roles such as Sieglinde, Marguerite and Elisabeth de Valois in *Don Carlos*. These were prestigious engagements, some of them with Russia's most renowned singers such as Chaliapin and Erschov. When she left Russia, amid the post-war revolutionary chaos, she made for Berlin where reputedly she sang with success (though details are elusive). At any rate her reputation was sufficiently sound for Diaghilev to recommend her for the leading soprano role of Parasha in Stravinsky's *Mavra*, which was to have its world premiere at Paris in 1922. This in turn must have shown that here was a soprano, still young at 33, who in addition to her merits as a singer had the distinction of being a thoroughly reliable musician. It might have been supposed at this point that some opera house would have welcomed her and that she for her part might have welcomed a period of steady employment leading to an international career in a few years' time. Offers did indeed come her way, but they were mostly for concert work. The period also brought an extension of her career, for these were the years of her American tours with the impresario Max Rabinoff. Yet in all this time a major operatic career was slipping from her grasp: doubly frustrating as, in the United States especially, it was the big operatic names that the public at large wanted to hear in concerts. In 1928 she opened a new chapter with a new name. At the Baltimore Music Hall, Rabinoff presented Odali Careno, a glamorous exile whose true identity as a Russian princess had to be kept secret from Bolshevik agents. She sang operatic arias, with 'Vissi d'arte' as her *cheval de bataille*, and included Mussorgsky's *Gopak* which she would dance as well as sing. It was an extremely successful act, remunerative too. It also led to her first engagement in London – not at Covent Garden but the Palladium. Here again she was enthusiastically received, her appearance (usually adorned with a dress of gold or silver) contributing almost as much as her voice. *The Stage* (January 1930) depicted her in one of its clever pocket cartoons, the legs and gown forming a slender pillar to support the profiled head, all nose and chin with black hair *à la russe*.

Then Oda Slobodskaya reappeared and Odali Careno vanished in good time for Chaliapin's last season in London. This also took place outside Covent Garden, a little further down the road at the Lyceum. By that time, July 1931, the name of Slobodskaya had become familiar to English audiences. In the January of that year she had sung in the first broadcast of Rimsky-Korsakov's *The Invisible City of Kitezh* conducted by Albert Coates (and severely criticised by Ernest Newman who complained that the opera had been 'hacked about in a way for which there can be no excuse'). She also proved useful as a soloist in the Wagner concerts which were given with fair regularity in both London and the provinces: 'She has enjoyed something of a vogue lately,' reported *Musical Opinion* under the heading of 'Music in Liverpool', 'and the voice itself, though lacking perhaps the amplitude required for the bigger dramatic roles of Wagner, is of a fine texture and full of colour.' It must have been a great satisfaction for her to be reunited with Chaliapin. She sang Natasha to his Miller in Dargomizhsky's *Rusalka*, and again won praise. The trouble was that the compliments to her were so incidental, hidden away among the discussion of Chaliapin and the opera, that this also turned out to be something of a dead end; and the opportunity for singing Russian opera in Russian was not likely to recur often in the London of those years.

Eventually she was to have two roles at Covent Garden: Venus in *Tannhäuser* (1932) and the half-caste heroine Palmyra in Delius' *Koanga* (1935). Her debut in the first brought mixed reviews: 'a most cultivated performance, though sensuousness was lacking in her refined singing' (Richard Capell in the *Daily Mail*), 'musically equal to her task, but she hardly incarnated for us the voluptuous Venus of the legends' (Newman in *The Sunday Times*). In the Delius premiere critics naturally concerned themselves with the work itself, Slobodskaya's share in it being described as finely sung but visually unconvincing ('even her art could not persuade us that she looked the part as Delius must have conceived it,' Newman wrote). In between these productions, she had travelled to South America and Italy with a Russian company assembled by Emil Cooper (conductor in 1909 of the premiere of *The Golden Cockerel* and the conductor who in the 1940s was to introduce *Peter Grimes* and *Khovanshchina* to the Metropolitan). *Tsar Sultan*, *Boris Godunov* and *The Invisible City* were the operas in which Slobodskaya sang, *Kitezh* being also given at La Scala.

Again the episode was a feature but not a foundation. She returned to England where she now remained and became a regular soloist at Promenade concerts, usually singing such heavy stuff as Brünnhilde's Immolation and the closing scene in *Salome*. She took part in some important broadcasts: *The Love for Three Oranges* in 1934, *Lady Macbeth of Mtsensk* and *Oedipus Rex* (1936), *Boris Godunov* in the original version (1937). In 1941 she joined up with other Russian singers to perform Mussorgsky's *Sorochintsi Fair*, 'a marvellous thing to happen in wartime' as the *Musical Times* commented. By then the voice had deepened, and it is interesting that the reporter wrote of 'the well-known contralto of Oda Slobodskaya, who added to good singing a fine character sketch as the amorous termagant mother'. The opera was conducted by Anatole Fistoulari, with a three-week season at the Savoy followed by a tour of the provinces. After that it seems that she sang on stage only once more, at the Royal Academy in 1964 in a performance of *Mavra*, an historic survivor from the premiere but now in a small character part and, like most of the soloists, overwhelmed by the loudly playing orchestra. Earlier, in 1950, she had sung the part of the old Countess in a broadcast of *The Queen of Spades*, and Cedric Wallis wrote: 'Those of us who saw as well as heard her broadcast could not but realise what she would make of it on the stage. In the bleak surroundings of the Camden theatre the chorus itself was carried away by the atmosphere she managed to create. At her Wigmore Hall recital a few weeks later, they sent her a bouquet of flowers as an acknowledgement of the pleasure she had given them – surely an unusual tribute for a singer to receive after a broadcast?'

Such an event was unusual, and yet it was also typical of the effect Slobodskaya had on people as she grew into old age. By 1950 she was 62, and it was at about this time that Britain woke up to what it had got and had had for so long. The Wigmore Hall recital of 1950 had a still more remarkable successor in 1960. Cedric Wallis was now the *Musical Times* critic for the occasion and, summing up, he wrote that Slobodskaya's most remarkable gift of all was 'her ability to convey simplicity – whether that of the peasant or of the child – without ever striking a false note of archness or condescension'. He was almost echoing the words of a predecessor, H.J. Kimbell, who in the same magazine in 1932 had written: 'There was an entire absence of fuss in her performances. She was too intent on doing her music full justice to flaunt a "personality".' But this writer analysed a little further: 'Her full use of the palatal sounding-board gave to her voice a dome-like character. It made for majesty.'

'Majesty' is probably not a word that would suggest itself now when we listen to the voice on records. For the whole span of her life and for the still vivid picture of her character it may indeed be the word; but the records show, first, a thrillingly pure quality caught in the nick of time at an age of just over 40, then, with a more mellow beauty in 1938 by which time she was 50. Again the impression is of a singer not so much regal in tone or manner as very human in both. Perhaps finest of her many admirable features is the legato; a marvellously bump-free progression of notes. Recent dips into the archives have come up with some fascinating things such as Cassandra's solo from *Les Troyens* taken from a broadcast in 1947. But essentially Slobodskaya had to wait till she was over 70 to catch the interest of a major recording company. In 1961 'The Art of Oda Slobodskaya' appeared on the Decca label, the second side of the long-playing record comprising a collection of songs newly recorded, with introductions spoken in the style of the lecture-recitals which she gave almost to the end of her life.

It is perhaps not surprising that the record companies neglected her, and that she was similarly overlooked by opera-house and concert managers too. The fact is that Slobodskaya (like her contemporary Nina Koshetz and her junior Kyra Vayne) was a displaced Russian living abroad at a time when knowledge of Russian music and demand for it were far less widespread than they are now. She was also an individualist who was never for long a member of a company. Yet she was also one of the most accomplished singers of her time, with a musicianship that involved to the end of her life an insatiable appetite for new repertoire; and in its prime her voice had that fine glistening beauty that is distinctively East European.

The irony is that when in old age she did come to be recognised, it was predominantly as a 'personality'. In those recordings of 1961 the great joy is her story-telling. Of 'Tilim-bom' she says 'Den dey all sit arrount ant sink', and introducing Stravinsky's *Three Tales for Children* like the most adorable mamushka that ever was, 'Here is de bear's paw for our dinner: cook it woman.' She was a wonderful old lady, and after all a great singer is not only a singer. John Lade, who produced her on BBC radio, tells of her laughter which joyfully but agonisingly prolonged the live transmissions beyond their scheduled time; of her fur coat opening to envelop him on a cold night at the Festival Hall; and of her description of an English contralto's singing 'as mud, as mmmuddd!'

For myself, I think of her now as I heard her most recently, through headphones, at the National Sound Archive where they have her lecture-recitals of 1962. There were four of them, one a week, devoted to Russian song. At first, when it comes to singing, she is careful and 'takes the temperature' before risking more in range and volume. But gradually all is opened up. Top notes are taken fearlessly and never from below. The tone at a mezzo-forte is still velvety, and intonation is still faultless. She explains that she loves best the character-songs, but the purely lyrical ones still preserve the true legato, in which consonants seem never to impede the vocal line. She spares nothing: a dozen, twenty songs may be sung in the course of an evening's 'lecture', and at the end she is ready for more. The septuagenarian lives a more intense artistic life than do most in their natural prime. 'She would seize a song by its throat,' as her pupil Yvonne Fuller recalled. This too survives vividly in those lecture-recitals, together with a kind of passion for music and life as one and the same thing. Among her Desert Island Discs she chose the Credo in its choral setting by Grechaninov. 'I shall play it,' she said. 'And as I play it ... I shall walk ... slowly ... into ze sea.'

CHAPTER 46

# Dmitri Hvorostovsky and
# Pavel Lisitsian

'What Lisitsian was in mid-century Hvorostovsky is today.' Discuss.

So might a question run in the Russian paper ('Candidate's special choice' list) of the Finals Examination of a university course entitled *The History of Singing*.

'Compare and contrast' are implied instructions, and the model answer would no doubt begin with a comparison:

Pavel Lisitsian (born 1911) and Dmitri Hvorostovsky (born 1962) have been among the most notable descendants in the line of Russian lyric baritones from Oscar Kamionsky ('the Russian Battistini', 1869-1917) and Mikhail Karakash (1887-1937). In style they have maintained the close connection established in the nineteenth century between the Russian school and the Italian. In the Russian repertoire they have both specialised in roles such as Onegin and Yelitsky (*Queen of Spades*), and the songs of Tchaikowsky and Rachmaninov have been prominent in their recitals. Lisitsian's most admired role of Germont in *La traviata* is also in the steadily growing Italian repertoire of Hvorostovsky, and in French opera a role they have in common is that of Valentin in *Faust*. Both have supported relatively modern composers, with Hvorostovsky incorporating song-cycles by Georgi Sviridov into his programmes and Lisitsian playing an important part in a number of world-premieres, most memorably as Napoleon in Prokoviev's *War and Peace*. Both singers have bequeathed a valuable legacy of recordings, Lisitsian's being as extensive for its period as is Hvorostovsky's for his age.

[If the examiner were to annotate the margin of such an opening paragraph with queries like 'Ots?' (referring to the Estonian baritone) and 'Where do Mazurok, Chernov and Leiferkus stand in relation to this?', the candidate might reply 'Hang on, can't do everything at once!' And the model essay would probably go on its way, comparing origins and early careers. Thus:]

232

Dmitri Hvorostovsky

Both came from a provincial background, Lisitsian from an Armenian
family in Vladikavkas in the deep South, Hvorostovsky in Krasnoyarsk in
central Siberia. Music was part of their lives from early on. Lisitsian, son
of a drilling engineer, joined a local church choir as a boy; Hvorostovsky
studied the piano and thought of becoming a choirmaster and conductor.
It seems that, while he was orientated from the first towards a musical
career, Lisitsian went about it cautiously, working at a full-time job and
singing in his spare time. His voice must have been something special even
as a teenager, for the Tblisi Geological Board helped him to a course of
study at the Leningrad Conservatoire while continuing as a metalworker.
Hvorostovsky also developed his baritone voice early, going to a local
teacher who tried to make a tenor out of him but successfully taught him
about breath-control. At the age of twenty, he then began working with the
teacher to whom he attributes much of his success, Yekaterina Yofel. She
and her methods are regularly mentioned by Hvorostovsky in his inter-

233

views, especially with reference to her way of developing powers of expression, so that even a scale would have emotional connotations. Lisitsian must have learnt something of the kind too, but no individual teacher seems to be accredited with his progress, which must also have been rapid. He sang with the Leningrad Youth Opera and made his debut at the Malyi, one of the smaller Leningrad houses, in 1935. Hvorostovsky was similarly at the age of 24 when he joined the Krasnoyarsk Opera as a soloist in 1986.

It is at about this time that their paths diverge and larger historical forces begin to take effect.

[Examiner in margin: 'Begin? In 1917 Lisitsian was five. Was his life unaffected by the Revolution?']

For Lisitsian, war broke out just as his career had begun to prosper; for Hvorostovsky, the freedoms of the new post-Soviet era enabled him to travel and develop his career abroad. Lisitsian joined the Bolshoi at Moscow in 1940, but on his own request was drafted to the Front as an entertainer, singing as many as three or four times a day to different units and giving altogether more than 500 concerts. From that time onwards till 1960, he rarely if ever left the Soviet Union, so that during his best years as an opera singer such international reputation as he acquired was made essentially through records and reports. With Hvorostovsky, conditions promoted faster development. At 25, he won first prize in the national Glinka Competition, at 26 another but international one at Toulouse, and at 27 was proclaimed 'Singer of the World' at Cardiff. From that time onwards his career has been based in the West, with all the advantages of western publicity as backing.

[Examiner: 'Are you sure they are advantages?']

With Lisitsian established as principal lyric baritone at the Bolshoi and Hvorostovsky as a baritone in whom all the impresarios and record producers were interesting themselves

[Examiner: 'Aren't you jumping ahead rather? Have you forgotten the apprenticeship years, L. with the opera at Yerevin, 1937-40, Hv. at Krasnoyarsk, 1985-87?']

both careers seemed well set up for success. Here too the parallels dissolve. In his mid-thirties at the end of the war, Lisitsian did indeed have a stable career ahead: he remained with the Bolshoi and celebrated his 25th anniversary there in 1966. A busy round of concert-work then kept him active for many more years. His family joined him to form the Lisitsian Quartet, three of his four children having become singers, and the eldest, an actor, sometimes joining the group to sing bass. He has been many

Pavel Lisitsian     Lisitsian as Amonasro in *Aida*

times honoured ('People's Artist of the USSR'), has been of service to his native Armenia, and, though the opportunities were late in arriving, eventually travelled widely, singing (it is said) in as many as thirty countries. In all that time his voice never failed him and he has been reported as being in fine form well into old age.

Hvorostovsky's career may well turn out to be as enduring, but the conditions which favour brilliance and international excitement do not necessarily make for stability. The years immediately following his triumph at Cardiff disappointed some of the high hopes that were by then perhaps prematurely pinned to him. Some of the reactions of critics were of the kind that almost by reflex follows what is considered to be media-hype.

[Examiner: 'Jargon. Define term. Is the widespread enthusiastic reporting of an artist for whom there is widespread enthusiasm inevitably excessive ("hyper")?' Candidate: 'And is a recent, and possibly useful, critical coinage inevitably "jargon"?']

In part, the reaction was personal, or had to do with personality, there being a somewhat mean-spirited view that the good-looking young prize-winner looked too pleased with himself when he came on to the platform. Partly, there was a not unfounded concern that his high notes, the Fs especially, were already losing precise focus. Then came the discovery that this was not a voice that sounded big or that penetrated brightly in a large opera house. Nor, more surprisingly perhaps, did the good looks ensure an effective stage-presence. In London, the city of his adoption, the disappointment was genuine when his Covent Garden debut as Riccardo in *I puritani* brought no great satisfaction on any account. At the same time, word also began to spread that his expressive powers in Russian song (increasingly important to him if his operatic future was in some doubt) were themselves limited and were inferior to those of other singers, such as Sergei Leiferkus, who were not the beneficiaries

[Examiner: 'Victims?']

of such media-hype. At the present time of writing, in 1998, in the general balance of critical opinion, Hvorostovsky seems to have regained approval; and perhaps at this point a few personal observations may be permitted to intervene.

[Examiner: 'Don't apologise! And don't tell us what you're going to do. Just do it.']

Almost without exception, Hvorostovsky's recitals have been among the richest pleasures for a lover of singing in the past nine years. Most have confined themselves, for the printed programme at least, to Russian song. Always the first sound of his voice has brought the recognition and confirmation that here is something special in the warmth, depth and resonance of timbre. It is not merely in degree but in kind that the sound distinguishes itself among the baritones likely to be heard in the course of a year or so. The high-placed, frontal, hard-palate production seems not to govern here, but instead a method nearer to that of Italian baritones such as Ruffo, Granforte, Bechi and Gobbi: that is, a richer, more vibrant sound-quality, more sensuous in appeal even at the risk of being found backward or throaty. That is purely as to timbre (no affinity with what is sometimes called the 'snarling' sound of those baritones). With Hvorostovsky (as opposed to Mazurok and Chernov) another common initial reaction is surprise at the depth of his tones. In usage, as the singer binds his notes into phrases, the affiliations (apart from those with Russians such as Kamionsky and Lisitsian and the Estonian Georg Ots) are with the older Italian school, of Ancona and De Luca, where genuine smoothness of line is a prime concern. In range of volume almost any individual song will show him capable of all gradations, rarely resorting in his quiet singing to a falsetto-mix; as to the vocal range, that too is very ample, and, though in programmes with a fairly low tessitura the top notes have had no special glory, when he sings a programme of Italian arias the high notes of 'Eri tu' or the Prologue to *Pagliacci* can ring out with thrilling fullness and ease. Often they will also be taken (as in Rodrigo's death scene in *Don Carlos*) within amazingly broad phrases. In all of this, Hvorostovsky 'live' has impressed as one of the modern singers whom it is possible to relate most closely to great baritones of the past as heard on records.

Among those, Lisitsian is sure of an honoured place. In a collection of songs by Tchaikowsky and Rachmaninov, transferred to compact disc, we hear a voice which, as introduced in a recording from 1961 made when he was fifty, is still of unimpeachable firmness and closely-woven texture. Going back then to 1956 and 1946 in the next tracks, we hear hardly a change, just a little more juice in the voice as the years drop away. The clarity of diction made compatible with evenly flowing, instrumental tone is admirable too. As a Verdi singer he shows himself capable of some most delicate and lovely touches, with fine, fluent cadenzas and a two-octave range that presents no local weaknesses. In the Russian operatic repertoire, excerpts such as Yelitsky's aria in *The Queen of Spades* and the Venetian Guest's song in *Sadko* are models of their kind.

A model has also been Lisitsian's role in the professional life of Hvorostovsky (he has said as much in interviews). It is difficult to estimate such things, but, apart from their other likenesses, they may be very comparable in volume or 'size' of voice: in his single appearance at the Metropolitan, in 1960, Lisitsian was greatly admired but his voice, in the role of Amonasro in *Aida*, was found small for the house. There is also something about his later records that brings into play the word 'throaty', though not necessarily as a criticism. As to their powers of expression – the aspect of their singing that has been least discussed in these pages –

[Examiner: ' "Least"! You mean "not".']

this can be tested and will not be found wanting in such recordings by Lisitsian as those of Tchaikowsky's 'Reconciliation' and Rachmaninov's 'Excerpt from Musset'. I do not know whether he included Mussorgsky's *Songs and Dances of Death* in his repertoire, but Hvorostovsky does so, and, in the concert hall, with profoundly moving effect. The changing face of Death in the 'Serenade' is depicted in the voice with chilling mastery; the pallid tones of the last lines in 'Trepak' evoke a shudder even now; and the ruthless hardening of voice in 'The Commander-in-Chief' transcends any notion that the singer's business is merely to sing – though in my opinion such a limitation would not be so totally dishonourable as is often assumed.

The Examiner's final comments and assessment are illegible. Readers who wish to know more about the *History of Singing* course are advised that it has been discontinued, having been judged élitist. A paper entitled *The Ethnic Diversity of Rhythm and Blues* has been introduced under the same press-mark.

# CHAPTER 47

# Mario Sammarco and Mariano Stabile

'She was of the old school, content to stand and deliver.'

'For expression, he relied on the semaphoric method which once passed for acting on the operatic stage but does so no more.'

'The progress of the past thirty or forty years seems to have bypassed this company, whose singers might be still in the age of Caruso and Melba for all the interest they show in the characters they are supposedly portraying.'

'This was a throw-back to the pre-war age when the success of a performance depended on the soprano's trills and the tenor's top C.'

'They seemed to have forgotten Maria Callas, who taught singers to act.'

These are variants of a peculiarly irritating commonplace: the notion that before the 1950s opera singers merely donned costume and make-up, advanced to the footlights, waved their arms around and addressed their arias to the gallery. There was certainly much to deplore, as there is now (though the forms of offence on stage have changed). Singers were not schooled in acting as they are now. They rarely had adequate rehearsal for the dramatic side of their work, and, individually, they were rarely part of a properly thought-out production. But the great majority, then as now, cared for their singing as an expressive art, and many acted conscientiously and well. Critics and audiences were not indifferent to what they saw. Sometimes, as when Caruso and Melba sang together, they accepted a visual absurdity for the sake of an aural splendour, but customarily they required a fair balance, and (at the very least) preferred a singer who 'looked the part' to one who did not.

The Italian baritones who share this chapter are examples of singers who in the first half of the century were appreciated quite as much for their acting as for their singing. At this distance of time Stabile is the better remembered, most especially for his performances as Verdi's Falstaff,

Mariano Stabile as Scarpia in *Tosca*

which he is said to have played more than 1,200 times. Sammarco has a place in the annals as the first Gérard in *Andrea Chénier* (1896). Other world premieres in his career were those of Leoncavallo's *Zazà* (1900), Franchetti's *Germania* (1907) and Victor Herbert's *Notoma* (1911). Essentially he was the reliable and popular house-baritone, serving in this capacity at La Scala, Covent Garden and Hammerstein's Manhattan. He had a large repertoire, kept his place throughout a career which lasted some thirty years, and proved his worth alike in his singing and acting.

Both baritones were born in Palermo, Sammarco in 1867, Stabile in 1888. Their careers were continuous, overlapping in the years around 1920, which is when we hear the last of Sammarco and when Stabile was approaching full recognition of his abilities, chosen by Toscanini in 1921 to play Falstaff in the re-opening of La Scala after the war. One would suppose their paths must have crossed at some time, for Stabile made his debut in their native city as early as 1909. That, however, was the time which for Sammarco saw the beginning of the American years, when he became known as a member of the Tetrazzini 'Triumvirate', the other male being John McCormack. Sammarco had sung with the famous soprano first in Buenos Aires in 1898, and his own career dates back another ten years. With Sammarco giving his first stage performances in 1888 and Stabile his last in 1961, the two Sicilians between them cover a sizeable period in operatic history: Sammarco came into the business before Enrico Caruso, and Stabile lived to share the stage with Maria Callas.

Sammarco's fame as an actor-singer was shared with another of the leading Italian baritones of their age, Antonio Scotti. Of the two, Sammarco seems to have had the better voice, but in conjunction they very effectively give the lie to the idea that in those days singers won a way to the head of their profession by voice alone. Scotti is the subject of a separate study in *Singers of the Century*, Volume 1 (no. 22) where the point is made by quotations from (among others) Puccini, who found Scotti's voice 'bad' but still welcomed him gratefully as a magnificent Scarpia – the magnificence evidently lying in his distinction as an operatic actor. Sammarco was also an admired Scarpia, of less aristocratic subtlety but still fit for comparison with Scotti who by general consent was the greatest of all. In London at Covent Garden these two were for many years the house-regulars of the main Italian wing. Between 1899, when Scotti made his debut, and 1919, when Sammarco sang there for the last time, other baritones who came and went included Maurel, Renaud, Battistini, Amato, Ruffo, Stracciari, Gilly and De Luca, yet Scotti and Sammarco remained the steady favourites.

Recalling Sammarco's London debut in 1904, P.G. Hurst (*The Age of Jean de Reszke*, London, 1958) wrote: 'as Amonasro in *Aida*, he made an instant success, for this was one of his most effective roles. Although actually short in stature, so formidable was his aspect that, added to the breadth of shoulder and depth of chest, he never appeared to be so.' As Scarpia in *Tosca,* Hurst thought him 'perhaps better suited than the more admired Scotti'. 'Not especially pleasing vocally,' he concludes, 'he was a superb actor.' On his return the following season, the *Illustrated London News* (8 July 1905) reported that Sammarco 'fulfilled all expectations. From the moment when he appeared on stage as Amonasro he claimed the closest attention of the house, and in a performance where all the music was well sung ... he remained the dominant figure.' Particularly admired was his Tonio in *Pagliacci*: 'he gave an exquisitely finished portrayal and sang the Prologue superbly' (*The Times*, 10 June 1907). His Rigoletto in that season was 'beyond praise', and in these and many other roles he strengthened his position from year to year. By 1919, his last season, his voice had deteriorated. 'We had him in a part that he always made great,' wrote A.P. Hatton, the opera critic ('Figaro') of *Musical Opinion*, 'and great his impersonation of it still is, but Time is relentless and unsparing in its toll, and Mario would not thank me (or believe me) if I said that he had all his old time compelling power that used to astonish one by its absence of effort, its consummate assurance ... There were glad moments enough that had the old unique Sammarco hallmark, especially the "Pari siamo", and his acting was more polished than ever.'

240

Mario Sammarco

Of Stabile, the same critic wrote that he was 'an artist to his fingertips ... the subtlety of his acting equalled by the dramatic elegance of his singing'. That was in 1930, when Stabile's Scarpia in *Tosca* was said to have quite eclipsed the Cavaradossi of Beniamino Gigli. He had made his debut in the house four years earlier as Iago. Herman Klein listed 'youth, good looks, height, intelligence, alertness of gesture and mobility of feature' among his assets, together with a fine voice that 'only needed greater amplitude for things like the Credo or the Brindisi' (*Gramophone*, June 1926). In the famous revival of *Don Giovanni* under Bruno Walter he was 'brilliant', and in 1927 he and Kipnis were the only singers whose performances did anything to redeem a dreadful evening with *Les Huguenots*. As the years went by, critics noted more detail; thus *The Times* in 1931 described Scarpia's ruthlessness 'expressed in those dry, swiftly spoken comments, or in those moments where he does nothing but sip his wine or look out of the window or gloat over Tosca'. In that season Stabile added a greatly admired Gianni Schicchi to his repertoire (these were his first performances in the part). And of course there was the supreme revelation of his Falstaff, experienced first in London at Covent Garden in 1926 and last in the memorable seasons of 1946 to '48 at the Cambridge Theatre and the Stoll. Lord Harewood, in a tribute to Stabile in *Opera*, May 1956, wrote that Falstaff 'has run like a thread of gold through the whole of his career', enriched by his affection for words and the infinite detail characterising 'one of the greatest performances of our time in one of the greatest roles'.

241

Among the very few dissenting voices was that of Ernest Newman. Having welcomed Stabile in 1926, he noted a deterioration of voice the following year: a 'strong vibrato' had developed, disfiguring his Rigoletto which Newman thought well acted apart from the first scene in which he 'exaggerated grossly the effects of Monterone's curse'. A few weeks later he reported that Stabile had 'developed so strong a vibrato that legato singing is almost impossible for him, and a Scarpia who cannot sing legato cannot be suave, and consequently is no longer Scarpia'. By 'vibrato' he cannot have meant the fast, reiterative sort, for there is nothing remotely of that kind audible in Stabile's records; it must therefore have been the slow, uneven type, nearer to 'wobble', and, although by today's standards the criticism may seem harsh, records do give some support to that. So does my own memory, though it catches only the Stabile of twenty years later. His Malatesta in *Don Pasquale* came to me as something of a shock, for I had not heard his records and was expecting something different. The first sounds remain vivid with me, a voice which even in the phrase from off-stage I recognised as disappointingly thin and unsteady and which in his 'Bella siccome un angelo' simply confirmed the initial disappointment. The polish of his acting remains vivid too: he was the complete master of gesture and facial expression, exercising a kind of magnetism I had not known before. Yet the total impression was not endearing.

Sammarco too was a singer for whose records I have still no great liking. In those he made between 1902 and 1910 his voice is impressive in fullness and resonance though not notably individual in timbre. There is more of conviction and energy in his singing than there is of expression, and, whereas Stabile's records show a vocal make-up artist of the highest quality, Sammarco's are those of a man whose changes from one character to another must have been achieved by appearance rather than sound. In the notes for a compilation of his records transferred to compact disc, the producer of the record, Keith Hardwick, quotes an interesting memorandum written in 1908 from the head of the Gramophone Company's Italian branch. He reported that Sammarco had 'made a very good name for himself on his own merits and in spite of his defects of voice. He is a very clever actor, makes up extremely cleverly and is a clever vocal artist and a good musician. By this combination he has succeeded in masking the poor timbre of his voice.' If asked to guess at the identity of the Italian baritone thus described I would have said 'Mariano Stabile'.

One small postscript on Sammarco. In 1910 he gave a recital at London's Wigmore Hall, the programme of which included 'Lament and Hymn' from Monteverdi's *Orfeo*. This also appears to have been the opera in which he was heard for the last time, at the Milan Conservatory in 1919. It is not what one might have expected, and it is good to know; not many star singers, either in Italy or elsewhere, took an interest in Monteverdi in those days.

242

CHAPTER 48

# Gerhard Hüsch and
# Hermann Prey

From the first I was singing German Lieder; they should come before learning a role in opera. (Hüsch, quoted in *The Times*, 2 February 1981)

As a human being I need both those things: opera and Lied. But if you were to hold a gun to my head and say that, in the future, I should devote myself only to one of them, it would be Lied. (Prey, quoted in *Bravo*, Helen Matheopoulos, Gollancz, 1989)

Doubtless one should not put words into other people's mouths, but it is highly likely that many of the century's best-known German baritones would agree. Hüsch had in mind the start of a career, Prey its later stages. Hüsch's point was specific and practical: 'opera-singers who take up Lieder afterwards don't sound at home. The frame is smaller, and must come naturally, not as a shrinking of the limits.' Prey was making a statement about his personal needs and taste, though a more general aesthetic, intellectual and spiritual judgement is implied. He also says that it is better for young singers to come to the main nineteenth-century operatic repertoire through Mozart, 'and even better if they come to him through Lieder-singing, through Bach, Beethoven and Schubert, as I did'.

There is an essential continuity here. Between them, the careers of these baritones covered a large part of the century, Hüsch making his debut, in opera, in 1923, Prey his, in concert, in 1950. The voices of both singers lasted well, as was evident when Hüsch returned to sing in Britain in the mid-1950s, and when Prey at the age of 65 gave a generously programmed recital in 1994 at London's Queen Elizabeth Hall with James Levine as his pianist. Prey was not, so to speak, a continuation of Hüsch, but they were both good, central representatives of their times, and they embody a tradition, albeit a developing one.

In his autobiography (English translation, Calder 1986), Prey talks of the antipathy which the German youth of his generation had towards nineteenth-century art-song, principally on account of its associations: 'Many people had become so horrified at what their fathers' generation had done, that they had come to reject all that their forebears had stood for, while welcoming with open arms anything they knew to have been rejected in the past'. He says that this was not true of himself but that peer-pressure caused him to adopt the 'cool' approach. He sang popular songs and joined with friends to form a group called The Rhythm Trio. When he sang Lieder it had to be in the more impersonal modern way: 'Deep down inside, I wanted to put my whole heart into these songs, but feared that this would conflict with the spirit of the age.'

The fathers' generation was of course Hüsch's; and yet, if what is in immediate question here is style in Lieder singing, Hüsch was himself a modern singer. Prey says that, partly because of fashion and post-war opinion, he avoided like the plague anything that could be accused of sentimentality or even emotionalism; but Hüsch himself was never of the old-fashioned 'romantic' persuasion. More decisively than contemporaries such as Schlusnus and Janssen, Hüsch was a singer whom Prey's own generation would have seen as disciplined, non-indulgent and 'modern'. An interesting study of style and performance-practice can be found in Edward E. Kravitt's *Mirror of Late Romanticism* (Yale, 1996). Two features of late-romantic style are identified as the subordination of rhythm to 'feeling', and, in vocal music, the cult of personality, involving a licence for singers to use portamento (a curve or 'slide' between notes) whenever they felt like it. As a modern reaction against the first, Kravitt quotes Prey in a masterclass of 1992 insisting on strict tempo in Schubert's 'Erlkönig' ('To maintain tempo, Prey urged students to clap'). On the second, he refers to Hüsch. Even when the composer of the songs being rehearsed, Richard Trunck, suggested 'a tiny *gefühl* (expressive) portamento', Hüsch declined. Kravitt shows that both doctrines – the primacy of rhythm and the elimination of portamento – contradict what we know of romantic nineteenth-century practice. Hüsch no less than Prey was reacting against the 'emotionalism and sentimentality' of his predecessors.

Where Hüsch is likely to show himself the earlier and, in these particular respects, the better singer is in his evenness of texture and line. Prey also cares for beauty of tone (his was the more ringing, vibrant sound) and for a well-preserved legato, and it is notable that critics of Fischer-Dieskau will often express a preference for Prey. But compared with Hüsch, his vigour has a roughness about it, and his quiet singing is a degree looser. It is clearly so if one plays a record of Hüsch's after one of Prey's: Prey's may have the more expressive manner, but the finer finish, in purely vocal terms, belongs to Hüsch. Hüsch can himself be surprisingly emphatic and declamatory when he tries his luck with Italian opera, but in that central part of his repertoire, which overlaps with Prey's, the voice-production is that of an earlier generation, one which made sheer evenness of emission a top priority.

They were, however, alike in their care over repertoire, making a realistic assessment of their rightful territory, staying within it (by and large) and exploring with an eye for development. Prey identified his *Fach*,

Hermann Prey

or voice-type, as what used to be termed the *Kavaliersbariton*, with Mozart's Count Almaviva as its archetypal role. Don Giovanni, Guglielmo and Papageno were other Mozart roles at the centre of his repertoire, as they were of Hüsch's. Similarly, they would sing Valentin in *Faust*, Wolfram in *Tannhäuser* and as many of the appropriate roles in the nearly

245

forgotten operas of Lortzing as there were available performances. Both tried some Verdi – Hüsch in *La traviata*, *Il trovatore* and *Un ballo in maschera*, Prey in *Don Carlos* and *La forza del destino* – but such roles were not theirs by nature or inheritance. Both were clear-sighted about it, and about attendant dangers. Hüsch said: 'I refused Rigoletto ... because I knew that would lead to Amonasro, Iago and a quick vocal decline.'

The main extensions to their core-repertoire were enterprisingly chosen. Hüsch became a specialist in the songs of Yrjö Kilpinen; Prey built up a large repertoire of early German song, going back to the Middle Ages. Hüsch sang in the Berlin productions of several operas that have disappeared from the general view (Dressel's *Armer Columbus*, Graener's *Friedemann Bach*, Gurlitt's *Die Soldaten*, for instance). Prey's discography includes rarities such as Cavalieri's *La rappresentazione di anima e di corpo* (1600) and the Weber-Mahler *Die drei Pintos*. We also have to remind ourselves that the Schubert cycles, the Wolf songs and even the *St Matthew Passion*, works that we take for granted when a singer of Prey's generation records them, were all pioneered so many years before, with Hüsch prominently involved.

Where the two singers have a different story to tell lies with the difference in their dates of birth and their ages at the time of the Second World War. Hüsch, born in 1901, was of military age in 1939, but was exempt from call-up because of his musical activities as singer and teacher. The war nevertheless made a nasty hole in his career. He had scored a success at Covent Garden in 1938 with his Papageno in *Die Zauberflöte* and would certainly have been invited back. The famous recording of the opera under Beecham spread his name internationally, and at just about the right age of forty he would in the normal course of events have launched a promising international career. Instead, as he said to William Mann who wrote the article on him in *The Times*, he was commuting between Berlin and Munich 'mostly on unheated trains in the middle of the night, during an air-raid with buildings burning in the big towns'. Among those going up in flames one night in 1943 was the home of the twelve-year-old Hermann Prey. He too escaped military duty, but only just. In the last frantic months, young and old were conscripted, and call-up papers did arrive by a circuitous route, thence to be hidden away by Prey's father ('Now that the war was nearly over, he wanted his son to stay alive'). Then, while Hüsch was facing the denazification courts (quite needlessly, he said, though it was probably as well that the officials had not come upon his 1933 recording of 'Das Hakenkreuz' and 'Deutschland erwache'), young Prey was picking up the songs of the occupying forces and turning his voice to good account with anything from the Volga Boatmen to 'Give me five minutes more'.

The end of the war did not see the end of Hüsch's career, as he went on in the 1950s to sing, as did Prey many years later, to enthusiastic audiences in Japan. For Prey, the occupation brought vital assistance as in

# ITALIAN PIZZAS

**ALL PIZZAS ARE FRESHLY BAKED IN STORE**

| | 10" | 12" | 16" |
|---|---|---|---|
| JUST CHEESE | £4.45 | £5.45 | £8.45 |
| DONNER PIZZA | £5.45 | £6.50 | £9.45 |
| SPICY CHICKEN | £5.45 | £6.50 | £9.45 |
| SPICY MINCE | £4.95 | £6.50 | £9.45 |
| HAWAIIAN | £5.45 | £6.50 | £9.45 |
| MEAT FEAST | £6.45 | £6.95 | £10.95 |
| Chicken, ham, pepperoni & lamb | | | |
| VOLCANO | £6.45 | £6.95 | £10.95 |
| Spicy chicken, mushroom, onion, jalapenos & mixed peppers | | | |
| ROOSTER BOOSTER | £5.45 | £6.95 | £10.45 |
| Chicken, sweetcorn, peppers & mushroom | | | |
| PEPPERONI PASSION | £5.45 | £6.95 | £10.45 |
| HOT & SPICY | £6.45 | £6.95 | £10.45 |
| Spicy chicken, spicy mince & green chillies | | | |
| FOUR SEASONS | £6.45 | £6.95 | £10.95 |
| Chicken, chicken tikka, sweetcorn & mushroom | | | |
| TORNADO | £6.45 | £6.95 | £10.95 |
| Chicken tikka, peppers, onions, jalapenos, green chillies & fresh tomatoes | | | |
| VEGGIE DELUXE | £5.95 | £6.95 | £10.95 |
| Peppers, onions, mushroom, sweetcorn & fresh tomatoes | | | |
| INDIAN FEAST | £5.95 | £6.50 | £10.45 |
| Chicken tikka masala topped with cheese | | | |
| FULL BHUNA | £6.45 | £6.95 | £10.45 |
| Chicken & lamb bhuna | | | |

## EXTRA TOPPINGS

CHICKEN TIKKA, CHICKEN, CHILLIES, PEPPERONI, PEPPERS, SALAMI, SPICY CHICKEN, SPICY LAMB, DONNER, MUSHROOMS, ONIONS, SWEETCORN, TOMATO, PINEAPPLE, GARLIC

### VEG TOPPING

10" +£0.50 • 12" +£0.70 • 16" +£1.00

### MEAT TOPPING

10" +£0.70 • 12" +£1.00 • 16" +£1.50

CURRIES · KEBABS · PIZZAS · CALZONES · BURGERS

Introducing the Masala Zone
Indian takeaway and delivery service.
Our master chef has created using a selection of speciality dishes that
will take your taste-buds on an incredible culinary journey. Using only
the freshest ingredients & many years of experience, highly
recommended.

# Masala
# Zone

## FINEST INDIAN CUISINE

Quality & Service is our business.

## 227 MAIN STREET, WISHAW ML2 7NE

# 01698 351 414

Home Delivery Service Available to:
**wishaw, netherton, overtown, new mains, muirhouse,
waterloo, cleland, motherwell, morningside**

## Open 7 Days
Sun - Thurs 4pm - 11.30pm
Fri - Sat 4pm - 12am

حلال

VICTORIA & ALBERT MUSEUM

SOUTH KENSINGTON, S.W.7

*By kind permission of the Director.*

## MUSEUM GALLERY CONCERTS

THE BOYD NEEL CONCERT SOCIETY

presents

## GERHARD HÜSCH

*Pianoforte:* GEOFFREY PARSONS

**SUNDAY, OCTOBER 16th, 1955 at 8 p.m.**

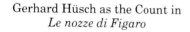

Gerhard Hüsch as the Count in
*Le nozze di Figaro*

1952 he won the American-sponsored Mastersingers of Nuremberg competition, one of the prizes for which was a visit, with singing engagements, to the States. And from there, with remarkably few setbacks, his career went its distinguished way.

We now remember both singers with affection. I only wish, for myself, that I could remember Hüsch more clearly 'in the flesh'. Awful truth to tell, his *Winterreise* on a Sunday evening in 1955 left no lasting impression at all. The voice was perfectly firm, but I could hardly identify it otherwise with the pre-war recordings; and it is quite probable that the restraint and refinement of his performance were too good for me. Of Prey I have many memories, joyful ones in the opera house, and in the concert hall most happy when strong-toned and vigorous, least when quiet and with a tendency to lose colour and pitch. The last time of all, a Schubert recital in 1994, ending with 'Was ist Silvia?' for encore, two verses in German, one in English, was a warmly remembered occasion, the 65-year-old a still-handsome presence with a smile in his voice and a fund of rhythmic life in his system. Hüsch and Prey between them span many of the years, and typify much of the best, of their country's school of singing in the twentieth century.

CHAPTER 49

# Bryn Terfel

A report on a concert:

> Bryn Terfel's voice, his musicianship, presence, vitality – the list could
> continue – are all special. But his genius lies in his intelligence. Things we
> have heard a hundred times take on not so much a new meaning as a real
> life. We all know, for instance, the words of 'Who is Sylvia?' and 'It was a
> lover and his lass', but the notion that the first is genuinely raising a
> question and that the second might actually be true (in the sense that it has
> just happened, and here is someone who saw that couple, this afternoon let's
> say, and who wants to tell us). This is Terfel's doing. He persuades us that
> these poems were not written, the words immutable for centuries in print:
> they are new and now. Another example. We all know what Corinthians 13
> has to say about which is the greatest ('charity' the King James Bible calls
> it but nowadays it's 'love'). I suppose we assume that St Paul had made his
> mind up all along: 'Faith, hope and charity, but the greatest of these is
> charity.' When Terfel sings Brahms's setting, he makes the other, more
> interesting assumption: that Paul was a thinking man and that he did not
> subordinate the other two (faith and hope) without a second thought. For a
> moment, a lightning mental operation surveys them, lovingly it would seem,
> and then (but only then) awards the prize – 'Aber die Liebe ist die grösste
> unter ihnen.'

Written the day after the concert, which was in London at the Wigmore
Hall on January 16, 1998, the account is still a trifle breathless. Writing
now some months later, one is ready to try out a little scepticism. Was it
really so good? And – more concerned now for critical balance and responsibility – is 'genius' indeed the word?

We'll step back, then, from that concert and return to it later, having
drawn breath. 'Genius' was a word that was not uttered and yet was not
far off when the first, relatively obscure, Terfel solo disc came to me for
review in *Gramophone* five years earlier. In it he sang an entirely Welsh
programme. Here is part of the review:

> Rather as some of the singers of old (Chaliapin pre-eminently, but, nearer
> home, an old-fashioned 'ballad' singer such as Harry Dearth), he has a
> confidence in instinct, a fresh willingness to show what the voice will do (a

248

solid bass at one time, almost a silvery tenor at another, a mighty opening-up of tone or a mere intimation), and he puts all these arts to good purpose. (*Gramophone*, August 1993)

He was not new to us then – had been the magazine's 1992 Young Artist of the Year, and the name was turning up all the time in the record lists – so no claim can he made for talent-spotting. But the reference to Chaliapin stands out, and again raises a question about critical responsibility. It was the second song in the programme, 'Cwynfyd' ('Paradise'), that brought the great Russian to mind. The song itself seemed musically very ordinary, but there was conviction in the singing, a quiet passion and an imaginative seizure of the opportunities. Possibly the Welsh language, as foreign to me as Chaliapin's Russian, brought the suggestion closer; and yet I rather fancy that what was then in view were the songs Chaliapin sang in English, 'The Blind Ploughman' and 'O, Could I in Song tell my Sorrow', also not the greatest music (and in some respects quite badly sung) but transfigured by the singer's way with them. And of course, where Chaliapin was concerned, the word 'genius' was never far off.

Perhaps we should brush away the comparison before it gets out of hand. It lingers, though. We know the Welsh are a singing nation, but it is a long way from 'Land of our fathers' to (say) the songs of Debussy, Poulenc and Ibert, in which Terfel first made a really strong impression upon me as a listener in the concert hall. Chaliapin travelled a greater distance, in all senses, but both singers brought with them something of their background, which was not metropolitan or industrial, sophisticated

249

or fashionable. Both were (are), physically, big men. Chaliapin was essentially a singer-actor and needed the stage, where he was, by all accounts, a figure from whom you did not take your eyes – any more than you do from Terfel on the concert platform. But there: that goes far enough.

On the whole, critics tend to be suspicious of an outstanding success. It sometimes appears easier to go through all the forms and phases of the canonisation process than to gain, while young, and living, a place in the line of great singers (at least there is only one Devil's Advocate appointed by the Vatican, while the critics are almost professionally bound to probe each weakness, scrutinise every recording and every review, examine their own memories and impressions). Terfel has come a long way in a short time, yet it has been by stages and degrees. In 1992, when he won the Young Artist Award, he made his debut at Covent Garden: the role was the suitably modest one of Masetto in *Don Giovanni*, but this was a Masetto who held the stage whenever he was on it. He came to that from appearances with the Welsh and English National Opera Companies and after experience abroad in Spain and America. This was doing things the right way. He had trained conscientiously, winning prizes as he went along, culminating in the Guildhall's Gold Medal for their best singer. With this as encouragement he entered for the Cardiff Singer of the World competition in 1989, where the result was probably the best thing that could have happened to him. Instead of winning outright over Dmitri Hvorostovsky (when the knowing-lobby would have said 'The Russian should have won'), he came second, leaving it to the whole television-viewing audience to say, 'Well, of course the Russian was very good, beautiful voice, very gifted, but personally I preferred the Welshman.'

Many of that original audience will have been back at their television sets for a programme about him which came out late in 1996. By then he was an international star, seen in rehearsal at Salzburg and with a Metropolitan debut behind him that made front-page headlines in the *New York Times*. But two other, more personal, aspects must have impressed many viewers. One was the vitality of the man; the other concerns his background. We saw a home-movie made of him as a youngster, singing with a light voice and a figure to match, then another, singing, mostly in thirds, with a young tenor: almost the only immediately recognisable features were the eyes and the smile. Then we recalled that that was 1982, and though I have forgotten what they were singing it certainly was not rock-and-roll. Even in those days, and well before, it was a miracle if a teenager with looks, personality and a voice did not make straight for an electric guitar and a microphone. Apparently the Terfels had always had music in the home, and that presumably meant for the most part songs round the piano. There was nothing quaint or dowdy about the home or the family, but in its North Wales setting among fields and mountains it was representative of a civilisation that is fast disappearing. In the film, showing him in his daily routine at Salzburg, he would hum along to

Terfel with Catherine Malfitano

'Hound Dog' on the car radio or play a twelve-bar boogie on the rehearsal-piano before getting down to work – nothing about him suggested a rejection of the modern world and its ways. But he chose Mozart, and that, these days, is remarkable. Moreover, he would have long ago found out that Mozart and the central 'classic' repertoire are the plums of the profession, the rewards: there is all the sheer hard grind, mastering difficult modern scores, memorising texts, learning languages. It would also be cheering to think that Terfel's achievements and the way he has carried them (as seen in that film) would inspire the following generation; but the likelihood is that they are at the disco, and that, whatever 'music in the home' may mean to them, it will not mean songs round the piano.

To hear and see Terfel at the recital of French song mentioned earlier was to know the exhilaration of release. For him there was no doubt the release inherent in the public performance of hard-learnt songs, but many

251

in the audience must have shared a sense that the songs themselves had been liberated. French song is a private preserve: authenticity is the password, and that is identified with the subtlety of nuance, the raising of an eyebrow, the curling of a lip. Della Jones was the other singer in this particular programme, part of a series devised by the accompanist Malcolm Martineau and presented in London at St John's, Smith Square in 1991. Both are exuberant singers with a lively sense of the ridiculous – and the lifting of an eyebrow, the curl of a lip, can be richly comical, however finely nuanced. They went about it another way, singing out, using their good voices and, instead of pursing their lips even closer in the interests of refinement, opening up in the interests of humanity. There was no crudeness about it; time and again the ear was delighted by phrases of a beautifully sustained legato and softness, while the mind took satisfaction in sensitive, well-pointed expression. But the abiding memory is of the repertory let out of its cage to enjoy a larger life, as if on holiday.

So, back (or forward in time) from that to the Wigmore recital of 1998. The programme began with a drinking song by Schubert, hardly more than a minute long. And again memory retains it very vividly, for he began straight-in with a sense of occasion and a zest of attack: it was like the way he launches 'Non più andrai' in *Le nozze di Figaro*, with a humorous unpremeditated relish. At the Wigmore, the Schubert and Schumann groups were followed by Brahms' *Serious Songs*, and those by Finzi's Shakespearean settings in *Let us Garlands Bring*. In that last work, the combination of such music, such words and such a voice could hardly have failed to be moving. But this was deeply so, with a marvellous unity of singer and audience, an intense engagement of the whole sensibility. Thus: in 'Come away, death' the line 'Fly away, fly away, breath' was not a rhetorical figure, but as though lightly, letting a butterfly free from cupped hands, he saw it go. In 'Fear no more the heat o' the sun', the line 'Thou hast finished joy and moan' was not a verbal formula but an instant survey of those twin poles of human experience in a compassionate impulse of pity and consolation. The shadow of mortality that lies over 'O mistress mine' finds its pensive recognition in Finzi's setting, but again it was Terfel's special gift to raise it from what is nominal to what is real and felt. He does the same with Vaughan Williams' *Songs of Travel*; and in a song as well-worn as Ireland's 'Sea Fever' every item of *desiderata* ('all I ask is a windy day ... and the seagulls crying') is freshly minted. Even with the shopping-list in Walton's *Belshazzar's Feast* ('gold and silver ... and the souls of men') he makes each item in turn pass before our eyes as no one else I can think of has done. Essentially, it is a virtuosity of the mind, a rapid, flexible, intense concentration. And if it is not a kind of genius, then, as Dickens' lisping, circus-master in *Hard Times* would say, 'then, Thquire, I'm bletht if I know what to call it'.

CHAPTER 50

# Maria Callas[*]

The recent play about her did Callas the great disservice of restoring her to life. That is no longer her element, and she is well out of it. While she was with us, doing the work for which she is properly remembered, common sense and good taste were frequently repelled by claims and counter-claims, scandals real or manufactured, and, in reported speech, a nauseous alternation of rudeness and pious platitude. When her singing days were over, the more unpleasant associations of her active career would probably have prevented her from making an unostentatious, stead-ily useful contribution to musical life, even if it had been within her power and inclination to do so. Once indeed she did emerge from retirement to try her hand, spending twelve weeks at the Juilliard School in New York listening to young singers and working with them on their music. This provides the setting for Terence McNally's play *Master Class*. Sadly, it gives little idea of what was valuable about those Juilliard sessions, and directs attention back to where it came from: to the woman, the associates, the life.

Callas is now beyond these things, and for the time being it would be better that she should remain so. Essentially, just as surely as Rembrandt is his paintings and Shakespeare his plays, Callas is her recordings. Beside them, the personal things – the mother, the ugly-duckling youth, the horrible millionaire and the riff-raff of gossip columnists, big spenders and big spongers that battened on him and his kind – they all pass as in a dream. The *Norma* remains, the *Medea*, the *Traviata*; and with them, or out of them, distilled as an essence, the real personality, that of the artist who gives life to all these, themselves fat copy for tabloid defamation but instead ennobled by the music of Bellini, Cherubini and Verdi.

Perhaps to the sound-recordings should be added the written records, the filmed 'evidence' and the additional matter of historical 'significance'. Yet, on the whole, it is a sterile heap that accumulates as we work our way through these. This 'significance', for instance. Callas' influence was po-tent in three principal respects: she created, willy-nilly, a school of singing

* Article published in *Opera Now*, Sept/Oct 1997. Terence McNally's *Master Class* was playing in London at the Queen's Theatre.

by inspiring a generation of imitators. She also showed, by her brilliantly successful example, the need for an operatic artist to combine the skills of musician and actor, and she helped decisively to reveal strengths in a part of the operatic repertoire which many had dismissed as worthless or impracticable. Of these, the first can now be relegated as a matter of temporary importance (though it spoilt some promising careers). The second and third are indeed valid, but too much has been made of them. The claim that operatic acting can be divided into periods BC (before Callas) and AC (after) is so facile that it hardly merits the space needed to clear it up; a moment's thought will suggest that, as the whole movement of operatic production from the 1930s onwards tended towards a more integrated, dramatically conceived performance, so an ever-growing emphasis would be placed upon the dramatic side of the singer's art. Similarly, with the redirection of repertoire; this rediscovery of the 'bel canto' repertory was something that was coming (the conductor Tullio Serafin, for instance, had it in mind and used Callas for the purpose, which would otherwise have been served by others who would have brought conviction if not genius). The filmed and written records similarly have a place, a validity and usefulness, though they seem to me less than one might hope and expect. The one gleaming trophy of Callas on film is her smile. Smile is not quite the right word, for that might suggest closed lips, and Callas' are open, brilliantly on the way to laughter. It is there in the filmed concerts which have her singing Rosina's 'Una voce poco fa' and Carmen's 'Habanera'. Anyway, it is an aspect of Callas, the performing artist, at which one might not have guessed, and it leavens the total impression so that one hates to think how very easily it might have gone into oblivion.

But really, it is possible to harvest a very few moments of Callas on film and find that the rest has not much to add: even the famous Act 2 of *Tosca* yields less than we may expect of it – and very naturally so, as we are seeing on film a performance acted on stage in a large opera house. What is perhaps more surprising is that the written words of critics and others yield so little truly 'enabling' matter. I would have hoped, through the on-the-spot accounts, to hear and see Callas in the imagination; and this so rarely happens.

In the valuable critical anthology compiled by David A. Lowe in his *Callas As They Saw Her* (Robson, 1987), one can read for a long time before coming upon a vivid pictorial detail, such as that of a moment in *I puritani* at Chicago in 1955 recalling 'how she took the wreath of white roses from her hair and her anguish when, as if by accident, it dropped to the floor'. It may not be much, but is worth pages of generalisation: one is, ever so briefly, present, and with a moment to remember. Claudia Cassidy's account of the *Madama Butterfly* in that same season tells something too: 'It set the mounting ardour of the man against the muted ecstasy of the

Callas as Norma (Covent Garden 1952)

woman – and in its way told which one kissed and which one turned the cheek.'

Looking outside that anthology, certainly, one can come upon more detail, and indeed the late Covent Garden Toscas were covered almost as with a verbal camera ('a teasing sense of humour in the scene with the

255

blue-eyed Magdalene', 'her sudden intense stillness as she looks down at the table and sees and understands the presence of the knife and remains poised as if suspended in time over the enormous question' (Philip Hope-Wallace in the *Guardian*, 22 January 1964, and David Cairns, *Spectator*). There is also what I think deserves the status of a classic in operatic criticism, Peter Heyworth's piece in the *Observer* on *La traviata* at Covent Garden on 20 June 1958. Her understanding of the great role, he says, 'finds its way into the smallest gesture and movement, into the nervous passage of a hand around the face, the terrible fragility of body that in the last act turns every movement into a labour, and the fearful abruptness with which the gaping image of death is all at once there in her staring eyes'. He also picks up what he calls 'perhaps the most marvellous moment of the evening'. This was the sustained note before 'Dite alla giovine', 'The moment of decision on which the whole opera turns ... By some miracle, Callas makes that note hang unsuspended in mid-air; unadorned and unsupported she fills it with all the conflicting emotions that besiege her. As she descends to the aria, which she opened with a sweet, distant *mezza voce* of extraordinary poignancy, the die is cast.' This is just the kind of thing one hopes to find somewhere in the writings of those who should be the eyes, as well as the ears, of posterity: it is rare enough.*

One other kind of record should be considered before we turn to the gramophone where the real living Callas is to be found. Now, the BC/AC people, who seem to believe that up till Callas' time singers 'stood and delivered' without bothering to act, have had plenty of time to think what to say when the name of Chaliapin is mentioned (he's 'the exception that proves the rule'). There can be few people alive now who saw Chaliapin on stage, but, though it was always said that you had to see him with your own eyes to know just how great he was, it is still quite possible, even at this date, to feel that one *has* seen Chaliapin. For one thing, his records are powerful dramatic events; for another, critics wrote about him in a way that renders him visible. But then there are the books, and you have only to turn the pages of illustrations to see, in astonishing photographic sequence, the range and individuality of his portrayals. The camera makes a vital contribution to the Chaliapin museum. It is (I think) not so with Callas. Turning the illustrative pages in Lowe's anthology or in George Jellinek's biography or John Ardoin's study of the Callas legacy on disc, one rarely comes upon a face, an expression, that is peculiar to the character involved, or indeed that would not pass, in a book of operatic photographs, as a standard operatic pose. For instance, in Lowe there is a fine photograph of her at the agonised moment of choice in *La traviata*: it

---

* In a more irreverent vein, Philip Hope-Wallace, staying on this occasion to the end of the opera and beyond, wrote in his notice of this same *Traviata* for the *Guardian*: 'As for her curtain calls, they are a thing of wonder. She allows the first storm to subside before gliding out, a shy schoolgirl unable to believe that this tumult is for her. The extent of her triumph is then seen to daze her. The violet shrinks, the gazelle flees – and the public yells for more.'

At the theatre                    Recording session with Walter Legge

is fine, yet, oddly, belonging to a line, almost a school (Bernhardt, Garbo), and in a collection of operatic photographs others of Galli-Curci and Selma Kurz (neither of them famous tragediennes) would be just as eloquent.

At this point, I very much wish it were possible to throw in tuppence of my own; but I saw Callas only once. For *Norma* in 1952 I easily, cheaply and quite uncharacteristically bought a good stall; thereafter it was the extreme gallery slips where everything that mattered on stage took place over the side of which one had no view. Memories of the *Norma* are principally of the singing and the glimpse of a desperately tired, white-faced woman outside the theatre later on; but of her acting, I gained no very favourable impression. There was a strong stage-presence but too much striding, too much accusatory arm-extension pointing either to two o'clock or five. The last scene was carried with an intense tragic dignity, but the sheer vocal and physical endurance seemed tried to the limit.

That is by the way. Essentially, my Callas (like everybody else's who comes after us) is on records. A great deal survives, including 'live' recordings many of which have still not entered the 'mainstream' commercial lists. *I vespri siciliani*, from Florence in 1951, was to have been added in this commemorative year, but apparently was considered too badly flawed in the quality of recorded sound. The role of Elena in this opera is not among the most interesting of Verdi's heroines, and the performance comes early in the great Callas decade. Even so, the hallmarks are there: instant and thrilling recognition of the voice in Act 1, an intuitive raising

257

above convention of the emotional tug-of-war, and then, in Act 4, that essential response to the agony of a soul under pressure and the sure grasp of a crucial moment to which all of this is tending. The aria addressed to her lover Arrigo is a most lovely example of her habitual feeling for *rubato*, the give-and-take of rhythm, and of a sympathetic collaboration with the conductor, who is Erich Kleiber. Previously, the duet had shown exactly the art (restrained anger, softening sweetness) which was to illumine all she touched, often at quite unexpected moments.

Walter Legge, the man who produced almost the whole run of Callas' recordings for EMI, had it in mind, after his retirement, to open a school for singers; and Callas was to have been invited to give a course – in recitative. It was an inspired notion. So much of her genius lay in her perception of a crucial point, which she would then endow with such life that the whole opera would be transformed (how, for instance, the first emotional climax in her *Lucia di Lammermoor* comes not with the aria but with the avowal in recitative, 'Egli è luce ai giorni miei'). This runs through her recordings and is one of the reasons why the sound of her singing is also visual. The recordings are no second-best. When people say of Callas, 'Oh but of course you had to see her!' the answer is 'I can! I do!'

Was it, I wonder, so deliberately exclusive a proposition (this invitation to teach recitative) as it sounds? Did it, in other words, imply: 'Hands off the voice, and leave the real business of singing to others'? It may have been so, for Legge became increasingly intolerant of Callas' vocal deficiencies: 'Why should I have to be fearful of every next high note?' The whole question of Callas' voice and its production is of course material for an essay on its own. Even in 1952 the tone itself had only a compromised kind of beauty, unequal to the purity and warmth of Ebe Stignani, the Adalgisa of those *Norma* performances and twenty years her senior. Later on in the '50s, notes above the stave sounded worn, and as the vibrations loosened so the famous 'flap' widened on the high Bs and Cs, and assuredly one flinched. Causes may have had at their root the imperfect equalisation of the voice throughout its range (a fault of training). The ruthless exploitation of her early years, with those Isoldes, Brünnhildes and Turandots, was compounded by the abrupt imposition of a totally different kind of technical requirement, in *Puritani*, *Lucia* and so forth, with the upper register heavily, and perhaps disastrously, overworked. The wonder is that she survived as long as she did.

Anyway, the time of mournfulness for Callas is surely past. When she was still before the public, and in later years when her influence over young singers was at its height, there was a point. Yet even then a certain complacency attended the Jeremiads. 'Isn't it a tragedy!' exclaimed an implacable golden-ager – but he said it in the tones of one who cries checkmate. My own view is that her glory grows greater by the year. The defects are real, but very often turn out to be less glaring than as remembered, while on the other hand memory is often found to have underrated the firm basis of legato. It was this which enabled her to use her full gift for expressiveness in a melody such as 'Qui la voce' in *I puritani* without pulling or melting it out of shape. Her brilliance as a virtuoso is still astonishing in its combination with the timbre of a dramatic soprano – the Rossini *Armida* aria sung in concert at San Remo, at the end of 1954, fair races the blood with its scales and triplets, its athleticism and emotional eloquence.

Perhaps such examples are themselves sufficient to explain the fame and the enduring fascination. There is of course more. Like most (all?) of the greatest singers, she is instantly recognisable, and the recognition itself brings that frisson which is the tribute our instincts pay to genius. A devil's advocate might urge that what we recognise with such a thrill is only a peculiarity: and certainly there was a peculiarity of voice, even of structure, which I used to think of as the 'muzzle' effect and which Walter Legge ascribed to the high palate – 'like looking up at a gothic arch'. No trick of physiognomy or mannerism will account, however, for the emotional power of those tones or for the sure sense of style or the sudden flash of imagination. Listen to her in the 'Suicidio' aria from *La Gioconda*: only a great artist of the operatic stage is heard there.

It is also notable, when you go back to a familiar recording such as this, that memory has again played tricks. Generally, it enlarges, thickens, underlines, almost caricatures. Those chest notes, for example. They're not half so big, black and chesty as one thought. Callas is, in fact, to quite a remarkable extent an artist in restraint. That is one of the lessons of her Juilliard classes. The most telling example is in her session on the Letter scene from *Werther* ('not more voice, more intensity'), but it is evident throughout. Evident too, as one hears the record or reads the book of these masterclasses is the genuineness – and usefulness – of her teaching, which again was not apparent in McNally's play.

What the play did concoct was a mixture, probably not far from truth, of the comic and the tragic, the repellent and the sympathetic. Flashbacks exposed the woman's agony and the artist's ecstasy. And at the end of it: 'So that's that.' Those were her last words at the Juilliard. Previously, McNally had shown her contemplating the unloveliness of 'Mut', the German word for courage. 'I don't like many things German, but I do like Mut.' She recalls singing *Fidelio* at eighteen (actually twenty), and that too must have taken courage. About a singer's life she says, 'There are no short cuts. There is only discipline, technique and Mut.'

There are also, if you're Callas, the clapping hands and upturned faces, the happy ghosts of great composers, the thrill of your voice in somebody's ears, perhaps daily and from now until the ending of the world.

And *that's* that.

# Dates, Books and Records

The singers are found here in alphabetical order. After the name (professional name only) their chapter number in this book is given in brackets, and the biographical information which follows is limited mainly to dates, names of teachers, place and role of operatic debut, important first appearances abroad, and world premieres. The list of books and records is selective. Autobiographies are included, though not all will be currently in print. The recordings listed are on compact disc unless otherwise stated, and catalogue numbers have been added where it is thought they may be useful; but of course many are deleted, often with a new reissue on a different number and sometimes another company label. The *Gramophone* Classical catalogue is the best guide to what is available. Of general reference books the most comprehensive is the *New Grove Dictionary of Music and Musicians* (Macmillan 1980) or for opera singers the *New Grove Dictionary of Opera* (1992). Among many other helpful books is the *International Dictionary of Opera* (St. James's Press 1993) which will be found to have interestingly written discursive articles on several of the singers listed here. On the earlier singers and their recordings Michael Scott's *The Record of Singing* (Duckworth, 2 volumes 1977, 1979) can usually be relied on for an informative and stimulating entry, and for the art on records of singers up to 1970 there is *The Grand Tradition* (Duckworth 1974, reprinted as a second edition 1993) by the present writer. Where a number has been dedicated to a particular singer in this series, reference is always given to the *Record Collector*, an invaluable specialist magazine available on subscription and published quarterly. Information from the Editor, 111 Longshots Close, Broomfield, Chelmsford, Essex CM1 5DU, England.

ALLEN, Thomas (19) English baritone. b. Seaham Harbour, Co. Durham 10 Sept. 1944. Studied Royal College of Music, London. Debut Welsh National Opera 1969 (D'Obigny, *Traviata*). Cov. Gdn. 1971. Glyndebourne 1973. Metropolitan 1981. Salzburg 1985. Scala 1992. Also Vienna, Munich, Paris, Chicago, San Francisco. Premiere: *The Voice of Ariadne* (Musgrave, Aldeburgh 1974). Won Laurence Olivier Award for performance as Busoni's *Dr. Faust* 1986. Many song recitals.
  Autobiography: *Foreign Parts: A Singer's Journal* (London 1993).
  Many recordings inc. the main Mozart roles, *Billy Budd, Eugene Onegin, Elijah*, song recitals esp. British song and Schubert (vol. 16 of Hyperion Schubert song ed.).

AMELING, Elly (41) Dutch soprano. b. Rotterdam 8 Feb. 1934. Studied in Rotterdam and Paris (w. P. Bernac). Concert debut 1953. Won 1st prize Geneva

1958. Career confined to concert work, w. appearances as Ilia (*Idomeneo*) Amsterdam 1973. Premiere: F. Martin's *Mystère de la Nativité* 1959.

Prolific recording artist inc. Lieder (inc. vol. 7 Hyperion Schubert song ed.), mélodies (EMI Fauré and Poulenc eds.), Bach cantatas. Seek on LP *After Hours* (Philips 6514 284) and *Souvenirs* (76738).

ARKHIPOVA, Irina (9) Russian mezzo-soprano. b. Moscow 2 Dec. 1925. Studied Moscow Conservatory. Debut Sverdlovsk and won international Warsaw prize 1954. Bolshoi 1956 (*Carmen*). Appearances abroad inc. Naples and Milan, Cov. Gdn. (1975 and 1988), USA, Japan. Song recitals, masterclasses and awards. Premiere: *War and Peace* (Bolshoi 1959).

Autobiography: *My Muses* (Moscow 1992).

Recordings inc. Russian song and opera recitals, *The Tsar's Bride*, *Carmen* 'live' from Bolshoi (Revelation RV20001).

BAKER, Janet (20) English mezzo-soprano. b. Hatfield, Yorks 21 Aug. 1933. Studied in London winning Ferrier award 1956. Opera debut 1956 (Oxford University Opera Club). Handel Opera Soc., English Opera Group, Glyndebourne, then Cov. Gdn. 1966. Premiere: *Owen Wingrave* (as Kate) 1971. Cressida in the revised version of Walton's opera 1963. Extensive concert, oratorio work inc. USA. DBE 1976.

Autobiography: *Full Circle* (London 1982).

Many recordings inc. *Dido and Aeneas, Orfeo ed Euridice, Dream of Gerontius*. Seek compilations which inc. *Sea Pictures*. Recitals inc. vol. 1 Hyperion Schubert song ed.

BATTISTINI, Mattia (10) Italian baritone. b. Contigliano nr. Rome 27 Feb. 1856; d. nr. Rieti, Italy 7 Nov. 1928. Studied w. Persichini. Debut Rome 1878 (*La favorita*). Scala 1888, St. Petersburg 1892, Moscow and Warsaw, S. America. Cov. Gdn. 1883, then 1905-6. Returned London in concerts 1922-4. Massenet adapted *Werther* for him.

See: J. Chuilon: *Battistini: le dernier Divo* (Paris 1996, superbly illustrated). Also S. Levik: *The Levik Memoirs* (London 1995); *Record Collector* vols. 8 and 29; Shawe-Taylor: *Opera* 1957; Steane: *Voices, Singers and Critics* (London 1992).

Records: CD reissues on Marston, Nimbus, Pearl. Seek complete ed. (7 LPs) EMI EX 290790.

BJÖRLING, Jussi (14) Swedish tenor. b. Stora Tuna 5 Feb. 1911; d. Stockholm 9 Sept. 1960. Sang as boy w. father's Björling Quartet. Studied Stockholm w. Forsell and Hislop. Debut Stockholm 1930 (Ottavio in *Don Giovanni*). Vienna 1936. London concert debut 1937, Cov. Gdn. 1939 and 1960. Metropolitan 1938.

See: Anna-Lisa Björling and A. Farkas: *Jussi* (Oregon 1996).

Many recordings. Seek esp. 'live' recordings (opera and concert), performances in Swedish and early recordings from 78s.

CALLAS, Maria (50) Greek soprano. b. New York 2 Dec. 1923; d. Paris 16 Sept. 1977. Studied in Athens w. Elvira de Hidalgo. Debut 1942 Athens (*Tosca*), Verona (*Gioconda*) and Venice (*Tristan* and *Turandot*) 1947, Buenos Aires 1949, Scala (*Aida*) 1950, Cov. Gdn. 1952 and Metropolitan 1956 (both *Norma*). Retired 1965. Reappearances in concert 1973-4 w. Giuseppe Di Stefano. Masterclasses NY 1971 and 1972.

See: J. Ardoin: *Callas at Juillaird* (London 1988). Also J. Ardoin: *The Callas Legacy* (London 1977 4th ed. 1995), M. Scott: *Maria Meneghini Callas* (London 1991), J. Kesting: *Maria Callas* (Germany 1990, Eng. trans. 1992).

Records: EMI ed. of complete operas in 30 vols. (1997), w. separate recital discs. Ardoin's *Callas Legacy* is an invaluable guide esp. to 'live' pirated recordings.

CLÉMENT, Edmond (26) French tenor. b. Paris 28 March 1867; d. Nice 24 Feb. 1928. Studied Paris Conservatoire. Debut Opéra-Comique (*Mireille* 1889). Premieres: 1892 *Phryné* (Saint-Saëns), *L'attaque du moulin* (Bruneau). Paris premieres: *Falstaff* and *Butterfly*. Metropolitan 1909. Boston 1911. Last concert 1927.

Records: Romophone 82002 has the 1905 Odeons and 1911-13 Victors. Pearl GEMM CD 9161 has a good selection of Victors and some Pathés.

COLLIER, Marie (35) Australian soprano. b. Ballarat 16 April 1927; d. London 7 Dec. 1971. Studied and debut Melbourne (*Cav. Rusticana* 1954). Cov. Gdn. 1956-71. Vienna, San Francisco, Metropolitan 1967. Premieres: *King Priam* (Hecuba, Coventry 1962), *Mourning Becomes Electra* (Christine, Met. 1967). Title role in British stage premiere *Katerina Izmailova*.

See: A. Blyth: *Marie Collier* (*Opera* Dec. 1968).

Records: very few. Chrysomethis in *Elektra* cond. Solti (Decca). Excerpts *Madame Butterfly* in English, some 'live' performances inc. Strauss' *Guntram*.

CORELLI, Franco (1) Italian tenor. b. Ancona 8 Apr. 1921. Studied at Pesaro. Debut Spoleto (*Carmen*, 1951). Scala 1954. Cov. Gdn. 1957 and 1966. Metropolitan 1961-74. Vienna, Berlin, Japan (concert tours). Retired 1975.

See: M. Boagno: *Corelli* (Italy 1990, Eng. trans. 1996).

Records: the biography has an excellent CD with many 'live' excerpts. Studio recordings inc. *Turandot, Andrea Chénier and Pagliacci* (all EMI).

CUÉNOD, Hugues (42) Swiss tenor. b. Corseaux-sur-Vevey 26 June 1902. Studied Geneva, Vienna. Operatic debut 1928 (Paris, *Jonny spielt auf*). Sang w. Boulanger Ensemble. Premiere: *Rake's Progress* (as Sellem, Venice 1951). Glyndebourne 1954-87. Cov. Gdn. 1954. Metropolitan (Emperor in *Turandot* 1987). Many composers wrote for him inc. Stravinsky (*Cantata* 1952).

See: J. Spycket: *Un diable de musicien* (Lausanne 1979).

Records: six-volume ed. on Lys includes troubador songs, Bach, Couperin, Poulenc and some made in his eighties. With the Boulanger group: Monteverdi madrigals (EMI CDH7 61025), Brahms *Liebeslieder* (CDH5 66425). Also fine recital on Nimbus NI5337.

DESTINN, Emmy (2) Czech soprano. b. (Ema Kittl) Prague 26 Feb. 1878; d. Ceské Budejovice 28 Jan. 1930. Studied w. Marie Loewe Destinn. Debut 1898 (*Cav. Rusticana*, Berlin). Bayreuth 1901. Cov. Gdn. 1904. Metropolitan 1910. Premieres: *Roland von Berlin* (Leoncavallo, 1904), *Fanciulla del West* (1910). Retired opera 1921, concerts 1926.

See: A. Rektorys: *Ema Destinova, Record Collector* vol. 20.

Records: complete ed. on Supraphon, Victors on Romophone.

DOMINGO, Placido (28) Spanish tenor. b. Madrid 21 Jan. 1941. Studied w. Carlo Morelli. Debut as baritone in zarzuela 1957, as tenor 1961. Israel National Opera 1962-5. Metropolitan 1968. Scala 1969. Cov. Gdn. 1971. First *Otello* Hamburg 1975 (Zeffirelli film 1986). Also Wagnerian roles (inc. *Parsifal*) and conducting.

Autobiography: *My First Forty Years* (NY 1983). See also D. Snowman: *The World of Placido Domingo* (NY 1985).

Many recordings inc. 18 Verdi operas and the Requiem, all of Puccini, 4 Wagner, many collections. Good videos inc. *Otello* (Cov. Gdn. 1992 cond. Solti).

EAMES, Emma (31) American soprano. b. Shanghai 13 Aug 1865; d. New York 13 June 1952. Studied in Paris w. Marchesi. Debut 1889 (*Roméo et Juliette*, Paris). Cov. Gdn. 1891. Metropolitan 1891-1909. Premiere: *Ascanio* (Saint-Saëns, 1890). Retired 1912.

Autobiography: *Some Memories and Reflections* (NY 1927, reprinted 1977). See also: J. Dennis and L. Migliorini *Record Collector* vol. 8 (Apr. 1953), D. Shawe-Taylor: *Emma Eames* (*Opera* Jan. 1957), P.G. Davis: *The American Opera Singer* (NY 1997).

Records: complete Victors on Romophone. Seek also Mapleson cylinders on LP (IRCC).

FASSBAENDER, Brigitte (22) German mezzo-soprano. b. Berlin 3 July 1939. Studied with father W. Domgraf-Fassbaender. Debut Munich 1961 (*Contes d'Hoffmann*) Cov. Gdn. 1971. Salzburg 1973. Metropolitan 1974. Premiere: *Kabale und Liebe* (von Einen, Vienna, 1976). Concerts, masterclasses and directing.

See: S. Gould: *Brigitte Fassbaender* (*Opera* 1981).

Many recordings inc. *Rosenkavalier* (cond. E. Kleiber), *Winterreise* (EMI CDC7 49846), vol. 11 Hyperion Schubert song ed. Seek *Die schöne Magelone* (Brahms).

FUGÈRE, Lucien (25) French bass-baritone. b. Paris 22 July 1848; d. Paris 15 Jan. 1935. Appeared in café-concert 1871. Operatic debut 1871 (Opéra-Comique where last 1932). Cov. Gdn. 1897. Premieres inc: *Le roi malgré lui* (1889), *La Basoche* (1890), *Cendrillon* (1899), *Louise* (1901).

See: R. Duhamel: *Lucien Fugère* (Paris 1929), V. Girard: *Lucien Fugère* (*Record Collector* vol. 8).

Records: 1902 Zonophones, but best remembered for Columbia 1928-30 collected on Symposium 1125.

GARDEN, Mary (5) Scottish soprano. b. Aberdeen 20 Feb. 1874; d. Aberdeen 3 Jan. 1967. Studied w. Fugère in Paris. Debut 1900 (*Louise*, Opéra-Comique). Cov. Gdn. 1902. Manhattan 1907. Chicago 1910 (Director 1919-20). Retired 1934. Premieres inc. *Pelléas et Mélisande* (1902) and *Chérubin* (1905).

Autobiography: *Mary Garden's Story* (London 1951). See: M. Turnbull: *Mary Garden* (Aldershot 1997), J. McPherson: *Mary Garden* (*Record Collector* vol. 41).

Records: complete Victors on Romophone 81008. Good selection 1903-29 Pearl GEMM CD 9067.

GERHARDT, Elena (40) German mezzo-soprano. b. Leipzig 11 Nov. 1883; d. London 11 Jan. 1961. Studied Leipzig Conservatory. Concert debut w. Artur Nikisch 1903. Only operatic appearances Leipzig 1903-4. London 1906. First American tour 1912. Retired 1947.

Autobiography: *Recital* (London 1953). See: D. Shawe-Taylor: *Elena Gerhardt* (*Record Collector* vol. 32).

Records: vol. 1 Hugo Wolf Soc. (EMI). Seek LP HLM 1436031 (*A Centenary Tribute*) and LP album Schumann and Brahms Lieder RLS 1547003.

GRÜMMER, Elisabeth (39) German soprano. b. nr. Diedenhofen 31 March 1911; d. Warendorf 6 Nov. 1986. Studied Aachen. Debut 1940 (Flower Maiden, *Parsifal*). Berlin 1946-72. Bayreuth 1957-61. Cov. Gdn. 1950. Edinburgh 1952. Metropolitan 1967.
See: A. Blyth: *Elisabeth Grümmer* (Opera 1987).
Recordings inc. complete *Meistersinger* (cond. Kubelik), *Lohengrin* (cond. Kempe), operatic collection EMI CDM7 63137, song and opera Testament SBT 1086.

HAGEGÅRD, Håkan (17) Swedish baritone. b. Karlstadt 25 Nov. 1945. Studied Stockholm. Debut 1968 (*Zauberflöte*). Glyndebourne 1973. Metropolitan 1978. Cov. Gdn. 1987. Premiere: *Ghosts of Versailles* (Met. 1991). Many concert tours. Papageno in Bergman film *Magic Flute* (1975).
Records: *Don Giovanni* (cond. Oestman), opera and song Caprice CAP 21362, Lieder BIS CD54. Also video *Ghosts of Versailles*.

HAMMOND, Joan (35) Australian soprano. b. Christchurch (NZ) 24 May 1912; d. Bowral (NSW) 26 Nov. 1996. Studied Sydney Conservatorium. Debut 1928 (Giovanna, *Rigoletto*). Vienna 1938 (State Opera 1939). Carl Rosa Co. (England) 1942-45. Cov. Gdn. 1948. NY City Center Opera 1949. Leningrad and Moscow 1957. DBE 1974.
Autobiography: *A Voice, A Life* (London 1970).
Records: a good collection on Testament SBT 1013.

HORNE, Marilyn (34) American mezzo-soprano. b. Bradford Pennsylvania 16 Jan. 1934. Studied University S. California. Sang w. Roger Wagner Chorale 1953. Operatic debut 1954 (*Bartered Bride*, LA Guild). Gelsenkirchen Opera 1956-9. San Francisco 1960. Cov. Gdn. 1964. Scala 1969. Metropolitan 1970 where she was honoured 1998. Sang voice of Carmen in film *Carmen Jones* 1954. Concerts Europe and USA.
Autobiography (w. J. Scovell): *My Life* (NY 1983).
Records: early recitals inc. *Age of Bel Canto* w. Sutherland, are reissued fairly frequently. Also complete *Norma, Lucrezia Borgia, Semiramide*. Seek La Scala recital 1983 (LP CBS M 37819).

HOTTER, Hans (23) Austrian bass-baritone. b. Offenbach am Main (Germany) 19 Jan. 1909. Studied w. M. Römer. Debut Troppau 1930. Munich 1937. Salzburg 1944. Cov. Gdn. 1947. Metropolitan 1950. Bayreuth 1952. Retired opera 1972. Much concert work, also as director and teacher. Premieres inc. *Friedenstag* (1938), *Capriccio* (1942), *Die Liebe der Danaë*.
Autobiography: *Der Mai war mir gewogen* (1996). See also: P. Turing: *Hans Hotter: Man and Artist* (London 1983).
Records: Wotan (*Walküre* and *Siegfried*) in Solti *Ring* Cycle (Decca). Good collections inc. early records on Preiser. Also Koch-Schwann *Vienna State Opera Live* vols. 3, 8, 15, 21, 22, 24.

HÜSCH, Gerhard (48) German baritone. b. Hanover 2 Feb. 1901; d. Munich 21 Nov. 1984. Studied w. H. Emge. Debut 1923 (*Waffenschmied*, Osnabrück). Cologne 1927. Berlin 1930-44. Cov. Gdn., Bayreuth 1930. Much concert work inc. Japan.

See: P. Rodden: *Gerhard Hüsch* (*Record Collector* vol. 36 no. 4).
Records: Papageno in *Zauberflöte* cond. Beecham. Songs of Schubert, Wolf, Kilpinen. Good collections on Preiser.

HVOROSTOVSKY, Dmitri (46) Russian baritone. b. Krasnoyarsk, Siberia 16 Oct. 1962. Studied and debut Krasnoyarsk 1986. St Petersburg 1987. Won Cardiff Singer of the World Competition 1989. Cov. Gdn. 1992. Chicago 1993. Much concert work.
Records: complete operas include *Eugene Onegin* (cond. Bychkov), *Queen of Spades* (cond. Ozawa), *Don Carlo* (cond. Haitink). Russian songs inc. folk songs (Philips 434 0801).

JERITZA, Maria (11) Czech soprano. b. Brno 6 Oct. 1887; d. Orange NJ 10 July 1982. Studied Prague. Debut 1910 (*Lohengrin*, Olmütz). Vienna 1912. Metropolitan 1921. Cov. Gdn. 1925. Occasional post-war appearances in Vienna and NY. Premieres inc. *Ariadne auf Naxos* (Ariadne in both versions, 1912 and 1916), *Frau ohne Schatten* (Empress 1919). First Vienna and NY Jenufa. First NY Turandot.
Autobiography: *Sunlight and Song* (NY 1924). See also: N. Douglas: *More Legendary Voices* (London 1994).
Records: good selections on Preiser and Pearl. Vienna State Opera 'live' vol. 14.

JOURNET, Marcel (24) French bass. b. Grasse nr. Nice 25 July 1867; d. Nittel 2 Dec. 1933. Studied Paris. Debut 1891 (Béziers). Brussels and Paris 1894. Cov. Gdn. 1897. Metropolitan 1900. Monte Carlo 1914. Chicago 1915. Scala 1917. Premiere: *Nerone* (Boito 1924). Fr. premiere *Bohème* and *Parsifal*.
Records: complete solo recordings 1909-33 Marston 52009. Selections on Nimbus and Pearl; also duets w. Caruso, Farrar etc. Complete *Faust* 1932, *Roméo et Juliette* (Pathé).

LEMNITZ, Tiana (38). German soprano. b. Metz 26 Oct. 1897; d. Berlin 10 Feb. 1994. Studied w. A. Kohmann, Frankfurt. Debut 1921 (*Undine*, Heilbronn). Hanover 1928. Berlin 1934. Cov. Gdn. 1936, 1938. Salzburg 1939. Retired 1957.
See: R. Seeliger and W. Park: *Tiana Lemnitz* (*Record Collector* vol. 15 no. 2).
Records: Pamina in Beecham *Zauberflöte* (1937), good collections EMI and Preiser.

LISITSIAN, Pavel (46). Armenian baritone. b. Vladikavkaz 24 Oct. 1911 (6 Nov. Russian style). Studied and debut Leningrad (1935). Yerevan, Armenia 1937. Bolshoi (*Eugene Onegin*) 1940-66. Concert work inc. USA tour 1960 (Amonasro in *Aida* at Met.). Premiere: Napoleon in Prokoviev's *War and Peace* (1955).
See: N. Linnel: *Pavel Lisitsian* (*Record Collector* vol. 28 nos. 5-6).
Records inc. complete *Queen of Spades* and 'live' *Carmen*. Solo collections Preiser and Memoria labels.

MAUREL, Victor (30). French baritone. b. Marseilles 17 June 1848; d. NY 22 Oct. 1923. Studied Paris Conservatoire. Debut Marseilles 1867 (*Guillaume Tell*). Paris Opéra 1868. Scala 1870. Cov. Gdn. 1873. Ac. Music NY 1873. Metropolitan 1894. Concerts till c. 1910. Taught London, NY. Premieres inc. *Simon Boccanegra* (rev. ver. 1881), *Otello* (1887), *Pagliacci* (1892), *Falstaff* (1893).
Autobiography: *Dix ans de carrière* (Paris 1897). See also G.B. Shaw: *Music in London* (1890-94); D. Shawe-Taylor: *Victor Maurel* (*Opera* 1955).

Complete recordings 1903-07 Pearl GEMM CD 9027, and (coupled w. Patti's) Marston 520112.

PAVAROTTI, Luciano (29). Italian tenor. b. Modena 12 Oct. 1935. Studied E. Campogalliani. 1961 International Award and debut (*Bohème*) Reggio Emilia. Cov. Gdn. and Glyndebourne 1964. Australian tour w. Sutherland 1965. Scala 1966. Metropolitan 1967. World Cup *Nessun dorma* 1990. Concert performance *Otello* Chicago 1991. Continuing operatic, concert work up to present time w. particular interest in fund-raising for cultural centre in Mostar, Bosnia.

Autobiography: *My Own Story* (London 1981).

Many recordings inc. almost all the main roles in Verdi and Puccini. Essential: *Fille du régiment, Guillaume Tell*. Many recitals, innumerable re-issues, several fine pirated 'live' operas and excerpts.

PEARS, Peter (7). English tenor. b. Farnham 22 June 1910; d. Aldeburgh 3 Apr. 1981. Studied London w. E. Gerhardt, D. Freer and L. Manen, NY w. T. Behr-Schnabel. BBC singers 1935. New English Singers 1936. 1937 Britten wrote song in *The Company of Heaven*: after that every relevant Britten premiere involved Pears (e.g. *Peter Grimes* 1945, *Billy Budd* 1951, *Death in Venice* 1973). Sadlers Wells 1943. Cov. Gdn. 1947. Metropolitan 1974. Also premiere Walton's *Troilus and Cressida* 1955. Much concert, oratorio work. Co-founder w. Britten of the English Opera Group and Aldeburgh Festival; also the Britten-Pears School at The Maltings. Knighted 1978.

See: C. Headington: *Peter Pears* (London 1992), P. Pears (ed. P. Reed): *The Travel Diaries* 1936-78 (Woodbridge 1995).

Many recordings: almost everything of Britten (his role in *Gloriana* an exception). Bach Passions, Schubert Lieder, English song.

PREY, Hermann (48). German baritone. b. Berlin 11 July 1929; d. nr. Munich 23 July 1998. Studied Berlin w. H. Gottschalk. 1952: debut (*Tiefland*, Wiesbaden), won Meistersinger Competition, appeared first in USA and sang first *Winterreise*. Hamburg 1953. Salzburg 1959. Metropolitan 1960. Edinburgh 1965. Cov. Gdn. 1973. Bayreuth 1981. Busy concert-operatic career, masterclasses.

Autobiography: *First Night Fever* (Munich 1981; Eng. trans. 1986).

Many records inc. good collections of German baritone arias, a many-volumed edition of German song from Middle Ages onwards, much Bach and Mozart, and an attractive *Barbiere* (DG cond. Abbado).

QUILICO, Gino (4). Canadian baritone. b. NY 29 Apr. 1955. Studied Toronto w. parents. Debut 1978 (*The Medium* on Canadian TV). Paris 1980. Cov. Gdn. 1983. Metropolitan 1987. Premiere: *The Ghosts of Versailles* 1991.

See: R. Mercer: *Les Quilico* (Quebec 1991).

Recordings: mostly of French opera (inc. Mercutio in *Roméo et Juliette*), also Rossini (*Cenerentola* and *Conte Ory*).

QUILICO, Louis (4). Canadian baritone. b. Montreal 14 Jan. 1930. Studied NY w. M. Singher. Won Canadian singing prize 1952. Debut 1953 (NY City Opera). Cov. Gdn. 1961. Paris 1962. Metropolitan 1972 and still singing there in the late 1990s. Also Bolshoi and Colón. Premieres inc. *La mère coupable* (Milhaud 1966).

Autobiography w. Christina Petrowska: *Mr Rigoletto* (Ontario 1996). See also R. Mercer: *Les Quilico* (Quebec 1991). Note that this book was written when the first Mrs. Q., Lina Pizzolongo, was alive; the later book, written w. L.Q.'s second wife, puts his career and personal feelings in a different light. The chapter in *Singers of the Century* came out before the publication of *Mr Rigoletto*.

Recordings inc. *Gemma di Vergy, Esclarmonde* (w. Sutherland), and 'live' *Rigoletto* (NY 1973 SRO 843).

SAMMARCO, Mario (47). Italian baritone. b. Palermo 13 Dec. 1868; d. Milan 24 Jan. 1930. Studied Palermo and Milan. Debut 1888 (*Faust*, Palermo). Scala 1894. Cov. Gdn. 1904. Manhattan 1907. Chicago 1910. Also S. America. Premieres inc: *Andrea Chénier* (1896), *Zazà* (1900*)*, *Germania* (1902), *Natoma* (1911).

Records: a good selection (1902-11) on Pearl GEMM CD 9181. Seek also duets *Barbiere, Bohème* and *Gioconda* w. McCormack.

SCHIØTZ, Aksel (44). Danish tenor and baritone. b. Roskilde nr. Copenhagen 1 Sept. 1906; d. Copenhagen 19 Apr. 1975. Studied Copenhagen w. V. Lincke and J. Forsell. Concert and oratorio work. Operatic debut 1939 (*Così fan tutte*, Copenhagen). Glyndebourne 1946 in first performances of *Rape of Lucretia*. Concert tours USA. Retired from singing 1948 after operation. Taught, masterclasses USA and Denmark.

Wrote *The Singer and his Art* (NY 1969).

Records: 1933-46 in fine 10 vol. ed. on Danacord. Selection on Pearl.

SCHIPA, Tito (43). Italian tenor. b. Lecce 2 Jan. 1888; d. NY 16 Dec. 1965. Studied Milan w. E. Piccoli. Debut 1910 (*Traviata*, Vercelli). Scala 1915. Chicago 1919. Metropolitan 1932. Also S. America. Concert tours inc. Russia and Australia. Last performance opera 1955 (*L'elisir d'amore*, Bari). Last concert 1963 (Lisbon). Appeared in many films. Wrote operetta *Principessa Liana* (Rome 1929). Premiere: *La rondine* (Monte Carlo 1917).

Autobiography: *Tito Schipa: Si confessa* (Genoa 1961). See also Tito Schipa jnr: *Tito Schipa* (Italy 1993, Eng. trans. 1996); R. D'Andrea: *Tito Schipa nella vita, nell'arte, nel suo tempo* (Italy 1981); N. Douglas: *Legendary Voices* (London 1992); J. Steane: *Voices, Singers and Critics* (London 1992).

Many records inc. complete *Don Pasquale*. Collections on EMI, RCA, Pearl, Nimbus.

SCHLUSNUS, Heinrich (18). German baritone. b. Braubach 6 Aug. 1888; d. Frankfurt 18 Jun. 1952. Studied Frankfurt. Debut 1915 (*Lohengrin*, as Herald, Hamburg). Berlin 1917-45. Concert tours Europe, USA, S. Africa.

See: E. von Naso and A. Schlusnus: *Heinrich Schlusnus, Mensch und Sänger* (Germany 1957) and S. Smolian: *Heinrich Schlusnus: A Discography* (*Recorded Sound* 1959).

Many recordings opera and song best represented on Preiser. Also complete *Tannhäuser, Rigoletto, Vespri siciliani* and *Traviata* (all in German).

SCHORR, Friedrich (6). Hungarian bass-baritone. b. Nagyvárád 2 Sept. 1888; d. Farmington Connecticut 14 Aug 1953. Studied Brno w. A. Robinson. Debut 1912 (*Walküre*, Graz). Berlin 1923. Cov. Gdn. and Metropolitan 1924. Bayreuth 1925. Retired 1943 and taught in USA.

See: A. Frankenstein and others: *Friedrich Schorr* (*Record Collector* vol. 19). D. Shawe-Taylor: *Friedrich Schorr* (*Opera*, May 1965)

Best recordings: HMV c. 1927-31. Collections on Pearl. 'Live' recordings mostly

Wagner, most from Met. late 1930s. Seek LP boxed set: Wagner on Record (1926-42) EMI RLS 7711.

SCOTTO, Renata (16). Italian soprano. b. Savona 24 Feb. 1933. Studied Milan w. M. Llopart. Debut 1952 (*Traviata*, Savona). Scala 1954. London and Edinburgh 1957. Chicago 1960. Cov. Gdn. 1962. Metropolitan 1965.
Autobiography (w. O. Roca): *Scotto: More Than a Diva* (USA 1984).
Many recordings inc. *Butterfly* (cond. Barbirolli), *Traviata* (cond. Votto), recitals (best on CBS) and video operas inc. *Bohème* Met. 1977, *Otello* (w. Vickers) 1978.

SEINEMEYER, Meta (38). German soprano. b. Berlin 5 Sept. 1895; d. Dresden 19 Aug. 1929. Studied and debut Berlin (1918). Dresden 1925. Vienna 1927. Cov. Gdn. 1929. Also N. and S. America. Premiere: *Dr Faust* (1925); German premiere *Andrea Chénier* (1926).
See: J. Dennis: *Meta Seinemeyer* (*Record Collector* vol. 14).
Records: good collections on Preiser and Pearl.

SEMBRICH, Marcella (31). Polish soprano. b. Wisniewczyk, Galicia 15 Feb. 1858; d. NY 11 Jan. 1935. Studied piano, violin and voice, Lemberg and Milan w. B. Lamperti. Debut 1877 (*Puritani*, Athens). Dresden 1878. Cov. Gdn. 1880. Metropolitan 1883-1909. Concerts till c. 1920. Taught Philadelphia and NY.
See: G. Owen: *Marcella Sembrich* (*Record Collector* vol. 18); W. Henderson: *The Art of Singing* (NY 1938).
Records: complete Victors on Romophone. Columbia 1903 Grand Opera Series (Sony NH2K 62334). Seek LP IRCC L7037 includes last records 1919. Also Mapleson cylinders on IRCC LP transfers, or on Romophone Vol. 2.

SLOBODSKAYA, Oda (45). Russian soprano. b. Vilnius 10 Dec. 1888; d. London 29 Jun. 1970. Studied St Petersburg. Debut 1919 (*Queen of Spades*, Mariinsky). Paris 1922. Tours N. and S. America. London 1931. Cov. Gdn. 1932. Scala and Colón BA 1933. Sang in music halls etc. as Odali Careno 1930-2. Gave lecture recitals and taught almost to time of death. Premieres: *Mavra* (Stravinsky, Paris 1922), *Koanga* (Delius, Cov. Gdn. 1935).
See: M. Leonard: *Oda Slobodskaya* (London 1979).
Records: Russian songs Pearl GEMM CD 9021. Essential seek LP Decca LXT 5663 (or SXL 2299). Lecture series in National Sound Archives.

STABILE, Mariano (47). Italian baritone. b. Palermo 12 May 1888; d. Milan 11 Jan. 1968. Studied Rome w. A. Cotogni. Debut 1909 (*Aida*, Palermo). Scala 1921 (*Falstaff* cond. Toscanini). Chicago 1924. Cov. Gdn. 1926. Salzburg 1931. Glyndebourne 1934. Edinburgh 1948. *Turco in Italia* w. Callas, Scala 1955. Retired 1961 (*Falstaff*). Premiere: Respighi's *Belfagor* (1923).
See: G. Gualerzi: *Stabile – A Centenary Tribute* (*Opera* vol. 39 1988).
Records: Salzburg *Falstaff* cond. Toscanini (Grammofono), early Columbias on Preiser, also some postwar recordings (*Falstaff* and *Don Pasquale*).

SUPERVIA, Conchita (3). Spanish mezzo-soprano. b. Barcelona 9 Dec. 1895; d. London 30 Mar. 1936. Training uncertain. Debut 1910 (*Los amantes de Teruel*, BA). Rome 1911 (*Rosenkavalier*). Chicago 1915. Scala 1925. Paris 1929. London concert debut 1930, Cov. Gdn. 1934. Also popular in Spain and S. America.

See: Barnes and Girard: *Conchita Supervia* (*Record Collector* vol. 6 no. 3); D. Shawe-Taylor (*Opera* 1960).

Records: reissues EMI, Preiser, Pearl, Nimbus inc. Rossini arias and much of the role of *Carmen*. Seek also song recitals. Brief appearance in film *Evensong* (1933).

TAMAGNO, Francesco (30). Italian tenor. b. Turin 28 Dec. 1850; d. Varese 31 Aug. 1905. Joined opera chorus Turin where solo debut 1870 (Nearco in *Poliuto*). Scala 1877. London (Lyceum) 1889, Cov. Gdn. and Metropolitan 1895. Also S. America, Spain, Russia. Premieres inc: *Simon Boccanegra* rev. ver. (1881), *Otello* (1887), de Lara's *Amy Robsart* (1897) and *Messaline* (1899).

See: *Il titanico oricalco: Francesco Tamagno*: Turin 1997. A. Favia-Artsay: *Francesco Tamagno* (*Record Collector* vol. 7).

Records: 1903-4 14 pub. titles, some in several versions. Complete on Symposium 1186/7.

TEBALDI, Renata (32). Italian soprano. b. Pesaro 1 Feb. 1922. Studied Parma w. C. Melis. Debut 1944 (Elena in *Mefistofele*, Rovigo). Scala 1946 (opening concert cond. Toscanini). Cov. Gdn. 1950. Paris 1951. Metropolitan 1955. Chicago 1956. Also S. America and concert tours inc. Japan and Russia. Retired 1976.

See: C. Casanova: *Tebaldi* (Dallas 1995).

Many recordings (Decca) and reissues inc. *Aida, Otello, Tosca, Butterfly*.

TE KANAWA, Kiri (36). New Zealand soprano. b. Gisborne, Auckland 6 Mar. 1944. Trained in NZ, Australia and London Opera Centre w. V. Rozsa. Debut 1969 (*Donna del lago*, Camden Fest.). Cov. Gdn. 1970. Glyndebourne 1973. Metropolitan 1974. Paris 1975. Scala 1978. Also Salzburg, Vienna, Sydney, Chicago. DBE 1982.

See: D. Fingleton: *Kiri te Kanawa* (London 1983).

Many recordings inc: *Nozze di Figaro* (cond. Solti), *Così fan tutte* (cond. Levine), *Otello* (w. Pavarotti, cond. Solti, also videos of performances Cov. Gdn. and Vienna). Song recitals, *Les nuits d'été, 4 Last Songs*, and Mozart concert arias all desirable.

TERFEL, Bryn (49). Welsh bass-baritone. b. Pwllheli, Gwynedd 6 Nov. 1965. Studied Guildhall London w. A. Reckless. Ferrier Scholarship 1988. Cardiff Singer of the World Lieder prize winner 1989. Operatic debut 1990 (*Così fan tutte,* Welsh Nat. Op.). Eng. Nat. Op. 1991. Cov. Gdn. 1992. Metropolitan 1994. Also Salzburg, Vienna, Chicago, Scala. Many concert and oratorio performances.

Records: essential recital Eng. song (*The Vagabond*), also Schubert, Handel, German opera recital, Mozart operas, *Elijah, Belshazzar's Feast*.

THILL, Georges (27). French tenor. b. Paris 14 Dec. 1897; d. Paris 17 Oct. 1984. Studied Paris and Naples w. F. De Lucia. Debut 1924 (*Thaïs*, Paris Opéra). Cov. Gdn. 1928. Metropolitan 1931. Many concerts inc. tours Australia, Canada, N. Africa. Appeared in films inc. *Louise* w. Grace Moore. Retired 1956.

See: A. Segond: *Georges Thill ou l'âge d'or de l'opéra* (Lyons 1980); D. Shawe-Taylor: *Georges Thill* (*Opera*, 1985).

Records inc. complete *Werther, Carmen*, abbreviated *Louise*. Many reissues EMI, Pearl, Nimbus. Seek: LP album (5 recs.) w. fine booklet EMI 2901933.

TIBBETT, Lawrence (13). American baritone. b. Bakersfield, Cal. 16 Nov. 1896; d. NY 15 Jul. 1960. Studied LA, then w. F. La Forge in NY. Debut 1923 (Levitsky in *Boris Godunov*, Met.). Cov. Gdn. 1937. Many concerts inc. tours Europe, USA, Australia. Films and musicals. Premieres: Taylor's *King's Henchman* (1927) and *Peter Ibbetson* (1931), Gruenberg's *Emperor Jones* (1933), Goossens' *Don Juan de Mañara* (1937).

Autobiography: *The Glory Road* (Brattleboro, Vermont, 1933). See also H. Weinstat and B. Wechsler: *Dear Rogue* (Oregon 1996); A. Farkas: *Lawrence Tibbett: Singing Actor* (Oregon 1989); T. Bullard: *Lawrence Tibbett* (*Record Collector* vols. 23 & 24).

Records: 'live' *Simon Boccanegra*, *Otello* (w. Martinelli), abbr. *Emperor Jones*. Many reissues RCA, Nimbus, Pearl (exc. selection on GEMM CDS 9452).

TOUREL, Jennie (21). Russian-born mezzo-soprano (Amer. cit. 1946). b. Vitebsk 9/22 Jun. 1900; d. NY 23 Nov. 1973. Studied Paris w. R. Hahn and A. El-Tour. Debut 1926 (Opéra Russe, Paris). Chicago 1930. Opéra-Comique 1933. Metropolitan 1937. Concert tours Europe and Israel. Taught at Juilliard NY. Premieres: *Rake's Progress* (Venice 1951), Stravinsky's *Cantata* 1952.

Records: recital at Tully Hall NY 1970 (Vox Box CDX 5126). Seek: Rossini, Offenbach, Rachmaninov solos on 78s, Stravinsky's *Cantata* on LP, pirated *Rake's Progress* premiere.

TUCKER, Richard (33). American tenor. b. NY 28 Aug. 1913; d. Kalamazoo 8 Jan. 1975. Trained as cantor, studied w. P. Althouse. Debut 1943 (*Traviata*, NY). Metropolitan 1945-75. Verona 1947. Cov. Gdn. 1958. Scala 1969. Tours Far East and Israel.

See: J. Drake: *Richard Tucker* (NY 1984).

Records: RCA reissues of broadcast *Aida* 1949 cond. Toscanini. Also *Aida* and *Forza* w. Callas (EMI). Selections *La Juive* (1974, RCA). Carnegie Hall concert w. R. Merrill (1973, Decca). As cantor: Passover, Seder Fest (1962, CBS).

TURNER, Eva (15). English soprano. b. Oldham 10 Mar. 1892; d. London 16 Jun. 1990. Studied w. A. Broad. Debut 1916 (*Tannhäuser* w. Carl Rosa co.). Cov. Gdn. 1920; reintroduced in *Turandot* 1928. Scala 1924. Chicago 1928. Also S. America and Germany. Taught Oklahoma and London. DBE 1962.

See: J. Richards: *Eva Turner* (*Record Collector* vol. 11), and tributes in *Opera* vol. 41 (1990).

Records: excerpts *Turandot* 'live' Cov. Gdn. 1937 (EMI). Collection opera and song w. short talk (1989) EMI CDH 7 69791 2.

VALLIN, Ninon (27) French soprano. b. Montalieu-Vercien 8 Sept. 1886; d. nr. Lyons 22 Nov. 1961. Studied Paris w. M. Héglon. Debut as concert-singer 1911, operatic debut 1912 (Micaëla in *Carmen*, Opéra-Comique). Scala and Colón, BA 1916. Paris Opéra 1920. Tours N. Africa, Canada, Australia. Taught in Montevideo. Premieres inc: *Le martyr de Saint-Sébastien* (Debussy, 1911).

See: R. de Fragny: *Ninon Vallin, princesse du chant* (Lyons 1963), H. Barnes: *Ninon Vallin* (*Record Collector* vol. 8).

Records: complete *Werther* and abridged *Louise* w. Thill (reissued EMI and Nimbus). Pathés 1927-9 (Marston 52006 2). Good selection opera and song Pearl GEMM CD 9948.

VON STADE, Frederica (37). American mezzo-soprano. b. Somerville, NJ 1 Jun. 1945. Studied NY w. S. Engelberg. Debut 1970 (3rd boy in *Zauberflöte*, Metropolitan). Paris and Glyndebourne 1973. Salzburg 1974. Cov. Gdn. 1975. Scala 1976. Many recitals. Premieres inc. Argento's *The Aspern Papers* (1988).

See: G. Movshon: *Frederica von Stade* (*Opera* Jan. 1980); P. Davis: *The American Opera Singer* (NY 1997).

Records inc. Cherubino in *Nozze di Figaro* (cond. Karajan, Decca), *Cenerentola* (video Scala cond. Abbado), Rossini's *Otello*, *Cendrillon*. Several song recitals inc. *Songs of the Auvergne*.


WELITSCH, Ljuba (12). Bulgarian soprano. b. Borisovo 10 Jul. 1913; d. 31 Aug. 1996. Studied Vienna w. T. Lierhammer. First major role Nedda (*Pagliacci*, Graz 1936). Vienna 1944 (*Salome* cond. Strauss). Cov. Gdn. 1947. Edinburgh and Metropolitan 1948. After c. 1954 sang 'character' roles, acted in stage plays and in films.

See: Harewood: *Ljuba Welitsch* (Opera 1953).

Records: Donna Anna in *Don Giovanni* (1950) cond. Furtwängler, Salzburg. Good selection on EMI CDH 7610072.


WIDDOP, Walter (8). English tenor. b. Norland, nr. Halifax 19 Apr. 1892; d. London 6 Sept. 1949. Studied locally then w. D. Gilly in London. Debut 1923 (*Aida*, Leeds). Cov. Gdn. (*Siegfried* w. Brit. Nat. Op. Co. 1924). Also concert, oratorio work. Premieres inc. E. Goossens's *Judith* (1929) and 1st British performances (on radio) *Wozzeck* (1934) and *Oedipus Rex* (1936). Last appearance Prom. concert 5 Sept. 1949.

See: A. Holler and J. Jarrett: *Walter Widdop* (*Record Advertiser* vol. 4).

Records: good collections Pearl and Claremont which have also reissued the abridged Wagner recordings cond. A. Coates.

# List of Singers in Volume 1

1. Richard Tauber
2. Emma Calvé
3. Elisabeth Schwarzkopf
4. Feodor Chaliapin
5. Amelita Galli-Curci
6. Tito Gobbi
7. Nellie Melba
8. Maria Ivogün
9. Fernando De Lucia
10. Marian Anderson
11. Renato Zanelli
12. Ezio Pinza
13. Kathleen Ferrier
14. Giuseppe di Stefano
15. Luisa Tetrazzini
16. Joseph Hislop
17. Geraldine Farrar
18. Giacomo Lauri-Volpi
19. Carlo Bergonzi
20. Régine Crespin
21. Kirsten Flagstad
22. Antonio Scotti
23. Boris Christoff
24. Adelina Patti
25. John McCormack
26. Victoria de los Angeles
27. Birgit Nilsson
28. Joan Cross
29. Aureliano Pertile
30. Antonio Cortis
31. Christa Ludwig
32. Dietrich Fischer-Dieskau
33. Titta Ruffo
34. Maria Cebotari
35. Rosa Ponselle
36. Florence Austral
37. Arleen Auger
38. Giovanni Zenatello
39. Galina Vishnevskaya
40. Giuseppe De Luca
41. Lucia Popp
42. Ernestine Schumann-Heink
43. Jon Vickers
44. Elisabeth Rethberg
45. Martti Talvela
46. Toti Dal Monte
47. Robert Merrill
48. Dmitri Smirnov & Leonid Sobinov
49. Gundula Janowitz
50. Joan Sutherland

# Index of Singers

Main entries are given in **bold** type. Pages in brackets contain illustrations.

# General Index

Works, arias, songs and operatic characters are indexed under the name of the composer; major works of opera composers have individual headings.

277